The Federal Resume Guidebook

A step-by-step guidebook
for writing a federal resume
in accordance with the
Office of Personnel
Management's flyer, OF-510,
"Applying for a Federal Job."

Kathryn K. Troutman

With material contributed by:

Michael Dobson / Sharon Harvey / Jo Lee Loveland Link / Edward J. Lynch, Ph.D. / Paul Radde, Ph.D.

The Federal Resume Guidebook

by Kathryn K. Troutman with materials contributed by:

Michael Dobson
Sharon Harvey
Jo Lee Loveland Link

Edward J. Lynch, Ph.D.
Paul Radde, Ph.D.

© 1997, 1995 JIST Works, Inc.

Published by JIST Works, Inc.
720 N. Park Avenue
Indianapolis, IN 46202-3490
Phone: 317-264-3720 **Fax:** 317-264-3709 **E-mail:** jistworks@aol.com
World Wide Web Address: http://www.jist.com

Other Books by Kathryn K. Troutman
The 171 Reference Book

> **See the back of this book for additional JIST
> titles and ordering information.
> Quantity discounts are available.**

Printed in the United States of America

1 2 3 4 5 6 7 8 9   02 01 00 99 98 97

Library of Congress Cataloging-in-Publication Data
Troutman, Kathryn K.
    The federal resume guidebook / Kathryn K. Troutman. — [2nd ed.]
      p.   cm.
    Includes bibliographical references.
    ISBN 1-56370-313-0
    1. Civil service positions—United States.   2. Résumés
(Employment)—United States.   I. Title.
JK716.T73 1997
808'.06665—dc21   97-2638
                            CIP

We have been careful to provide accurate information throughout this book, but it is possible that
errors and omissions have been introduced. Please consider this in making any career plans or other
important decisions. Trust your own judgment above all else and in all things.

ISBN 1-56370-313-0

Dedication

I dedicate this book to my children, Chris, Emily and Lori; to my mother Bonita and my deceased father Edward, who helped build up my confidence in owning my own business; and to my sister Bonny Kraemer Day, who has been an integral part of The Resume Place since 1980.

Acknowledgements

Human Resource Managers and Staffing Specialists who provided outstanding customer service and technical advice throughout the composition and review of this publication included: Jan Burchard, Janie Carr, Debbie Harlow, Sheila Johnson, Sandra Kopchick, Paul Krumsiek, Debbie Lee, Steven McGarry, Jim Patch, Carlifia Washington and Betty Waters.

Federal departments and agencies included: The Office of Personnel Management, Department of Justice, Department of Agriculture, Department of Defense, Immigration and Naturalization Office and the National Performance Review Office.

Editor: Michael Varhola

Book Design: Cary Creative Design
                                     9 Scotch Elm Court
                                     Catonsville, MD 21228
                                     (410) 744-8458

Cover Design: Wendy Prescott

Proofreading: Bonita Kraemer

Resume Designs and Appendix: Bonny Day

Editoral Assistant: Jeffrey Florian

Glossary: John Link

Table of Contents

Introduction viii
    Kathryn K. Troutman

National Performance Review Status Report x

Federal Personnel Review xii
    Paul Krumsiek, Federal Personnel Manager

Index of Federal Resumes and KSAs xiii

Chapter 1 1
    What is a Federal Resume?
    Comparison to a Private Industry Resume and the SF-171

Chapter 2 9
    Step-by-Step Guide to Writing a Federal Resume According to
    OPM Flyer OF-510, "Applying for a Federal Job"

    Step 1 11
    Job Information / Objective

    Step 2 11
    Personal Information

    Step 3 14
    Education

    Step 4 21
    Other Qualifications

    Step 5 30
    Work Experience

Chapter 3 59

Writing a Scannable Resume
Key Words & Phrases, Format Tips

Chapter 4 65

The New Federal Employment Process
Search • Application • Rating • Selection • Hiring

Chapter 5 77

Analyzing the Vacancy Announcement

Chapter 6 87

Writing Narrative Statements - KSAs

Chapter 7 97

Senior Executive Service - Five Executive Core Qualifications

Chapter 8 109

Introduction to T.A.P.E.S. (Total Army Performance Evaluation System)

Chapter 9 123

Write an Effective Cover Letter

Chapter 10 129

Developing a Positive Attitude About Yourself Before Writing Your Resume

APPENDICES 137

Appendix A: Federal Resume Samples 138

Appendix B: KSA Samples 172

Appendix C: OF-612 191

Appendix D: OPM's Guide to SES Qualifications. 194

Appendix E: OPM Qualifications Standards .207

Appendix F: OPM News Release 214

Appendix G: General Schedule Pay Scale, 1995 215

Appendix H: National Performance Review Resources 216

Glossary 217

Biographies of Contributing Authors 220

About the Author and the Company 222

Order Form 225

Introduction

When I first heard that the SF-171 was going to be eliminated, I simply did not believe it. I had grown accustomed to the 10 (or more) page form and we had purchased SF-171 software and two PCs just seven months before Vice President Gore recommended in the National Performance Review (excerpt reprinted on page v) that the federal personnel system should be reengineered and the application form was to be simplified.

As of Jan. 1, 1995, OPM became "customer-friendly" and a federal job applicant can now choose any written format to apply for a federal job, including the new OF-612, the SF-171, a resume, or any other written format.

Well, I recommend a resume —- what I now call a "federal resume," to distinguish it from a private industry resume. An individual's private industry resume does NOT usually include: Social Security number; citizenship; supervisor names and telephone numbers; high school with zip code; veteran's status; and many more important facts included in the federal resume OF-510 that the federal personnel staff will analyze, code and verify.

The Office of Personnel Management wrote and published the flyer, OF-510, "Applying for a Federal Job," to inform applicants of specific information that must be included in a federal resume. The flyer is really to the point. But with 35+ years of writing complete life stories in the SF-171, the applicants need more information and encouragement to change their writing style to the shorter, more targeted federal resume. Applicants need samples, explanations, ideas for language, formats and encouragement to use the new federal resume format.

In 1979, Pat Wood and I published *The 171 Reference Book* for the very same reason. The Federal government didn't provide any written instructions on how to write an excellent SF-171. Job applicants did not know they were able to expand the job pages to write more about their experience. I first designed the expanded job page in 1973 early in my business years. *The 171 Reference Book* was reprinted five times and was used as a training guide for federal career centers, personnel offices and individuals seeking advancement in the government and first time employment with the federal government.

Since I have been writing and designing resumes and SF-171s in Washington, D.C., for almost 25 years, I decided to design federal resume formats and publish them for trainers, personnel staff and applicants to follow.

A major point I want to bring out in this book is to use your judgment, common sense and creativity (following directions) to present your federal resume. For example, if you hold a certificate of training that is very important to your application, make sure it is listed on the top half of page one (not at the end where the reader might pass over).

Sometimes I feel like I'm an extension of the federal personnel system, since it is so difficult to speak to a person at the federal government's personnel office. I answer questions and advise clients on how to fill out a successful application. The OPM flyer does not say anything about the KSAs. I spoke to an OPM spokesperson and asked if the KSAs were still going to be a mandatory part of the application process. She replied that they definitely were - and will be more important than ever since the federal resume will be shorter and written to present the basic facts relevant to the vacancy announcement.

That did it. There was so much information that was not reaching the public, I felt it was my responsibility to find out the whole truth about the new application process and make it available to the people who are not in the government yet; to current government employees who need guidance for converting their SF-171 into a federal resume; to career development trainers and librarians. I also empathize with the personnel staff in the hiring agencies. I want to help them receive more organized and understandable resumes — that are complete. I believe this book will achieve that goal.

I asked for the help of The Resume Place's best professional writing staff from the past 15 years. I am pleased that Michael Dobson, Sharon Harvey, Jo Lee Loveland Link, Edward Lynch, and Paul Radde have researched and contributed information to this book. While the book was being written and prepared, I was still writing federal resumes, KSAs and private industry resumes every day in my offices in Baltimore and Washington, D.C.

Kathryn Troutman
Author/Publisher

National Performance Review
Status Report, September 1994

CREATING A GOVERNMENT THAT WORKS BETTER & COSTS LESS
Vice President Al Gore

EMPOWERING EMPLOYEES TO GET RESULTS

Change At The Top

In a new vision statement published in January 1994, the Inspectors General wrote, "We are agents of positive change striving for continuous improvement in our agencies' management and program operations, and in our own offices." The IG's reinvention principles talk about working with agency heads and Congress as well as building relationships with program managers.

Three accomplishments stand out (two relevant accomplishments are listed here):
1. Eliminating, effective Jan. 1, 1995, the infamous Standard Form 171, the imposing government job application form that prospective clients had to fill out, and that discouraged many good people from even applying for federal work.

It's not hard to figure out why King, a widely experienced federal, state, and local official before coming to OPM in April 1993, wanted to kill the 171; he needed three days to fill one out. When the 6-foot, 4-inch King unveiled his 171 at a public event in April, it "stretched from above his head to his feet, with a few pages to spare."

Not every federal worker completed such a lengthy application process.

OPM Director Jim King unfolds his Standard Form 171.

But the SF-171, in use since 1938, remained an archaic instrument of employment; job applicants took an average of eight hours to fill them out, while agencies needed 90 minutes to read and process each one. The SF-171 sought general information about the applicant and specific information about availability; military service; work experience, special skills, accomplishments, and rewards; references; and history of criminal and related problems. The form was so complicated that it spawned an industry of career counselors and other employment specialists to help applicants through it.

Not surprisingly, it also discouraged many highly qualified individuals from seeking federal employment. As Vice President Gore put it recently, "For many, it was their first dose of red tape. It was almost like saying to somebody who wanted to come to work for the federal government, 'Welcome to the fun house.'"

In its place, agencies will seek basic information from applicants, who will be able to use their resumes and should need no more than an hour to complete the process. Agencies' computer scanners will read 1,500 applications per hour. Also, OPM has created an automated phone system that enables anyone with a touchtone phone or a PC and modem to learn — at any time, day or night — about almost any federal job available and how to apply. Job-hunters can even apply for some jobs by phone.

2. Scrapping the Federal Personnel Manual, a 10,000-page behemoth of rules — nearly 10 times bigger than the Bible (Old and New Testaments included) and five times the size of an unabridged dictionary.

"The dinosaur is officially ossified and is going away," OPM Director James King announced in January as he took the helm of a wheelbarrow into which OPM employees had thrown parts of the manual. It was a dramatic ceremony. In the lobby of OPM's main building, King held the wheelbarrow. In front of him was a three-member fife and drum corps. Alongside were OPM employees, personnel officials from other agencies, and union officials who carried pieces of the manual. They marched outside and threw them into a waiting recycling truck.

The ceremony seemed fitting for an event of this long-term significance, which OPM accomplished a year ahead of NPR's schedule. Here, after all, was the document that, for the last half-century, instructed government managers and personnel specialists on the tiniest details of their jobs. No longer will these federal supervisors be subjected to a manual that dedicated a whole chapter to telling them how to label their file folders.

Immediately, the manual's demise will save federal agencies money. Its 610 subscribers, most of whom are agencies, paid $1,333 a year, plus up to $300 for each of 14 supplements. In one fell swoop, OPM scrapped 86 percent of the manual's pages. The other 14 percent will remain in existence for the rest of 1994, after which some will be repackaged as governmentwide regulations or handbooks.

Such large-scale change is part of OPM's effort to turn over such personnel strategies as recruiting, testing, and hiring workers to the agencies and assume a kind of consulting role for them. To further that transformation, the Administration plans to send Congress legislation to reform the civil service.

Federal Personnel Review

When the SF-171 was abolished in 1995, applicants were given, for the first time, choices in how best to present themselves for federal jobs. Choices, however, can be overwhelming to applicants seeking the answers to such basic questions as: "What does the employer want to know about me? What's important? How much should I say?"

The Federal Resume Guidebook answers these questions for the applicant. The *Guidebook* clues the applicant in to what is required and essential in applying for the job, and then reveals how to present this material so that it captures the attention of the employer.

With the mystery gone as to the content, the applicant is free to highlight his/her accomplishments.

As a personnel manager, I see hundreds of applications per year. Federal personnel staffing specialists, who do the screening of the resumes, see thousands. Yet, each of us can tell you that certain resumes jump out of the pack.

What makes these applications unique? Seldom are they the longest. Instead, they are well-organized, related to the stated job search criteria, and, most importantly, through an applicant's accomplishments, give the employer a sense of motion, making a difference — they make the reader <u>want</u> to meet the applicant.

The Federal Resume Guidebook instructs the applicant how to do this. It cuts away the unnecessary verbiage which can obscure the good applicant's message. It inspires the federal applicant to create that resume which will present to employers a special someone, someone whom they would want to work with.

Paul Krumsiek, Federal Personnel Manager

Index of Federal Resumes and KSAs

Refer to the pages indicated for resumes and KSAs that appear in this Guidebook.

FEDERAL RESUMES

Labor Economist, GS-0110-9/11
Recent Graduate Student in Economics
Gary L. Blankenburg, 138

Paralegal Specialist, GS 950-7
Private Practice Law Clerk
Elaine McCarthy, 141

Realty Specialist, GS-1170-9
Management Analyst, GS-7
Private Industry Property Management
Jessica L. Heil, 143

Realty Appraiser, GS 1171-9
Private Industry, Real Estate
Jerome V. Bushnell, 145

Program Assistant, GS-301-09
Department of the Navy
Donna Stephans, 148

Management Analyst, GS-343-9/11
Bureau of Naval Personnel
Margaret T. Thomas, 151

Computer Programmer Analyst, GS-334-11
Defense Investigative Service
Harold L. Walterson, 152

Child Development Specialist, GS-301-12
Department of Defense Schools
Caroline P. Dawson, 154

Engineering Technician, GS-802-12
Department of the Navy
John H. Smith, 159

Program Analyst, GS-301-12/4
National Cancer Institute
Michael L. Grenstar, 161

Computer Systems Specialist, GS 334-13
Private Industry Executive
Moses W. Jackson, 164

Inspector General for Investigations, GM-1811-15
General Services Administration
Timothy Hutton, 168

KSAS

Visual Information Specialist, GS-9
Knowledge of principals & methodology, 172

Security Specialist, GS-12
Knowledge of theories ... automated Information Systems, 173

Pharmacist, GS-12
Ability to apply concepts ... pharmacokinetic, 174

Chief of Medical Technical Equipment, GS-12
General knowledge ... health care facility, 175

Inspector General, GS-12
Analysis of multi-million dollar financial transactions, 176

Vocational Rehabilitation Specialist , GS-12
Promote the rehabilitation program, 177

Foreign Affairs Officer, GS-13
Ability to plan program activities, 178

Environmental Specialist, GS-13
Knowledge of hazardous materials transportation, 179

Construction Manager, GS-13
Expert level of engineering skills ... construction trades, 180

Attorney, GS-14
Ability to communicate orally and in writing, 181

Contract Specialist, GS-13
Knowledge of laws ... government contracting, 182

Procurement/Contract Specialist, GS-13
Experience with federal acquisition process, 183

Safety Manager, GS-13
Knowledge of principles ... highway safety, 184

Housing Specialist, GS-15
Knowledge of housing or community development programs, 185

Personnel Clerk/Assistant, GS 6/7
Knowledge of personnel rules
Ability to work with others
Ability to plan, organize and coordinate
Ability to communicate in writing, 186

Program Assistant, GS-9
Knowledge of government operations
Knowledge of rules governing disadvantaged business utilization
Ability to research, collect and analyze data
Ability to deal with senior members of public and private sectors, 189

xiii

Before - SF-171 - Block A

A Name and address of employer's organization (include ZIP Code, if known)

GSA Office of Inspector General
Washington Field Investigations Office
Rm 1915, Regional Office Building
7th & D Streets, SW, Washington, DC 20407

Dates employed (give month, day and year) From: 9/17/90 To: present

Average number of hours per week 55-60

Number of employees you supervise 13 - 18

Salary or earnings
Starting $ 66,125 per annum
Ending $ 80,800 per annum

Your reason for wanting to leave
Advancement/Become DHUD
Deputy AIGI

Your immediate supervisor Name
Albert B. Puglia

Area Code Telephone No. 202 501-1397

Exact title of your job
Regional Inspector General for Investigations

If Federal employment (civilian or military) list series, grade or rank, and, if promoted in this job, the date of your last promotion
GM-1811-15; 05-24-87

Description of work: Describe your specific duties, responsibilities and accomplishments in this job, including the job title(s) of any employees you supervise. If you describe more than one type of work (for example, carpentry and painting, or personnel and budget), write the approximate percentage of time you spent doing each.

During this tour of duty, I managed a staff of professional special agents ranging in grades from GM-14 to GS-07 (FTE between 13 and 18) as well as three support personnel. I managed the regional investigative program which, in the Washington Field Investigations Office (WFIO) covers both regional and national GSA programs and operations. I provided technical advice to supervisors and special agents; managed the administrative (budget, personnel, office automation, etc) and operational workload of the office and made long range investigative plans. During this tour, I carried out all phases of personnel management including hiring, firing, staff and career development, reassignments, personnel and program evaluations. I accepted and rejected highly complex and sensitive investigative work products and worked closely with OIG iquarters and regional management personnel to enhance and improve the investigative progra ersonally conducted sensitive and complex investigations of the highest level employee in the agency. During this tour I advanced the concept of cultural diversity in the OIG by hirin both minority employees and women. I promoted the first and currently only two female special agents to Assistant RIGI positions. I continue to promote and re- quire the use of information technologies in the investigative progr

After - Federal Resume - Current Position

EMPLOYMENT HISTORY

GENERAL SERVICES ADMINISTRATION
Office of Inspector General

May 1979 to present

Regional Inspector General for Investigations, GM-1811-15
Washington Field Investigations Office
Regional Office Building, Room 1915
7th & D Streets, SW, Washington, DC 20407
Supervisor: James E. Henderson (202) 501-1397   Yes, contact can be made.

9/90 to present
55-60 hours/week
Beginning Salary: $66,125/year
Current Salary: $83,614/year

Manage a staff of professional special agents ranging in grades from GM-14 to GS-7 (FTE have ranged between 8 and 18), as well as three support personnel. Responsible for hiring, staff and career development, reassignments, personnel and program evaluations. Management of the regional investigative program in the Washington Field Investigations Office covers both regional and national GSA programs and operations.

Managed the administrative (budget, personnel, office automation) and operational workload of the office and made long range investigative plans. Provide technical advice to supervisors and special agents. Continue to promote and require the use of information technologies in the investigative program.

Accept and reject highly complex and sensitive investigative work products. Work closely with OIG headquarters and regional management personnel to enhance and improve the investigative program. Personally conducted sensitive and complex investigations of the highest level employee in the agency.

Advanced the concept of cultural diversity in the OIG by hiring both minority employees and women. Promoted the first and currently only two female special agents to Assistant RIGI positions.

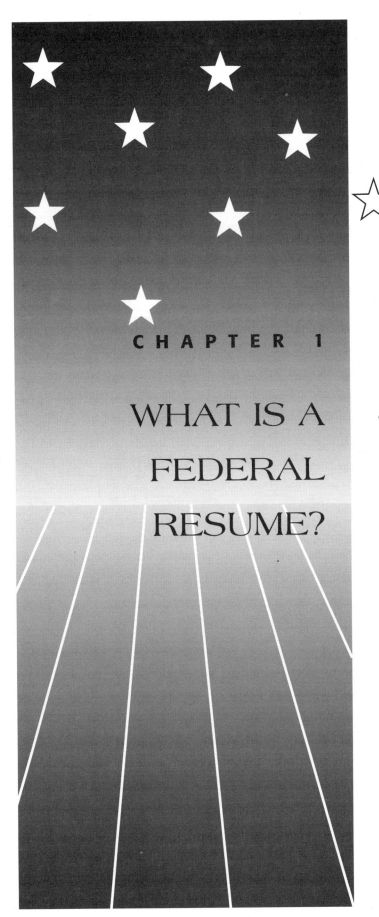

C H A P T E R   1

WHAT IS A FEDERAL RESUME?

- Everything Important from the SF-171 and <u>Less</u>...

- Same Text as a Private Industry Resume <u>Plus</u>...

Federal personnel staff and resume scanning project directors are asking the author of this Federal Resume Guidebook to emphasize the importance of including the following highlighted information in a federal resume:

CLARENCE CANNADY

U.S. Citizen
SS: 218-26-3666
Veteran's Preference: Air Force, 6/70-3/74
Highest Federal Civilian Grade Held: WS-5402-12

3600 Margaret Street
Baltimore, MD 21225
Home: 410-355-7277
Work: 301-394-2799

OBJECTIVE: **Engineering Technician (Project Manager) GS-802-12**
Announcement Number: 95-34-900

EMPLOYMENT EXPERIENCE:

Department of the Navy, Naval Surface Weapons Center 4/94 - Present

10910 New Hampshire Avenue
Silver Spring, MD 20910-5000
Supervisor: Mike Gamble Tel: (301) 394-1000
Yes, you may contact supervisor.

50 hours per week
$23.37 per hour

ACTING PROJECT MANAGER, MINOR SPECIFIC
CONSTRUCTION CODE 580, WS-5402-12

ENGINEERING TECHNICIAN, WS-5402-10
Project manager for Washington District-wide projects ranging from 1,000 to 80,000 sf and with budgets ranging from $25K to $700,000K. Manage an average of four to nine projects simultaneously on an ongoing basis. Customers include the U.S. Army, Navy, Marine Corps, Washington Naval District. Supervise an average of 20 to 40 tradesmen per project. Report to a Zone manager concerning minor specifics. Responsible for all aspects of project from intake, construction analysis, planning, scheduling, managing budget, customer liaison, quality control AND COMPLETING PROJECT ON TIME AND ON BUDGET.

CHAPTER ONE

What Is A "Federal Resume"?

A Federal Resume is not a Private Industry Resume.

Since the SF-171 was eliminated Jan. 1, 1995, **the Office of Personnel Management (OPM) is accepting resumes as federal applications.** OPM has adopted a new customer service orientation following the recommendations of Vice President Gore's National Performance Review. Now you have a choice of application format, including the new OF-612, the SF-171 or a resume format.

The Vacancy Announcement and OPM's flyer are very clear regarding the basic facts to be included in a federal resume, but federal staffing specialists explain that many applicants are leaving out information that will be required for a review panel, including veteran's status, civilian federal status, permission to contact the present supervisor, etc.

Debbie Harlow, Federal Staffing Specialist, has been receiving resumes as applications and offers this advice to applicants: 1) "Do not make your resume a life story" - the new resume format should present only relevant qualifications for the position; 2) make sure the staffing specialist can understand what you are "responsible for" in your jobs, i.e. "Manage a professional and administrative staff of 10 who administer accounting and budget services for the directorate;" 3) make your resume format easy to read and follow; 4) include your veteran and civilian federal status — this is very important!

> Federal Staffing Specialist says,
> *"Do not make your resume a life story."*

The federal resume format is an excellent application choice because you can "sell" yourself on paper to the government. You can use your common sense, formatting and organizing your resume background to fit the vacancy announcement. You can use your own computer at home or work with basic word processing software to produce and update your resume.

It is important that you realize that you cannot use your private industry resume for a federal application. A private industry resume would not contain the following mandatory details of a federal resume:

Social Security Number, Citizenship, Veteran's Preference; Federal Civilian Status; High School, date, address, zip code; addresses and zip codes for all employers and colleges; supervisor; names and telephone numbers; starting and ending dates of employment (month and year); hours worked per week; salary; indicating if they can contact your current supervisor.

The most significant differences between the old SF-171 and the new federal resume are the following:

- no birthdate (major success!)

- sections of the resume can be <u>interchanged</u>; i.e., education or experience, to highlight your best qualifications

- no references are needed, unless specifically requested from the job announcement

- <u>former</u> memberships, certifications or activities should not be included

- short-term positions that are not relevant do not need to be included

- creative and new sections can be added to highlight your major strengths; i.e., "Summary of Relevant Skills" or "Profile."

> Use your common sense and creativity to present your professional experience, education, interests, skills and accomplishments in a federal resume.

The goals of a federal resume are the following:

1. To meet the basic qualifications of the Vacancy Announcement.

2. To *sell* yourself more than the competition.

3. To impress the reader with the content, the look of the resume, and your organizational skills.

4. To keep the reader interested in your resume for more than 10 seconds.

5. To include key words and phrases for optical scanners.

6. To get you "best qualified."

Federal Resume Sample

> The same resume text can be used, but the federal resume includes other details.

CHRISTINE S. TAYLOR

8401 NewtonStreet
Chevy Chase, Maryland 20719
(301) 222-9999

Citizenship:	United States
Social Security Number:	222-22-5656
Veteran's Preference:	U.S. Army, 1971-1973
Federal Civilian Status:	Budget Analyst, GS-9, 5/91-present

PROFILE

Budget analyst with an effective record for detecting deficiencies in program operations and devising strategies to recover costs. Meticulous attention to detail and thorough understanding of both Federal and District financial regulations and procedures. Effective developing and delivering training to enhance team approach to financial operations. Recent professional education adds real estate focus to established analytical skills.

CURRENT EMPLOYMENT

Budget Analyst (DS-
614 H Street, NW, R
Washington, DC 200
Current Supervisor:
Starting Salary: $17,
This employer should

Budget Development

Collect, coordinate,
and regulatory prog
ensure consistency v
regulating insurance

Budget Execution

Receive, analyze, ar
funds and complian
Federal, and other r
develop alternative p
of procedures.

Financial Controls

Establish and monit
records of apportion
and report variations

Significant Accomplishmer

* Documented
Affairs, reco

* Conducted a

* Established
Department.

Private Industry Resume

CHRISTINE S. TAYLOR

8401 NewtonStreet
Chevy Chase, Maryland 20719
(301) 222-9999

PROFILE

Budget analyst with an effective record for detecting deficiencies in program operations and devising strategies to recover costs. Meticulous attention to detail and thorough understanding of both Federal and District financial regulations and procedures. Effective developing and delivering training to enhance team approach to financial operations. Recent professional education adds real estate focus to established analytical skills.

CURRENT EMPLOYMENT

Budget Analyst
DEPARTMENT OF CONSUMER AND REGULATORY AFFAIRS
May, 1986 - Present

Budget Development

Collect, coordinate, and consolidate financial and accounting data to develop and administer Washington, DC's consumer and regulatory programs and policies. Analyze operating programs' budget plans and estimates and evaluate changes to ensure consistency with legal requirements and program priorities. Develop projections and estimates from program records, and review programs' submissions for accuracy and sufficiency of justifications. Conduct cost-benefit analyses, assess program trade-offs, and propose alternative methods of funding where appropriate to formulation of the agency's budget. Recent accomplishments concentrated on commissions regulating insurance, real estate, housing, and other functions generating revenues for the District.

Budget Execution

Receive, analyze, and recommend approval of modifications of budget execution documents on the basis of availability of funds and compliance with regulatory requirements. Review personnel actions authorized through appropriated, private, Federal, and other non-District revenue sources to ensure compliance with spending plans. Recommend disapproval or develop alternative proposals to ensure personnel actions comply with legal requirements. Train staff to ensure knowledge of procedures.

Financial Controls

Establish and monitor financial management controls and documentary procedures to maintain thorough and accurate records of apportionments and obligations. Monitor obligations and expenditures to ensure timely disbursment of funds and report variations in excess of funding expeditiously.

Significant Accomplishments:

* Documented deficient payments from the Insurance Fund Bureau to the Department of Consumer and Regulatory Affairs, recovering a $6 million payment.

* Conducted an effective audit of the Uninsured Motorist Fund, resulting in a $150,000 reimbursement.

* Established a system for collecting on bad checks and established a profile of bad check writers for use within the Department. Reduced deficiencies attributable to bad checks.

> *How long can a federal resume be?* Customer service-oriented federal personnel staff say that the federal resume can be as long as you need it to be. An acceptable length is 2-6 pages.

Private Industry Resume

MICHAEL T. ROGERS
Page Two

Special project : Prepared a response to a question from the FY 1990 House Hearings on reduction levels in the NIH Research Centers Program by researching, preparing and analyzing information on the NCI Cancer Centers Program for FY 1987, 1988, 1989.

PENSION BENEFIT GUARANTY CORPORATION, Washington, DC   6/87 - 3/89

Budget Analyst
Prepared, evaluat
budget es
Account. P
material fo
in financial

Oversaw F
all departr
included a:

FEDERAL HIGHWAY ADMINIS

Budget Analyst
Prepared summa
Budget Fo
and progra
obtain info

INTERNAL REVENUE SERVIC

Tax Auditor, Examination Div
Analyzed individu
applied ap
proposed
reports.

EDUCATION:

B.S., General Bus
University of Mary

CONTINUING EDUCATION:

National Property

USDA Graduate

National Cancer I

National Institutes

COMPUTERS: Symphony, IBM

MICHAEL T. ROGERS

1010 Rockville Pike, Unit 102   Home: (301) 545-7878
Rockville, MD 20852   Work: (301) 676-8989

OBJECTIVE:

Seeking a professional position in Human Resources management where I can contribute expertise in personnel administration, computers and communications skills.

PROFILE:

Department manager with 16 years professional experience with an emphasis on personnel program development, budget and program analysis, research and preparation of reports and statements. Extensive computer skills utilized to research data via LAN and databases; analysis of data; and preparation of statistical reports. Department and program management   liaison concerning research and outcome of budget questions, report preparation and schedules.

PROFESSIONAL EXPERIENCE

National Cancer Institute, Bethesda, MD   12/90 to present

Program Analyst, Division of Cancer Prevention and Control (DCPC), Administrative Management and Planning Branch, (AMPB), Office of the Director.

Provide administrative and management programs support for the Director and divisional programs in areas of personnel management, administration, budgeting, property management and other related administrative areas.

Personnel management responsibilities include division responsibilities for Senior Executive Service personnel recruit actions; act as executive secretary for the Qualifications Review Committees and preparing official minutes from Qualifications Review Committee meetings. Maintain performance appraisal system management for divisional employees. Prepare and review special compensations. Member, National Cancer Institute Committee, that developed standard performance elements.

Execute, maintain and oversee the Personnel System Database on a personal computer connected to a LAN for the Division responding to requests for information, preparing and coordinating Personnel reports including current employees, recruitment actions and personnel ceilings. Member, National Cancer Institute Committee. Developed standard performance elements for various positions.

Update and maintain NIH Personal Property Inventory Data Base System for AMPB; decal new personal property; transfer and surplus personal property.

GrantsFinancialAnalyst   3/89 - 12/90
National Cancer Institute, Rockville, MD

Prepared and analyzed grant budgets involving multi-year budget projections for grant research programs: Cancer Centers, Clinical Cooperatives Group, Small Grants, Small Business Innovation Research, Instrumentation program and Scientific Review and Evaluation Programs.

Communicate with program directors and administrative officers concerning availability of funds for grant research programs. Prepare and analyze funds financial schedules reflecting a surplus or deficit; monitor current financial information and program information within the database system; conduct analysis on grant research programs to provide financial information on direct/indirect cost trends, grant award rates and balances. Reconcile and examine accounting reports of obligations and expenditures.

Federal Resume Sample

Note: Screened areas indicate information unique to a Federal Resume.

Michael T. Rogers page two
212-46-6731

Grants Financial Analyst (GS 12/20)   3/89 - 12/90
National Cancer Institute, 6120 Executive Blvd., Rockville, MD
Susan Thomas, Supervisor; Tel: (301) 787-8989
Beginning Salary: $45,999

> Prepared and analyzed grant budgets involving multi-year budget projections for grant research programs: Cancer Centers, Clinical Cooperatives Group, Small Grants, Small Business Innovation Research, Instrumentation program and Scientific Review and Evaluation Programs.

> Communicate wit
> research p
> current fina
> grant resea
> rates, gran
> expenditure

> Computers: Symp

> Special   projec
> (3/89
> 12/90):
> Prepared a
> response to
> a question

PENSION BENEFIT GUARAN-
TY COR-
PORATION

> from the FY
> ing, prepar

Budget Analyst (GS11/3)
> Prepared, evaluat
> budget est
> Account. P
> material fo
> severa

FEDERAL HIGHWAY ADMINIS-
TRATION

> department

> Oversaw F
> all departm
> ed assignin

Budget Analyst (GS 9/6)

MICHAEL T. ROGERS

1010 Rockville Pike, Unit 102   U.S. Citizen
Rockville, MD 20852   SS #: 212 -46-6731

Home: (301) 434-7878
Work: (301) 787-6665

Veteran's Status:
   Not Applicable
Federal Civilian Status:
   Program Analyst, GS-301 12/4, 12/90 to present
   National Cancer Institute, Bethesda, MD

OBJECTIVE:

   Program Analyst, National Institutes of Health, GS-12
   Announcement No. I-907

PROFILE:

   Program Analyst with 16 years Federal government experience with an emphasis on financial, budget and program analysis, research and preparation of reports and statements. Extensive computer skills utilized to research data via LAN and databases; analysis of data; and preparation of statistical reports. Communication with department and program managers concerning research and outcome of budget questions, report preparation and schedules.

PROFESSIONAL EXPERIENCE

National Cancer Institute, Bethesda, MD   12/90 to present
900 Rockville Pike, Room 10A50, Rockville, MD 20205
Nick Henderson, Supervisor; Telephone: (301) 778-8898
Salaries: $49,567 to $55,777
Yes, you may contact present employer.

Program Analyst, Division of Cancer Prevention and Control (DCPC), , (GS-12/4)
Administrative Management and Planning Branch, (AMPB), Office of the Director.

Provide administrative and management programs support for the Director and divisional programs in areas of personnel management, administration, budgeting, property management and other related administrative areas.

Personnel management responsibilities include division responsibilities for Senior Executive Service personnel recruit actions; act as executive secretary for the Qualifications Review Committees and preparing official minutes from Qualifications Review Committee meetings. Maintain performance appraisal system management for divisional employees. Prepare and review special compensations. Member, National Cancer Institute Committee, that developed standard performance elements and standards for various positions.

Execute, maintain and oversee the Personnel System Database on a personal computer connected to a LAN for the Division responding to requests for information, preparing and coordinating Personnel reports including current employees, recruitment actions and personnel ceilings. Member, National Cancer Institute Committee. Developed standard performance elements for various positions.

Update and maintain NIH Personal Property Inventory Data Base System for AMPB; decal new personal property; transfer and surplus personal property.

Checklist for your federal resume

What to Include:

If your resume or application does not provide all the information requested in the job vacancy and in the OPM flyer, OF-510, you may lose consideration for a job.

___ Announcement Number, title and grade of job applying for

___ Social Security Number

___ Country of Citizenship

___ Veteran's Preference

___ Federal Civilian Preference

___ High School (yes, this is required, even with higher degrees) and zip code (if known)

___ Zip codes for educational institutions and employers (for verifying purposes)

___ Supervisor's name and telephone

___ Yes or No - contact can (or cannot) be made with this supervisor (an important reference, if possible)

___ Address, phones and supervisors' names for other employers

___ Salaries and number of hours worked in all positions

___ Employment history and all of the other information that is important for the last 10 years and longer, if relevant.

Selecting an organizational format for your federal resume.

You can organize your major resume categories to best present your most important, recent and relevant experience on page one. Samples of major headings can include:

Format 1:	**Format 2:**	**Format 3:**
Education & certifications	**Education-employment**	**Employment**
Name (heading info)	Name (heading info)	Name (heading info)
Summary of Skills	Profile	Summary of Experience
Certificates	Education	Employment
Education	Employment	Education
Professional Training	Professional Training	Professional Training
Employment	Publications	Leadership Activities
Awards	Community Service	Computer Skills
Memberships	Languages	Personal Qualifications
Military Training	International Experience	

8

CHAPTER 2

STEP-BY-STEP GUIDE TO WRITING A FEDERAL RESUME

- Job Information

- Personal Information

- Profile

- Education

- Work Experience
  (and converting your SF-171 text)

- Other Qualifications

9

Applying for a Federal Job

United States
Office of
Personnel
Management

OF 510
(September 1994)

OPM's Guidelines, "Applying for a Federal Job," OF-510

Here's what your resume or application must contain
(in addition to specific information requested in the job vacancy announcement)

JOB INFORMATION

❑ Announcement number, and title and grade(s) of the job for which you are applying

PERSONAL INFORMATION

❑ Full name, mailing address *(with ZIP Code)* and day and evening phone numbers *(with area code)*
❑ Social Security Number
❑ Country of citizenship *(Most Federal jobs require United States citizenship.)*
❑ Veterans' preference *(See reverse.)*
❑ Reinstatement eligibility *(If requested, attach SF 50 proof of your career or career-conditional status.)*
❑ Highest Federal civilian grade held *(Also give job series and dates held.)*

EDUCATION

❑ High school
   Name, city, and State *(ZIP Code if known)*
   Date of diploma or GED
❑ Colleges and universities
   Name, city, and State *(ZIP Code if known)*
   Majors
   Type and year of any degrees received
   (If no degree, show total credits earned and indicate whether semester or quarter hours.)
❑ Send a copy of your college transcript only if the job vacancy announcement requests it.

WORK EXPERIENCE

❑ Give the following information for your paid and nonpaid work experience related to the job for which you are applying. *(Do not send job descriptions.)*
   Job title *(include series and grade if Federal job)*
   Duties and accomplishments
   Employer's name and address
   Supervisor's name and phone number
   Starting and ending dates *(month and year)*
   Hours per week
   Salary
❑ Indicate if we may contact your current supervisor.

OTHER QUALIFICATIONS

❑ **Job-related** training courses *(title and year)*
❑ **Job-related** skills, for example, other languages, computer software/hardware, tools, machinery, typing speed
❑ **Job-related** certificates and licenses *(current only)*
❑ **Job-related** honors, awards, and special accomplishments, for example, publica– tions, memberships in professional or honor societies, leadership activities, public speaking, and performance awards *(Give dates but do not send documents unless requested.)*

**THE FEDERAL GOVERNMENT IS
AN EQUAL OPPORTUNITY EMPLOYER**

Step-by-Step Guide to Writing a Federal Resume

According to OPM's Brochure OF-510, "Applying for a Federal Job"

Q: What is the main reason a federal resume is better than an OF-612 or SF-171?

A: Because you can organize resume sections to best present your related background to the announcement.

Editor's Note:
Examples shown are intended to provide you with both information and format ideas. The resume excerpts are varied with different types of resume language you may use in preparing your federal resume.

Step 1

JOB ANNOUNCEMENT

❏ Announcement number, and title and grade(s) of the job for which you are applying.

Step 2

PERSONAL INFORMATION

❏ Full name, mailing address *(with ZIP code)* and day and evening phone numbers *(with area code)*

❏ Social Security number

❏ Country of citizenship *(Most federal jobs require United States citizenship.)*

❏ Veterans' preference

❏ Reinstatement eligibility *(If requested, attach SF-50 proof of your career or career-conditional status.)*

❏ Highest federal civilian grade held *(Also give job series and dates held.)*

11

Example 1

EDWARD N. REYNOLDS
SSN: 454-89-7878
U.S. Citizen

2456 Edmondson Avenue
Arlington, VA 22234

Day: (202) 879-8989
Evening: (703) 787-7878

Announcement No. & Job Title:	Mitigation Program Specialist, GS-301-13 Vacancy Announcement No. 94-26411-CNB
Veteran's Status:	U.S. Navy, Lieutenant Junior Grade Honorably Discharged January 1990 - January 1995
Federal Civilian Status:	Department of Justice, Washington, DC Computer Programmer Analyst, GS 334/9 January 1988 - January 1990 Form 50 is attached.

Example 2

SUSAN M. TAYLOR
310 Arlington Boulevard
Arlington, VA 22203
Office: (202) 737-8637 • Home: (703) 666-8989

SS#: 445-78-8989   U.S. Citizen

Veteran's Status: None
Federal Eligibility Status: None

OBJECTIVE: To apply for the position of Management Analyst, GS-0343-9/11,
Office of the Secretary of Defense, Ann. No.: 140-A-94-250-LP

Application for Federal Employment—SF 171
Read the instructions before you complete this application. Type or print clearly in dark ink.

Form Approved.
OMB No. 3206-0012

GENERAL INFORMATION

1 What kind of job are you applying for? Give title and announcement no. (if any)
Asst. Inspector General for Investigations, ES-1811. Dept. of Transportation, Office of Inspector General. Ann. No. 1-95-30

2 Social Security Number
265-43-0987

3 Sex
[X] Male [ ] Female

4 Birth Date (Month, Day, Year)
3/15/49

5 Birthplace (City and State or Country)
Woodbridge, VA

6 Name (Last, First, Middle)
HUTTON, Timothy

Mailing address (include apartment number, if any)
13343 Triadelphia Mill Road

City
Alexandria

State
VA

ZIP Code
2 2 1 9 1

7 Other names ever used (e.g., maiden name, nickname, etc.)
None

8 Home Phone
Area Code 703 Number 744-4324

9 Work Phone
Area Code 202 Number 709-9874 Extension N/A

10 Were you ever employed as a civilian by the Federal Government? If "NO", go to item 11. If "YES", mark each type of job you held with an "X".
[ ] Temporary [ ] Career-Conditional [X] Career [ ] Excepted
What is your highest grade, classification series and job title?
Supervisory Special Agent, GM-1811-15
Dates at highest grade: FROM 5/87 TO Present

AVAILABILITY

11 When can you start work? (Month and Year)
2 wks. notice

12 What is the lowest pay you will accept? (You will not be considered for jobs which pay less than you indicate.)
Pay $_____ per _____ OR Grade 14

13 In what geographic area(s) are you willing to work?
Washington, DC, Northern Virginia

14 Are you willing to work:

	YES	NO
A. 40 hours per week (full-time)?	X	
B. 25-32 hours per week (part-time)?		X
C. 17-24 hours per week (part-time)?		X
D. 16 or fewer hours per week (part-time)?		X
E. An intermittent job on call/seasonal)?		X
F. Weekends, shifts, or rotating shifts?	X	

15 Are you willing to take a temporary job lasting:

A. 5 to 12 months (sometimes longer)?		X
B. 1 to 4 months?		X
C. Less than 1 month?		X

16 Are you willing to travel away from home for:

A. 1 to 5 nights each month?	X	
B. 6 to 10 nights each month?	X	
C. 11 or more nights each month?		X

MILITARY SERVICE AND VETERAN PREFERENCE

17 Have you served in the United States Military Service? If your only active duty was training for the Reserves or National Guard, answer "NO". If "NO", go to item 22.

	YES	NO
	X	

18 Did you or will you retire at or above the rank of major or lieutenant commander?

		X

THE FEDERAL GOVERNMENT IS AN EQUAL OPPORTUNITY EMPLOYER
PREVIOUS EDITION USABLE UNTIL 12-31-90
Page 1

FOR USE OF EXAMINING OFFICE ONLY

Date entered register
Form reviewed:
Form approved:

Option	Grade	Earned Rating	Veteran Preference	Augmented Rating

[ ] No Preference Claimed
[ ] 5-Point Tentative
[ ] 10 Pts. (30% or More Comp. Dis.)
[ ] 10 Pts. (Less Than 30% Comp. Dis.)
[ ] Other 10 Pts.

[ ] Disallowed [ ] Being Investigated

FOR USE OF APPOINTING OFFICE ONLY
Preference has been verified through proof that the separation was under honorable conditions, and other proof as required.

[ ] 5-Point [ ] 10-Point-30% or More Compensable Disability [ ] 10-Point-Less Than 30% Compensable Disability [ ] 10-Pt.
Signature and Title

Agency _____ Date _____

MILITARY SERVICE AND VETERAN PREFERENCE

19 Were you discharged from the military service under honorable conditions? (If your discharge was changed to "honorable" or "general" by a Discharge Review Board, answer "YES". If you received a clemency discharge, answer "NO".) If "NO", provide below the date and type of discharge you received.

	YES	NO
	X	

Discharge Date (Month, Day, Year)
6/1/78

Type of Discharge
Honorable

20 List the dates (Month, Day, Year), and branch for all active duty military service.

From	To	Branch of Service
6/1/67	6/1/78	USMC

21 If all your active duty was after October 14, 1976, list the full names and dates of all campaign badges or expeditionary medals you received or were entitled to receive.
3 Purple Hearts
1 Bronze Star w/ Combat V

22 Read the instructions that came with this form before completing this item. When you have determined your eligibility for veteran preference from the instructions, place an "X" in the box next to your veteran preference claim.

[ ] NO PREFERENCE
[ ] 5-POINT PREFERENCE – You must show proof when you are hired.
[X] 10-POINT PREFERENCE – If you claim 10-point preference, place an "X" in the box below next to the basis for your claim. To receive 10-point preference you must also complete a Standard Form 15, Application for 10-Point Veteran Preference, which is available from any Federal Job Information Center. ATTACH THE COMPLETED SF 15 AND REQUESTED PROOF TO THIS APPLICATION.

[X] Non-compensably disabled or Purple Heart recipient.
[ ] Compensably disabled, less than 30 percent.
[ ] Spouse, widow(er), or mother of a deceased or disabled veteran.
[ ] Compensably disabled, 30 percent or more.

NSN 7540-00-935-7150   171-109
Standard Form 171 (Rev. 6-88)
U.S. Office of Personnel Management
FPM Chapter 295

BEFORE - SF-171
Page 1

AFTER - RESUME
Page 1 - top third of page

TIMOTHY HUTTON

13343 Triadelphia Mill Road
Woodbridge, VA 22191
Home: (703) 744-4324
Work: (202) 709-9874

Social Security No:	265-43-0987
Citizenship:	U.S.A.
Federal Civilian Status:	Supervisory Special Agent, GM-1811-15 5/87 to present
Military Status:	U.S.M.C., 1967-1978
Veterans Preference:	10 Point Veteran (3 Purple Hearts and 1 Bronze Star w/ Combat V)

OBJECTIVE: Assistant Inspector General for Investigations, ES-1811 Department of Transportation, Office of Inspector General Announcement No: I-95-30

13

Step 3

EExport

EDUCATION

- ☐ High school
    Name, city, and state *(ZIP code if known)*
    Date of diploma or GED
- ☐ Colleges and universities
    Name, city, and State *(ZIP code if known)*
    Majors
    Type and year of any degrees received
    (if no degree, show total credits earned and indicate whether semester or quarter hours.)
- ☐ Send a copy of your college transcript only if the job vacancy announcement requests it.

Additional Notes:

- You do need to list high school even if you have higher degrees.

- Educational background may be listed in any location on the resume. Place it near the top if your application will rely more heavily on your educational accomplishments; i.e., a recent graduate who is looking for a job in the field of work supported by this degree. Otherwise, if your application weighs more heavily on your professional experience, education may be included later in the resume.

- Be sure to separate your college education and degrees from the continuing education. The college needs to stand out separately.

- "Job-related training courses" are typically listed in a separate section, and may directly follow "Education." This section can be called Professional Development, Continuing Education, Specialized Training, etc.

Example 1

EDUCATION

Washington State University, Pullman, Washington 06589
B.S. Degree, June 1976. Major: Construction Management

University of Idaho, Moscow, Idaho 08765, September 1972 to June 1974

Boise High School, Boise, Idaho 08652, Graduated 1972

Professional Development:
Autocad II Training, sponsored by Republic Research Training Center, October 1989
Autocad I Training, sponsored by Vycor Corporation, September 1988

Example 2

EDUCATION AND TRAINING

MASTER OF SCIENCE, International Agricultural Development, Specialization in Project Management. University of California, Davis, 89898, 1984. Project paper: A Management Systems Approach for Initiating a Revised Farming System in the Semi-Arid Region of Northern Nigeria.

SUMMER LANGUAGE INSTITUTE, University of California, Santa Cruz 67676, 1984. Successfully completed a nine-week Language Studies Program in French.

BACHELOR OF ARTS, MAGNA CUM LAUDE, INTERNATIONAL AFFAIRS, Minor in Economics. Florida State University, Tallahassee 34343, 1974.

GRADUATE, St. Petersburg High School, Florida 34240, 1971.

Professional Development:

IN-SERVICE TRAINING, Villeta, Paraguay, 1981. Intensive two-week training sessions in the Guarani language, cross-cultural studies, and specialized instruction in pest control, live-stock diseases, plant pathology, and apiculture.

PEACE CORPS VOLUNTEER TRAINING, Villeta, Paraguay, 1981. Intensive three-month training in the Spanish and Guarani languages, cross-cultural studies, and agricultural extension methodology with emphasis on organizing farmer cooperatives, promoting diversified food/cash crop production, controlling crop and livestock pests and diseases, and establishing small animal projects.

Financed entire education with my own funds.

Example 3

EDUCATION

Legal **AMERICAN UNIVERSITY**
WASHINGTON COLLEGE OF LAW, Washington, DC 20036
J.D. expected May 1996

College **BUCKNELL UNIVERSITY,** Lewisburg, Pennsylvania   17189
B.A., Economics and Philosophy degrees, May 1988
History minor; Bucknell University Track Team; Bucknell Rugby Football Club; Alpha Lambda Delta Freshman Honor Society; Theta Chi Fraternity, treasurer and brother

Overseas **INSTITUTO BRASIL - ESTADOS UNIDOS**
Rio de Janeiro, Brazil
Summer 1988
Six-week intensive Portuguese language course (90 class hours), sponsored by IBEU/University of Florida. Travelled afterward to the Brazilian states of Minas Gerais, Sao Paulo, Goias and Mato Grasso.

BUCKNELL UNIVERSITY SUMMER SCHOOL PROGRAM 1987: EASTERN EUROPE
Spent six weeks of accredited study in the communist bloc countries of Eastern Europe. Wrote a paper, "The Economic Systems of Eastern Europe: A Comparison of the East German and Hungarian Economic Models."

Example 4

EDUCATION **Georgetown University,** Washington, DC 20006
1981 -1985
Edmund A. Walsh School of Foreign Service
B.S.F.S. Comparative International Politics and Economics

The American University, Washington, DC 20036
1987-1991
Kogod College of Business Administration
M.B.A. Finance (Summer 1991 Graduate)

Georgetown Preparatory School, Rockville, MD 20815
Graduated 1980

16

Example 5

EDUCATION

NEW YORK UNIVERSITY, SCHOOL OF LAW   NEW YORK, NY 04332
Masters of Law in Taxation, 1991

> **Resident Director,** August 1990 - May 1991. Director of graduate residence hall.

THE GEORGE WASHINGTON UNIVERSITY,
NATIONAL LAW CENTER   WASHINGTON, DC 20006
J.D., 1989

> **Resident Director,** August 1986 - August 1989. Designed, organized and managed social, cultural and academic programs for 210 undergraduates through management of staff of six resident advisors.

> **Research Assistant, Government Contracts Program,** May 1987 - May 1988. Researched and drafted chapters in service, supply and construction contracting in both the private and government sectors for inclusion in scholarly text. Analyzed case law while noting variances among jurisdictions.

> Moot Court Semi-finalist.

> Tutored undergraduate students in macro and micro economics.

RIDER COLLEGE   LAWRENCEVILLE, NJ 07890
B.S., Commerce, cum laude, 1985

> Double major: Accounting and Finance; concentration in Economics
> President, Omicron Delta Kappa (National Leadership Honor Society)
> School of Business, Business Advisory Board
> DAARSTOC - Student Executive Development Program

CENTRAL HIGH SCHOOL   NEW HAVEN, NJ 07832
Graduated with Honors, 1980

> National Honor Society
> Debate Champion

> *Financed 100% of education through employment and scholarships.*

Example 6

EDUCATION:

JOHNS HOPKINS UNIVERSITY, Baltimore, MD 21218
B.A., Social Sciences, with Honors, 1992
GPA: 3.87

CATONSVILLE COMMUNITY COLLEGE, Baltimore, MD 21228
A.A. General Studies, 1985
GPA: 3.86

CATONSVILLE SENIOR HIGH SCHOOL, Baltimore, MD 21228
Graduated, 1965

Example 7

EDUCATION:

UNIVERSITY OF MARYLAND, UNIVERSITY COLLEGE, College Park, MD 21289
Graduate School of Management and Technology
Pursuing Masters of General Administration with a concentration in Finance
(three courses to be completed)

UNIVERSITY OF MARYLAND, UNIVERSITY COLLEGE, College Park, MD 21289
B.S., Business Management, 1985   Major: Accounting

NORTHWESTERN HIGH SCHOOL, Largo, MD 20879; Received Diploma 1981

Example 8

EDUCATION:

MSN, Community Health and Public Health, 1993
YALE UNIVERSITY, New Haven, CT 23489
Concentration: Maternal Child Health

BSN, 1987
UNIVERSITY OF MIAMI, Miami, FL, 34787

Diploma in Nurse Midwifery, 1980
Hospital of Obstetrics and College of Midwifery, Miami, FL 34642

High School Degree, 1976
North Central High School, Miami, FL 34878

Additional Training:
Diabetes Mellitus Optimizing Treatment, University of Miami Diabetes Research
    Center, Miami, FL, 1993
Dysrhythmia and Pacemaker Course, University of Miami, Miami, FL, 1984
Critical Care Nursing Course, Cedars of Lebanon Hospital, Miami, FL, 1983

Example 9

EDUCATION:

Bachelor of Arts, Political Science, 1978
UNIVERSITY OF MARYLAND BALTIMORE COUNTY, Baltimore, MD 21228

Additional Professional Training:
- "The Impact of Fiscal Constraints on Public Sector Industrial Relations,"
  Eighth Annual Conference of the Public Sector Labor Relations Conference
  Board, University of Maryland, University College, College Park, MD, 1979.
- Grievance Administration Arbitration Seminar, U.S. Department of Labor,
  Hagerstown, MD, 1979.
- Reinventing Government, AFSCME, Eastern Seaboard Annual
  Conference, New York, NY, 1994.
- Recognized for my expertise in labor relations by professional law enforce-
  ment officials. Guest speaker and panelist at the Maryland Criminal Justice
  Association, Ocean City, MD, October, 1994.

Graduate, 1973 BALTIMORE POLYTECHNIC INSTITUTE, Baltimore, MD 21289

19

BEFORE - SF-171
PAGE 3 + ATTACHMENT

◄ ATTACH ANY ADDITIONAL FORMS AND SHEETS HERE

EDUCATION

25 Did you graduate from high school? If you have a GED high school equivalency or will graduate within the next nine months, answer "YES".

YES **X** If "YES", give month and year graduated or received GED equivalency 6/63
NO ☐ If "NO", give the highest grade you completed .

26 Write the name and location (city and state) of the last high school where you obtained your GED high school equivalency.

Woodrow Wilson High School, Woodbridge, VA

27 Have you ever attended college or graduate school?   YES **X** If "YES", continue with 28.   NO ☐ If "NO", go to 31.

28 NAME AND LOCATION (city, state and ZIP Code) OF COLLEGE OR UNIVERSITY. If you expect to graduate within nine months, give the month and year you expect to receive your degree.

Name	City	State	ZIP Code	MONTH AND YEAR ATTENDED From	To	Semester	Quarter	TYPE OF DEGREE (e.g. B.A., M.A.)	MONTH AND YEAR OF DEGREE
1) Northern Virginia Community College	Alexandria	V,A	2,2,0,9,3	6/63	6/64	12			
2) Northern Virginia Community College	Annandale	V,A	2,2						
3) George Washington Univ.	Washington	D,C	2,0						

29 CHIEF UNDERGRADUATE SUBJECTS Show major on the first line

	NUMBER OF CREDIT HOURS COMPLETED Semester / Quarter
1) Data Processing	15
2) International Affairs	30
3) English	30

30
1)
2)
3)

31 If you have completed any other courses or training related to the kind of jobs you are app

NAME AND LOCATION (city, state and ZIP Code) OF SCHOOL		MONTH AND Y ATTENDE From
School Name 1) Computer East, Inc.		
City Washington	State ZIP Code D,C 2,0,3,2,1	2/92 2/
School Name 2) Franklin Planner Corp.		
City Bethesda	State ZIP Code M,D 2,0,8,1,4	1/91 1/

SPECIAL SKILLS. ACCOMPLISHMENTS AND AWARDS

32 Give the title and year of any honors, awards or fellowships you have received. List your sp Some examples are: skills with computers or other machines; most important publications (do professional or scientific societies; patents or inventions; etc.

Computer Information Systems Degree - Graduated
Certificate of Recognition for Outstanding Acade
Business Technologies - Northern Virginia Comm
IRS Certificate of Achievement - IRS Washington,

33 How many words per minute can you:
TYP
50
Agen
skills

34 List job-related licenses or certificates that you have, such

35 Do yo langu Engl

1)
2)

REFERE

36 List th At lea

1)
2)
3)

Page 3

ATTACHMENT PAGE   BURKE, JAMES G.
                                                        059-38-8174

31. OTHER JOB RELATED TRAINING

Date	Hours	Course	Provider	Cert
2/92	16 hrs.	Aldus Pagemaker	Computer Ease Inc. Washington, D.C.	N/A
11/91	8 hrs.	Franklin Planner	Franklin Planner Corp.	N/A
12/90	32 hrs.	TIC 2000 Advanced	VOTEK INC. Course at IRS	N/A
12/90	8 hrs.	TIC 2000 Autoreply	Service Ctr., Austin, TX	N/A
12/90	8 hrs.	Configuration Management	Quality Mgmt., Inc. Sterling, VA	N/A
11/90	40 hrs.	Project Management	Boeing Computer Services Vienna, VA	Cert.
2/91	8 hrs.	Harvard Project Manager	IRS In-house	
10/90	40 hrs.	TIC 2000 Training	Votek Inc. Austin, TX	N/A
			In-House	Cert.
			In-House	Cert.
			In-House	Cert.
			In-house	Cert.
			In-house	Cert.
			In-house	Cert.

JOHN SMITH   **PAGE 3**

EDUCATION:

NORTHERN VIRGINIA COMMUNITY COLLEGE, Annandale, VA 70305
A.A.S. Computer Information Systems, cum laude 1988
Certificate of Recognition for Outstanding Academic
Achievement in the Business Technologies.

A.S. English, 1985

UNIVERSITY OF SOUTH CAROLINA, Columbia, SC, 30357
B.A., International Affairs, 1980

PROFESSIONAL TRAINING:

Aldus Pagemaker, Computer Ease, Inc., 1992
TIC 2000 Advanced, Votek Inc., 1990
TIC 2000 Autoreply, Service Center, Austin, TX, 1990
Configuration Management, Quality Management, Inc., Sterling, VA, 199

IRS:
Project Management, Boeing Computer Services, 1990
Harvard Project Manager, IRS, 1990
BASIC Instructor Training, 1989
Team Leader Training Workshop, 1989
IPF (Interactive Processing Facility), 1988
Advanced COBOL Files Workshop, Structured Analysis,
     Analyst Techniques, Lotus 123 Structured Program Design,
     Advanced COBOL, DMS 1100 DML

AWARDS:
     IRS Certificate of Achievement - IRS, Kansas City, 1990
     IRS Special Act Award, Department of Treasury, 1992
LANGUAGE:
     French (conversant)

NOTE: References are not requested in the OF-510; personnel staff are calling supervisors for references.

AFTER - RESUME EDUCATION TRAINING AWARDS PAGE

☆

Step 4

OTHER QUALIFICATIONS & SKILLS

❑ **Job-related** training courses *(title and year)*

❑ **Job-related** skills, for example, other languages, computer software/hardware, tools, machinery, typing speed

❑ **Job-related** certificates and licenses *(current only)*

❑ **Job-related** honors, awards, and special accomplishments. For example, publications, memberships in professional or honor societies, leadership activities, public speaking, and performance awards. *(Give dates but do not send documents unless requested.)*

> Job-related training courses see Step 3 Education Section, page 14.

Examples:
Summary qualifications statements:

SUMMARY OF QUALIFICATIONS:
Healthcare Specialist with 10 years' experience in directing and developing clinical program for obstetrics, prenatal and maternal care. Expert in issues surrounding infant mortality with experience as coordinator for Yale University demonstration project. Skills include research, data development and authoring articles and protocols. Effective trainer and presenter before physicians and medical staff.
Expertise: Maternal and Child Health –Women and Child Advocacy

QUALIFICATIONS PROFILE:

Offer outstanding seven year record of accomplishment in Personnel/Labor Representation with the state of Maryland ... possess excellent skills in negotiation, communication and public relations ... career has been highlighted by founding a new union and by successful mediation of several major employee/employer disputes and recognition throughout the state ... possess the ability to readily adapt to changing situations and respond appropriately ... familiar with basic personnel activities ... articulate ... enthusiastic ... ambitious.

> As part of "other qualifications and skills" we are including **Profiles** and **Summaries of Experience** which have always been used for private industry resumes. This is an opportunity to set the tone and level of the resume as well as highlight key experiences and strengths. Writing a summary of your overall skills was not an option on the SF-171 form or the OF-612.

PROFILE:

Sixteen-year federal government career with an emphasis on financial, budget and program analysis, research and preparation of reports and statements. Extensive computer skills utilized to research data via LAN and databases; analysis of data; and preparation of statistical reports. Communication with department and program managers concerning research and outcome of budget questions, report preparation and schedules.

> The resume reader will understand your career and expertise in just five seconds with a summary intro paragraph.

OVERVIEW:

Technical/Operations Supervisor with 25 years' experience and versatile background in mechanical, hydraulic and electric machinery, from nuclear-grade valves to steam generators and turbines, air compressors, pumps, condensors, and more. Highly skilled in the full range of test and shop equipment, and in all facets of repair, maintenance and operation. Strong field supervisor and team leader, able to motivate, train, organize and direct technicians to perform quality work. Highest quality orientation — trained to meet nuclear-grade standards of excellence.

PROFILE:

Education Program Specialist with eight years' professional experience in child development programs and services for DoD child education programs. Experienced teacher with pre-school, elementary and secondary levels. Four years' experience as supervisor and instructor of teachers and staff. Consulting experience in curriculum and program development; assessing program quality and effectiveness; and selection of age-appropriate toys and materials. Skilled researcher, writer and presenter. Strong administrative, budget and program management abilities.

SUMMARY:

Administrative Support Professional with eight plus years' experience in the financial industry with increasing levels of responsibility. Skilled in organization and analysis of data; coordination, setting and evaluating of objectives; producing management reports and meeting briefings via computer spreadsheet and word processing software; able to compose and produce correspondence. Efficient, detail-oriented and possess excellent communications skills.

PROFILE:

Policy Researcher and Analyst with experience developing guidelines and procedures implementing the Americans with Disabilities Act for a major academic and professional association. Exceptionally well-organized in planning and implementing national conferences and advancing the association's goals and priorities. Prolific writer with extensive experience developing reports and program materials.

SUMMARY:

Nearly 20 years progressive experience in media relations; issues management; image building; crisis management; broadcast news. Skilled writer and public speaker. Extensive contacts.

PROFILE:

Over 10 years of professionally responsible technical management experience in the food industry, most recently as head of technical affairs of an international trade association whose member companies comprise 85% of a $2.1 billion segment of the bottled water industry. Responsibilities have included department direction, quality control, production, research/technical strategic planning, regulatory liaison, foundation fundraising, budget management, educational program development, product analysis and coordinating committee activities.

SUMMARY OF SKILLS:

Ten years' experience in payroll accounting, including handling of nationwide, multi-state tax preparation, withholdings, quarterly reports through year-end, and benefits allowances.

Ten years' administrative reception experience with expertise in file management, organizing office systems, appointment scheduling and telephone reception.

SUMMARY OF SKILLS:

Administration: • Nine years' professional experience in administrative positions in areas of publications, distribution, inventory control and accounting administration.

Accounting: • Nine years' experience in budgeting, contract compliance, accounts payable, accounts receivable, accounting system and spreadsheet reports.

Publication: • Eight years' experience in publication fulfillment, purchasing, distribution and customer service.

Summary of Qualifications:

• Experienced in mainframe system environment
• IBM/MVS/ESA System Architecture
• TSO, CICS/VS, COBOL/COBOL II experience
• Knowledge of A/P, A/R and accounting principles
• Ability to perform detailed system analysis
• Experienced working independently

Examples:
Specific technical and computer skills statements; foreign language skills

Computer Skills
Proficient in utilizing accounting and spreadsheet software, including LOTUS 1-2-3 and financial software packages.

COMPUTER SKILLS

Spreadsheet and word processing systems including Lotus 1-2-3, WordPerfect 5.0, PFS:Write, TSO, WYLBUR, IPS, Aldus PageMaker, MS-DOS, Q:Filer, and Convergent Technologies packages. Good computer skills and aptitude; able to learn new systems quickly.

COMPUTER KNOWLEDGE

Equipment: PCs, IBM 3800, 3203, 7700 NCR Ureck processor. Printers: 6262 High Speed printer, Xerox 9700 and 9790 duplicators, Data-Com microfiche processor; Kodak Komstar. Software: Word Perfect 5.1, Windows, Lotus and dBase.

Skilled in performing preventative maintenance of printing and other office equipment. Assist co-workers with training, troubleshooting and utilizing equipment and software.

COMPUTER SKILLS

- IBM PC, WP, Excel 4.0, Lotus 123, Quicken
- Utilize PCs networked to a mainframe
- Lexus-Nexus legal software

LANGUAGE PROFICIENCY

Language fluency in French, German and Italian
Three advanced level diplomas in Modern Language
Aldenham School, Elstree, Hertfordshire, England

LANGUAGE SKILLS AND INTERNATIONAL EXPERIENCE

Bilingual English/French.
Able to speak and understand conversational Spanish.
Fluent Portuguese and Spanish. Foreign Service Examination, Grade 4.
Moderate German and Italian.
Multi-linguist: French, Italian, Spanish and English. Simultaneous interpretation from French/English and Spanish/English; Translation and word processing in all languages.
Lived and traveled in Europe from 1975 to 1985 with Foreign Service Officer spouse.
Studied and lived in France and Belgium from 1975 to 1980 with family as part of the Diplomatic Corps. Traveled throughout Europe, Africa, Asia and the Middle East.
Studied German four years and French three years in high school and college; capable of learning languages easily.

Examples:
Job-related Certificates and Licenses

If the license you hold is required to perform your job, the acronym and license belongs at the very top of the resume. This is your no. 1 credential for performing your job.

RICHARD E. KRAEMER, J.D.
Member, Maryland and Colorado State Bars

CARLA T. YONKERS, M.S.W., L.C.S.W.-C

MATTHEW R. BENDETT
CLU, CFP

CHARLES T. GREEENE, CPA, MBA

Further in the resume, you can write the license or certificate in a separate section to add to the professionalism of the resume.

LICENSES:

> Certified Financial Planner
> Series 7 License, NASD
> Certified Public Accountant, State of Maryland
> Licensed Realtor, Commonwealth of Virginia

CERTIFICATIONS (examples):

> Certified Safety Manager, World Safety Organization, 1994
> Certified Planner, Asbestos Abatement Design, Environmental Protection Agency, 1992-present
> CPR, current
> Teacher Certification, District of Columbia, 1992-199
> Certificate of Completion, FEMA Management Intern Program

LICENSURE:

> RN Licensure, Connecticut State Board of Nursing, 1988
> Critical Care RN Certification (CCRN), Connecticut, 1985
> ASPO Lamaze Natural Childbirth Certification Course, Newark, N.J., 1988
> RN Licensure, Massachusetts State Board of Nursing, 1987
> Aero Medical Life Support Certification, Miami, FL, 1986
> Advanced Cardiac Life Support, Certified Licensure, Mt. Sinai Medical Center, Miami, FL, 1986
> Basic Cardiac Life Support Certification, Baltimore, MD, 1981 - present

Professional honors, awards, special accomplishments, publications, presentations, consultancies, volunteer activities, community service, special interests, media experience, and more.

This "catch-all" section can be lengthy or brief depending on each individual. If you are going to include this information, it is important to be thorough and well organized. Publications and presentations should be included, of course, because they demonstrate expertise in your field. You may shorten this section to include only recent or relevant written works or presentations. (i.e., full publication list is available upon request.)

> This section was formerly Attachment A to page 3 of the SF-171.

Examples:
Professional Publications & Presentations

PUBLICATIONS

Co-Author, *Non-Invasive Measurement of Platelet Kinetics in Normal and Hypertensive Pregnancies.* American Journal of Obstetrics and Gynecology (in press), 1993.

Author, *Women's Health Services Feasibility Study: Prenatal and Primary Care,* sponsored by Yale University (unpublished),1993.

Author, *Characteristics of Women With and Without Prenatal Care and Birth Outcomes* (unpublished Master's Thesis), Yale University, 1993.

Author, *A Support Group for HIV Positive Women* (unpublished), University of Miami, 1992.

PRESENTATIONS

Protocols on Preclampsia/Aspirin Prophylaxis Trials, Presentation to Staff, Department of Obstetrics/Gynecology, Yale University, St. Raphael's Hospital and Hill Health Center, New Haven, CT, 1990.

Participant in Meetings - National Institutes of Health for Review of Treatment Protocols and Tools for Aspirin Multicenter Trial, Bethesda, MD, 1990.

Volunteer Speaker. Presented Lecture Series on *Cardiac Risk Factors and Advantages of Eating Healthy,* Speakers Corner, American Health Association, Washington, DC, 1990.

Cardiac Enzymes and Myocardial Infarctions, Mt. Sinai Medical Center, New York, NY, 1986.

PUBLICATIONS

Chapter, "Drugs," *Products Liability Practice Guides,* New York Women's Medical College, New York, NY, 1986.

"A Decade of Consumer Protection Constraints," *Virginia Bar Journal,* Vol. 27, No. 2, March/April, 1994.

PRESENTATIONS & LECTURES

"Products Liability Law in Maryland," Women's Bar Association, July, 1993.
"Consumer Protection Law," American Bar Association, October, 1992.
"Home Improvement/Consumer Fraud," Maryland Institute for Continuing Legal
    Education, February, 1989.
Guest Lecturer, Georgetown University School of Law, Washington, DC, 1990 - present

PUBLIC SPEAKING

Teach continuing legal education courses on D.C. Rental Housing Law with
    Neighborhood Legal Services and the D.C. Bar Association, Washington, DC.
Testified before the District of Columbia City Council on Rental Housing issues.
Guest Lecturer, Legal Planning classes, Howard University Law School, Washington, DC.
Guest Lecturer, Department of Political Science, Howard University.
Member, Toastmistress Club, Civil Service Commission.
Panelist and Moderator on bar association committees on issues concerning federal
    criminal law revisions and Minority Women in Federal Government.

Examples:
Professional Memberships & Affiliations

MEMBER
American Nurses' Association (ANA)
American Public Health Association (APHA)
Connecticut Mothers' Healthy Babies Coalition
Yale New Haven Hospital Advanced Practice Nurses' Group
American Association for Critical Care Nurses (AACN)
American Academy of Nurse Midwives

PROFESSIONAL MEMBERSHIPS
Maryland State and District of Columbia Bar Associations
Maryland Trial Lawyers Association
American Trial Lawyers Association
National Association of Consumer Advocates

OTHER AFFILIATIONS
Omicron Delta Kappa (Leadership Honorary)
Outstanding Young Men of America - 1979
Vice President and Board Member, The League for the Disabled
Advisory Committee, George Washington Legal Services

PROFESSIONAL ASSOCIATIONS

American Association of Medical Society Executives (AAMSE)
  • Listed in **Who's Who in Medical Society Management**

American Society of Association Executives (ASAE)
  • Listed in **Who's Who in Association Management**

Maryland Society of Association Executives (MSAE)
  • Board of Directors - 1985-1989
  • Membership - 1989-present
  • Treasurer - 1988-1990

Greater Washington Society of Association Executives (GWSAE)
  • Membership - 1990 - present

Examples:
Honors & Awards

EMPLOYEE AWARDS & RECOGNITIONS

3250 Technical Training Wing
    Civilian of the Quarter (2 quarters)   1993, 1994
    Civilian Instructor of the Year, 1994
    Civilian Training Manager of the Year, 1993

Quality Salary Increase, 1992
Superior Performance Ratings, every year since 1989
Suggestion Awards, 1988, 1991, 1994
Letters of Commendation, 1989, 1991, 1994

Academic Honors:
B.A. with Highest Honors, 1982
M.A. with Highest Honors, 1989

ACCOMPLISHMENTS:

FEMA Certificates for Outstanding Performance, 1989-1992
Certificates of Appreciation for disaster activities during Hurricane Hugo
Received B.A. degree *Magna Cum Laude* (3.9/4.0)
    Phi Delta Kappa Honor Society
Who's Who Among American College Students
    Recipient of a four-year scholarship to University of Pennsylvania from the Youngstown Chamber of Commerce, Pennsylvania, for Outstanding Academic and Community Performance.

Examples:
Other - Community Service, Volunteer Experience

EEO VOLUNTEER DUTY
Conference Chairperson, Federally Employed Women, Inc. (1989-1990). Planned and managed the regional training program. Planned training needs and obtained speakers/instructors for workshop. Attendees included EEO specialists, civilian employees, military personnel and primarily female government employees. Promoted the training program on local "talk shows" and wrote press releases and materials to publicize the program nationally.

Chapter President, Federally Employed Women, Inc. (1987-1989). As a charter member, founded the chapter of FEW. Supervised five staff on the executive board and five on standing committees. Presided as parliamentarian during monthly meetings. Planned activities and programs of special interest to women and minorities. Wrote speeches on matters of interest to women and minorities.

MEDIA AND PUBLIC SPEAKING EXPERIENCE:

Quoted and featured in newspapers on the subject of resume writing, small business management and Washington, D.C., employment and politically-related issues in the *Washington Post, The Baltimore Sun, Warfield's Business Weekly, Patuxent Publishing Company, FEW News & Views.*

Guest on radio and television talk show programs on subject of resume writing, career change strategies and federal employment processes.

Guest speaker, keynote speaker, panelist and workshop leader with various non-profit associations, libraries, colleges, educational classes (elementary through college), corporations, government agencies. Topics include resume writing, federal employment processes, career change, strategies for job search, small business management and managing family and business.

COMMUNITY SERVICE:

Vice President, Patapsco Woods Homeowners Association, Catonsville, MD, 1992 - present
Chairperson, Annual Picnic; Co-Chair, Landscaping Committee
Planned and led annual homeowner association meetings and monthly board meetings; wrote and published quarterly newsletter. Managed a budget of $25,000 per year for 195 homeowners.

Fundraiser, Project Cradle, University of Miami, Fl, Christmas, 1993
Successfully raised $7,000 and donations of Christmas presents for pediatric aids clinic for 300 patients.

Volunteer, Emergency Food Ministries, Baltimore, MD, 1993 - present
Design and produce promotional materials; recruit volunteers; publicize food ministry service in local area.

VOLUNTARY LEADERSHIP ROLES

Member, Board of Directors, 1990 to present
Voluntary Action Center of Fairfax County Area, Virginia
Director of non-profit corporation to promote, support and increase effective volunteerism. Rewrote long-range strategic plan; evaluated referral service. Chair, Program Evaluation Committee; Member, Long-Range Planning Committee.

President/Trustee, 1983 to present
The McLean Orchestra, McLean, Virginia
Interim Executive Director (1990); President and Board Member since 1983. Administered 17-member board; promoted fundraising for $180,000 budget; developed long-range planning strategies; chaired numerous committees. Conducted staff assessment, developed job descriptions, recruited and hired permanent Executive Director. Founded community string ensemble for young musicians; obtained grant and oversaw promotion and marketing.

Member, Association of Volunteer Administrators, McLean, VA, 1989 - present

Step 5

WORK EXPERIENCE

❑ Give the following information for your paid and unpaid work experience related to the job for which you are applying. *(Do not send job descriptions.)*

> Job title *(include series and grade if Federal job)*
>
> Duties and accomplishments
>
> Supervisor's name and phone number
>
> Starting and ending dates *(month and year)*
>
> Hours per week
>
> Salary

❑ Indicate if we may contact your current supervisor.

Converting Your Lengthy SF-171 Job Description Into Succinct Federal Resume Language

I used to describe the old SF-171 to my clients as "a combination of a resume, a legal brief, and a college take-home exam." A first-rate SF-171 job description block needed not only to include information relevant to the position for which you were applying, but also information that simply described your job fully. Because many federal job applicants are not sure of the types of jobs they will apply for, we often took the "kitchen sink" approach—throw it all in on the grounds that some of it will be relevant. Since there was no penalty for excessive length, this was a good strategic approach.

> The new federal resume approach has the advantage of less actual writing. In reality, it forces you to focus on your goals, your relevant experience, and your ability to communicate that experience powerfully and clearly.

30

Mark Twain was once asked how long it would take him to prepare a three-hour lecture. "About a day," he replied. "How about preparing a 30-minute speech?" the questioner asked. "Oh, that would take me at least a week," Twain said. You may discover that writing a first-rate federal resume job description takes far more effort and time than the old "kitchen sink" approach.

Step 1: Get Organized

The first step in preparing a federal resume (or any employment document, for that matter) is to get all your paperwork together. Find your old SF-171 forms, private sector resumes, copies of notices of personnel action, your job descriptions, performance evaluations, letters of commendation and appreciation, details of major projects, military records, and anything else that is relevant. Clean off your desk and lay out the information in stacks. Take the time to read it all, making notes on a legal pad as you go.

Step 2: Plan

George Bernard Shaw once said, "I have made an international reputation merely by taking some time to think twice a month. Most people never take any time at all." Take time to think before you write. What should you think about?

Your Goals:

People with clear occupational goals who fall into easy categories have a tactical advantage in seeking federal employment. If you are an accountant, a computer programmer, an electrical engineer, or a secretary, you have skills that can be defined and compared with others in an objective manner.

> A great place to start your research is in the Government Printing Office (GPO). <u>The United States Government Manual</u> is a good guideline and resource for agencies and programs.

If you are a management or program analyst, a project leader, or fit in the "301" occupational series code (Miscellaneous Administrative and Program positions...also called the "lazy classifier's series"), you have a greater challenge ahead of you. You must work harder to identify your target positions and show how you satisfy the requirements. You may need to write more than one version of your federal resume—but not a separate version for every job (that way lies madness...!)

If you fall into the latter group, should you change your goals or give up? Not at all. It's no favor to you or your employer to get a job you're not well suited for or don't like. You will have to work a little bit harder on your resume, that's all.

Your Targets:

Identify areas in the federal government where you would like to work. You may be moving from position to position within your own agency, or trying to get in for the first time. Distinguish yourself from the competition by doing your homework. Call the Public Information Office in target agencies to request information.

If you are willing to work harder than the average person, and really want an edge, get a copy of the federal budget. This hefty tome is packed with information, although it's hard to extract. Among the resources in the budget is a table of expected employment levels in agencies and programs. You can discover which agencies are getting more people, and which are scheduled for major shrinking.

What if you are just answering a specific announcement or two? You may not need to do all this research, but it may benefit you anyway. You will be far more impressive on an interview if you have done your homework on the mission, programs, and future of an agency.

> Your federal resume first must help the personnel staffing specialist determine your relative qualifications.

Your Audience:

In the private sector, the audience for a resume is the hiring official. Personnel may do some preliminary screening, but that is all. The hiring official hires whomever she or he wishes, and personnel simply processes the paper-work. In the federal government, the personnel function is much more important. Since the founding of the Civil Service and the overturning of the "spoils system," a fundamental goal of the federal personnel process is to ensure that the most qualified candidate is selected, and that political and personal influences on the process are minimized, at least for so-called "statutory" positions. You must take seriously the role of personnel in the process, and realize that your federal resume must meet the needs of different audiences.

Personnel will determine that your stated qualifications fit the formal requirements of the position to classify you as "qualified." Depending on the number of qualified applicants, they will normally perform a deeper evaluation to select the "best qualified" candidates. Only the best qualified candidates are forwarded to the selecting official (your potential supervisor-to-be). The selecting official has some discretion in choosing the candidate she or he likes best from among the best qualified. Do not assume the staffing specialist is an expert in your career field, although many are quite knowledgeable. Help them understand and interpret your qualifications. Make their job easier and you will get more benefit of the doubt. Confuse or obscure your qualifications, and you will earn a lower score than your experience otherwise merits.

For the hiring official, think positively. When the hiring official sees your federal resume, it is in a folder along with resumes from other highly qualified candidates. The hiring official does not normally have to interview all highly qualified candidates. Who gets interviewed? Qualifications are important, of course. But so is the "feel" the hiring official gets from the resume. Is he a positive person? Is he hard-working? Will I like him? Will she fit my team? Is she going to be a threat to my job? You deal with these issues in a resume by watching the tone of what you write. Show your final version to friends and ask them how they feel about the person on that piece of paper.

Step 3: Research the Qualification Standards

You may already have the specific announcement in front of you. You still should do your homework about the agency, and you may also want to go one step further: visit your local Federal Agency Personnel Office or Federal Job Information Center to find the *Qualifications Standards Operating Manual* (formerly called the X-118). The qualification standards are intended to identify applicants who are likely to perform successfully on the job, and screen out those who are unlikely to do so. The "qualification standards" list basic descriptions of each major government position, which can help you write your federal resume and KSAs.

The occupational series code is the number between the pay plan ("GS") and the grade ("-11"), written "GS-334-11" for a Computer Specialist, Grade 11.

A major federal job series is the "301" (which is the code for "Miscellaneous Administration and Program.") Position titles in the 300 series include:

> *The Qualification Standards for General Schedule Positions* (formerly the X-118) contain qualification standards established by OPM for General Schedule (GS) positions in the federal government. This publication is available at a federal personnel office or a Federal Job Information Center.
>
> (see page 207 in Appendix for list of occupational series)

- Computer Specialist, GS-334
- Program Management, GS-340
- Administrative Officer, GS-341
- Management and Program Analysis, GS-343
- Logistics Management, GS-346
- Equal Opportunity Compliance, GS-346

WARNING: Occupational series codes ending in "01" are called "general" codes. The "301" series is "General Miscellaneous Administration and Program." The Qualifications Standards are of less help in "01" and especially "301," which is a catch-all for everything not in its own standard.

The position standards are written to assist personnel professionals first in classifying jobs, and second, in determining grade level. One Computer Specialist GS-334 designs local area computer networks for offices such as the Accounting Branch of a small agency. Another Computer Specialist GS-334 designs local area computer networks for all the scattered HHS offices in the Washington, D.C. metropolitan area. Both positions have similar technical requirements; however, one is a much bigger job and consequently should have a higher pay rate.

When you are describing your experience, a personnel staffing specialist may look for information to help determine whether what you do is equivalent to a GS-11 or GS-13 position. This is vital when coming into the federal government from outside. Even if you are already a graded Civil Servant in the proper series, you can still use this information. Perhaps you have done project work that is above your official grade level. This could help persuade a staffing specialist to put you among the best qualified candidates.

The final reason to check the official standards is for key words. Remember, some personnel staffing specialists are highly knowledgeable about your field they process applications all the time, but you shouldn't rely on this. Many staffing specialists look at positions falling in many different codes. They can't be experts on everything. If you have used the same language as the official standards for your series, it's easier for the staffing specialist to determine that you do possess the specific experience.

Step 4: Draft

Now you are ready to write. Get out a pad and pencil or boot up your word processor. We recommend doing a draft first, letting it cool at least overnight, then polishing it up.

Steve McGarry, an official with the OPM, told us that the first goal of the federal resume is simply to see that the candidate meets the basic qualifications for the vacancy announcement (e.g., academic degrees, years of experience, areas of expertise, technical capabilities). The actual KSAs tell if they are qualified to perform the specific position. The federal resume is more of a technical document with information. Personnel specialists want the hard facts—not a life story—that allow them to screen the resume quickly and see basic qualifications.

That is the goal. The first step in writing should be to get it all down on paper. A famous newspaper editor told a young reporter, "Don't put more fire into your work. Put more of your work into the fire." Write it all, go into excruciating depth, and cut from there. Your first draft should be a "life story" approach, which we will edit profusely in the next 10 pages. Write everything. *Just don't send it out!*

For each job, starting with the most recent and working back, write the following:

Job Title, (Series/Grade if federal), Computer Specialist GS-334-11
Employer, Internal Revenue Service
Address/City/State, Washington, DC 20037

Dates: (Month/Year to Month/Year or "Present") June 1991 to present

Supervisor's Name/Phone Number: Harry Singer, (202) 555-3131

Salary: $35,585

> Provide this information for each position.

Basically What The Job Was:
Write like you speak, at least in this draft. You might write something like this:

> I set up local area networks for offices in IRS headquarters.

Add some detail. Explain this as if you were writing for a total stranger.

> I set up local area networks for offices in IRS headquarters. Basically, my boss tells me which department is next. I go to the department and do a survey. I talk to the department head and others. I draw a map of the office and look at how I can run wires. I figure out when to do this so it won't interrupt anybody. Then I come in and actually run the wires and plug them in. I install the network software, and sometimes put in a server. Then I debug it and help people with their technical questions as they get used to it. I also answer telephone calls and sometimes go troubleshoot systems I put in previously.

Did you leave out any steps? Imagine your daily routine. For now, write it all down. We'll edit later.

I set up local area networks for offices in IRS headquarters. Basically, my boss tells me which department is next. I go to the department and do a survey. I talk to the department head and others. I draw a map of the office and look at how I can run wires. **I write up the work order and requisitions to buy the hardware and software.** I figure out when to do this so it won't interrupt anybody. Then I come in and actually run the wires and plug them in. **I have to go through ceilings, drill through walls, and do other work.** I install the network software, and sometimes put in a server. Then I debug it and help people with their technical questions as they get used to it. I also answer telephone calls and sometimes go troubleshoot systems I put in previously.

Next, quantify everything. Put in numbers that help flesh out the picture. How many, how big, how much?

I set up **1-2** local area networks **per month** for offices in IRS headquarters. Basically, my boss tells me which department is next. I go to the department and do a survey. I talk to the department head and others. I draw a map of the office and look at how I can run wires. **The offices usually have 15-20 workstations.** I write up the work order and requisitions to buy the hardware and software. **The cost of a project is normally $10-$15,000.** I figure out when to do this so it won't interrupt anybody. Then I come in and actually run the wires and plug them in. I have to go through ceilings, drill through walls, and do other work. I install the network software, and sometimes put in a server. Then I debug it and help people with their technical questions as they get used to it. I also answer **5-10** telephone calls **per day** and sometimes troubleshoot systems I put in previously (**usually at least once a week**).

We have now got a pretty good general description. Let's look for accomplishments. Are there any jobs you've done that are special? Problems you solved? Awards or recognition you received?

I set up 1-2 local area networks per month for offices in IRS headquarters. Basically, my boss tells me which department is next. I go to the department and do a survey. I talk to the department head and others. I draw a map of the office and look at how I can run wires. The offices usually have 15-20 workstations. I write up the work order and requisitions to buy the hardware and software. The cost of a project is normally $10-$15,000. I figure out when to do this so it won't interrupt anybody. Then I come in and actually run the wires and plug them in. I have to go through ceilings, drill through walls, and do other work. I install the network software, and sometimes put in a server. Then I debug it and help people with their technical questions as they get used to it. I also answer 5-10 telephone calls per day and sometimes go troubleshoot systems I put it previously (usually at least once a week).

The LAN for the Office of the General Counsel earned me a Letter of Commendation. I had to take on this project on a rush basis, because they had gotten funding to tie into the Tax Court database. The lawyers were working all hours and I had to work unusual shifts to fit in the work. They changed requirements on me six different times, and also added four new lawyers, each of whom had to be added to the network. I had to ensure compatibility with non-IRS software, debug a particular mess in one in-house software package, and deal with management problems. In spite of everything, I met a ridiculous deadline and came really close on the budget. The IRS General Counsel made sure I got a letter, saying "I wish all our support people had your positive attitude."

We want to make sure that we have addressed the various questions that personnel staffing specialists may have. To do that, we use a concept called the Factor Evaluation System (FES). The FES is used by OPM to assign grades to a position by using official classification standards. The nine FES factors are useful to you because they form a handy and logical checklist to ensure your job descriptions are effective and persuasive.

The FES is a technique for comparing apples to oranges. How do we determine that an accountant and a program analyst are both GS-12 positions? We do that by realizing that every position, regardless of subject, possesses the following common factors:

Factor 1.

Knowledge Required by the Position: What level of knowledge is required? Knowledge can be general ("a general knowledge of agency policies concerning computer procurement") or specific ("a detailed knowledge of Novell and Token Ring network design and implementation sufficient to design and install a network of up to 20 nodes with a central server"). This is a powerful factor, and explains why an entry-level lawyer is of a higher grade than an extremely experienced secretary, for example. Make sure you explain the level of knowledge required.

I set up 1-2 local area networks per month for offices in IRS headquarters. Basically, my boss tells me which department is next. I go to the department and do a survey.

To do this job, I need to know LAN systems in great detail, especially Token Ring. I know how to determine hardware and software requirements on my own, how to plan an installation start-to-finish, how to troubleshoot almost all technical problems, and how to do the actual work of installation. I also have to know agency policies on ADP to advise offices on what I can and can't do, and how people elsewhere are solving specific problems so I can do the same. I have to know about IRS and office missions and goals to do the work. I have to know how to implement customized solutions based on the technology.

The Factor Evaluation System (FES) is used by OPM to assign grades to a position by using the official classification standards.

The FES Criteria for each position:

1. Knowledge required for the position

2. Supervisory controls

3. Guidelines

4. Complexity

5. Scope and effect

6. Personal contacts

7. Purpose of contacts

8. Physical demands

9. Work environment

Factor 2.

Supervisory Controls: Everything else being equal, a person who has to check with the boss before spending $25 is of a lower grade than a person who gets a general assignment and runs with it. While job description language may go into a lot of detail, do not over-emphasize this area in your writing. A few key words ("substantial independence," "apply own judgment," "general guidance," "independently plan and execute") are all you need in your descriptive copy.

I set up 1-2 local area networks per month for offices in IRS headquarters. Basically, my boss tells me which department is next, **and I do the rest of the work independently, calling only if I run into a policy issue.**

Factor 3.

Guidelines: If you can look up the answers to all your problems in a book, you can not be handling very complicated problems. The availability and applicability of guidelines to your specific situation is another determining factor. What is there for you to use? General agency guidelines, detailed technical manuals, vendor instructions? Are the guidelines current, or are they inadequate and frequently inapplicable? Do you need to apply a lot of independent judgment and make difficult decisions?

I set up 1-2 local area networks per month for offices in IRS headquarters. Basically, my boss tells me which department is next, and I do the rest of the work independently, calling only if I run into a policy issue. The policies are pretty general and often don't apply to my situations. In most cases, I make my own decision unless there is a lot of money at stake or there is an issue of system compatibility that extends outside my work. I go to the department and do a survey. I talk to the ...

... customized solutions based on the technology.

There is quite a lot of technical documentation available. Most of the time I can find an answer to technical issues by doing research, but computer documentation is hard to read, badly indexed, and subject to interpretation. When I find an answer, I often have to use my judgment in deciding just how I'm going to make it work in the real world. Frequently, when I do the work, I end up creating my own answers.

The LAN for the Office of the General Counsel earned me a ...

39

Factor 4.

Complexity: What factors make this work complex, or is it really a simple job? Remember, simple and complex are in the eyes of the beholder. If you have 15 years' experience in highly technical work, hold a Ph.D., and are generally considered a national expert, you may think the problems and situations in your work are simple indeed. An outsider, comparing your work to that of other people, would conclude that your job was highly complex. Do not sell yourself short.

Some of your complexity issues are dealt with in knowledge and guidelines. Specific complexity issues include having to make decisions with insufficient data, dealing with competing interests and demands, changing of basic systems, responding to Congressional or public controversy or pressure, etc. Complexity can relate to office politics (and often does!), but you have to be careful in choosing your words.

... department head and others. **Often, I find that people in the department have strong and conflicting ideas about what they want and need. Sometimes, there is a lot of resistance about installing a LAN at all.**

The offices usually have 15-20 workstations. **They are older offices and often have problems taking the new wiring.** I write up the work order and requisitions to ...

... answers. **Every project I've ever done has posed at least a couple of unique technical challenges that made me go outside the standard procedures.**

Tax Court database. *(NOTE: All of this is complexity information, even though it was already in your copy.)* **The lawyers were working all hours and I had to work unusual shifts to fit in the work. They changed requirements on me six different times, and also added four new lawyers, each of whom had to be added to the network. I had to ensure compatibility with non-IRS software, debug a particular mess in one in-house software package, and deal with management problems. In spite of everything, I met a ridiculous deadline and came really close on the budget.**

Factor 5.

Scope and Effect: Scope and effect tell us how vast the work is. Our current situation involves 15-20 workstations in a single office. Someone else might do smaller offices; another might do far larger projects. Much of this information we have already described, so we highlight it.

I set up 1-2 local area networks per month **for offices in IRS headquarters.** Basically, my boss tells me which ...

The offices usually have 15-20 workstations. They ...

... hardware and software. **The cost of a project is normally $10,000-$15,000. I figure out when to do this so it won't interrupt anybody. Then I come in and actually run the wires and plug them in. I have to go through ceilings, drill through walls, and do other work. I install the network software, and sometimes put in a server. Then I debug it and help people with their technical questions as they get used to it. I also answer 5-10 telephone calls per day and sometimes go troubleshoot systems I put it previously (usually at least once a week).**

Factors 6 and 7.

Personal Contacts/Purpose of Contacts: These are really two different factors. The level of your work contacts tells us something about your grade. A secretary for a Branch Chief is a lower grade than the secretary for a Cabinet Secretary, because the ability to work effectively with VIPs is a specialized job skill. For most people, the purpose of contacts is more important. Who you talk with and what you talk about are both important.

I go to the department and do a survey. **I talk to the department head and others, usually working with branch chiefs (GS-13 and higher), and sometimes with senior agency officials at the SES level, listening to their objectives, offering technical solutions and options, and helping them gain familiarity and comfort with the new technology. Often, I find that people in the department have strong and conflicting ideas about what they want and need. Sometimes, there is a lot of resistance about installing a LAN at all. I have to deal with this in a diplomatic manner.**

41

... and sometimes put in a server. Then I debug it and **help people with their technical questions as they get used to it. I also answer 5-10 telephone calls per day from people at all grade levels in numerous departments** and troubleshoot systems ...

... and **deal with management problems such as lawyers trying to tell me how to program and wanting last-minute changes based on something they'd read in a magazine.** In spite of everything, I met...

The IRS General Counsel made sure I got a letter, saying "I wish all our support people had your positive attitude."

Factors 8 and 9.

Physical Demands/Work Environment:
Again, we lump together these two factors, because they do not apply to the majority of office positions. If there are unusual physical demands or the work environment is hazardous, this can increase your grade if the demands and environment are relevant to your new position. For most applications, ignore this.

Congratulations! You have now completed a first draft. It's too long and not yet written as powerfully as we want, but it's the first step. Take the rest of the day off and start again after your draft has had a chance to cool down.

Step 5: Rewrite

Your draft copy resembles an old-fashioned SF-171 experience block. If we were doing an SF-171, we would edit and clean up the copy and be finished. Remember that it takes more effort to write succinctly and clearly than to overwrite. Let's review the entire draft from our previous step.

> James Mitchener once said, "There are no great writers - only great rewriters."

I set up 1-2 local area networks per month for offices in IRS headquarters. Basically, my boss tells me which department is next, and I do the rest of the work independently, calling only if I run into a policy issue. The policies are pretty general and often don't apply to my situations. In most cases, I make my own decision unless there is a lot of money at stake or there is an issue of system compatibility that extends outside my work.

I go to the department and do a survey. I talk to the department head and others, usually working with branch chiefs (GS-13 and higher), and sometimes with senior agency officials at the SES level, listening to their objectives, offering technical solutions and options, and helping them gain familiarity and comfort with the new technology. Often, I find that people in the department have strong and conflicting ideas about what they want and need. Sometimes, there is a lot of resistance about installing a LAN at all. I have to deal with this in a diplomatic manner.

I draw a map of the office and look at how I can run wires. The offices usually have 15-20 workstations. They are older offices and often have problems taking the new wiring. I write up the work order and requisitions to buy the hardware and software. The cost of a project is normally $10-$15,000. I figure out when to do this so it won't interrupt anybody. Then I come in and actually run the wires and plug them in. I have to go through ceilings, drill through walls, and do other work. I install the network software, and sometimes put in a server. Then I debug it and help people with their technical questions as they get used to it. I also answer 5-10 telephone calls per day from people at all grade levels in numerous departments and sometimes go troubleshoot systems I put in previously (usually at least once a week).

To do this job, I need to know LAN systems in great detail, especially Token Ring. I know how to determine hardware and software requirements on my own, how to plan an installation start-to-finish, how to troubleshoot almost all technical problems, and how to do the actual work of installation. I also have to know agency policies on ADP to advise offices on what I can and can't do, and how people elsewhere are solving specific problems so I can do the same. I have to know about IRS and office missions and goals to do the work. I have to know how to customize solutions based on the technology.

43

There is quite a lot of technical documentation available. Most of the time I can find an answer to technical issues by doing research, but computer documentation is hard to read, badly indexed, and subject to interpretation. When I find an answer, I often have to use my judgment in deciding just how I'm going to make it work in the real world. Frequently, when I do the work, I end up creating my own answers. Every project I've ever done has posed at least a couple of unique technical challenges that made me go outside the standard procedures.

The LAN for the Office of the General Counsel earned me a Letter of Commendation. I had to take on this project on a rush basis, because they had gotten funding to tie into the Tax Court database. The lawyers were working all hours and I had to work unusual shifts to fit in the work. They changed requirements on me six different times, and also added four new lawyers, each of whom had to be added to the network. I had to ensure compatibility with non-IRS software, debug a particular mess in one in-house software package, and deal with management problems such as lawyers trying to tell me how to program and wanting last-minute changes based on something they'd read in a magazine. In spite of everything, I met a ridiculous deadline and came really close on the budget.

The IRS General Counsel made sure I got a letter, saying "I wish all our support people had your positive attitude."

While this is too long, it is at least complete. In cutting this down to size, remember that we have two objectives: making sure that the personnel staffing specialist can easily determine our qualifications, and persuading the hiring official to interview us.

We use a "bulleted format" for this purpose. Our job description begins with a general overview paragraph (1-2 sentences) to describe the work, then follows with a series of "bullet points," each helping to make the case for our qualifications. Remember to anchor your copy in the FES. You need not address each FES factor, only those that are key to your goals.

Let's try it.

Computer Specialist   *June 1991-present*
INTERNAL REVENUE SERVICE, Washington, D.C.

Establish 1-2 local area networks per month for offices in IRS headquarters, with independent responsibility for planning and executing projects of significant technical complexity, ranging from 15-20 workstations with budgets up to $15,000.

- Working directly with operating department heads, consult with them on management needs and technical solutions using cutting-edge PC technology.

- Independently solve complex technical problems in network implementation, normally not covered in manuals or published sources, using strong skills and good judgment to respond to unique technical challenges.

- Advise on sensitive management issues including technology resistance and agency policies regarding ADP, with diplomatic and interpersonal skills.

- Personally perform complex technical installations including running wires through older facilities, linking workstations of numerous brands and capabilities, installing software, and debugging setups.

- Ensure that department work continues uninterrupted during the installation process.

- Troubleshoot the full range of technical issues related to LAN installations by telephone and in person.

- Recognized as technical authority on Token Ring network; maintain high level of knowledge and skill relating to both technical and policy/agency issues.

Special Project/Accomplishment

- Working around the clock during a period of staff expansion and major projects, ensured compatibility of network with non-IRS software, debugged a non-LAN system to make it work, and dealt with a continual stream of last-minute change requests.

- Achieved on-schedule delivery and kept add-on requirements to minimal additional costs.

- Received a Letter of Commendation for successfully completing an interagency linking system for a LAN in the Office of the General Counsel, IRS. The General Counsel wrote, "I wish all our support people had your positive attitude."

Step 6: Edit

Our rewrite covers the critical points, but it is a bit too long. Let's consolidate a few bullet points, sweat out some extra words, and reduce its size.

Computer Specialist   *June 1991-present*
INTERNAL REVENUE SERVICE, WASHINGTON, D.C.

Establish 1-2 local area networks per month for IRS headquarters offices. Independently plan and execute projects of significant technical complexity, ranging up to 20 workstations with budgets up to $15,000.

- Consult with senior department heads on management needs and cutting-edge technical solutions. Advise on sensitive management issues including technology resistance and agency ADP policies, with diplomatic and interpersonal skills.

- Independently solve complex technical problems in network implementation, normally not covered in manuals or published sources, using strong skills and good judgment to respond to unique technical challenges.

- Personally perform complex technical installations including running wires through older facilities, linking workstations of numerous brands and capabilities, installing software, and debugging setups.

- Troubleshoot the full range of technical issues related to LAN installations by telephone and in person. Recognized as technical authority on Token Ring network; maintain high level of knowledge and skill relating to both technical and policy/agency issues.

Special Project/Accomplishment

- Working around the clock during a period of staff expansion and major projects, ensured compatibility of network with non-IRS software, debugged a non-LAN system to make it work, and dealt with a continual stream of last-minute change requests.
- Received a Letter of Commendation for successfully completing on-schedule an interagency linking system for a LAN in the Office of the General Counsel, IRS. The General Counsel wrote, "I wish all our support people had your positive attitude."

Better. A few of our points were not necessary, and others could be consolidated. As a final step, we'll use the power of the computer to shrink the actual size of the sample without cutting any more words. Appearance counts!

Computer Specialist   *June 1991-present*
INTERNAL REVENUE SERVICE, Washington, DC

Establish 1-2 local area networks per month for IRS headquarters offices. Independently plan and execute projects of significant technical complexity, ranging up to 20 workstations and budgets up to $15,000.

- Consult with senior department heads on management needs and cutting-edge technical solutions. Advise on sensitive management issues including technology resistance and agency ADP policies, with diplomatic and interpersonal skills.

- Independently solve complex technical problems in network implementation, normally not covered in manuals or published sources, using strong skills and good judgment to respond to unique technical challenges.

- Personally perform complex technical installations including running wires through older facilities, linking workstations of numerous brands and capabilities, installing software, and debugging setups.

- Troubleshoot the full range of technical issues related to LAN installations by telephone and in person. Recognized as technical authority on Token Ring network; maintain high level of knowledge and skill relating to both technical and policy/agency issues.

Special Project/Accomplishment

- Working around the clock during a period of staff expansion and major projects, ensured compatibility of network with non-IRS software, debugged a non-LAN system to make it work, and dealt with a continual stream of last-minute change requests.

- Received a Letter of Commendation for successfully completing on-schedule an interagency linking system for a LAN in the Office of the General Counsel, IRS. The General Counsel wrote, "I wish all our support people had your positive attitude."

A good federal resume can be three or four pages in length, as opposed to a traditional private-sector resume, which seldom exceeds two pages. Remember that previous positions will be described in progressively less detail.

Special Issues

What if your best job is not your most recent job?

The traditional career path, in which each subsequent position is better than its predecessor, does not describe as many people as it used to. When this happens, put the primary effort into your most *relevant* job, not your most *recent*.

What if you are applying to jobs in lots of different series?

Do you need to rewrite the federal resume each time? In general, one properly thought-out federal resume will work for just about every job for which you apply. I once had a client who had two career ideas: a spy for the CIA or a career in military music. If your career goals are that diverse, write two (or more) federal resumes, each with the appropriate focus. For most people, however, one is sufficient.

> Remember, the KSAs are the primary opportunity you have to tailor your background to the specific position.

Tip! If you are working on computer, and you do have different goals, write a few different approaches to your most recent or relevant jobs and paste and print each time. Do not do this unless you see a strong need; you can spend your time better in the job hunt by uncovering more job leads.

What about really old jobs? As you move back in your career, write less and less about each position. Jobs more than 10 years old can be summarized, thus: "Previous experience includes entry-level computer programming jobs with Smith Corp. and various part-time positions during high school and college." Put that at the end of your resume.

Examples

EEO Specialist GS-260-9. Target, GS-11, General Personnel or Management

<u>**OLD SF-171 COPY**</u>

Scope of Responsibility

As an **Equal Employment Opportunity Specialist** with the Federal Trade Commission, provide guidance and oversight to eleven EEO counselors in serving a 2,700-person staff. Extensive responsibility in training, program development and implementation, budget, and reporting.

Specific Duties, Responsibilities, and Accomplishments

- <u>Legal and Regulatory Issues</u>: Analyze and interpret applicable laws, regulations and decision impacting the EEO work environment.

  — Identify new issues and developments in EEO, personnel and labor law.

  — Interpret Equal Employment Opportunity Commission and Federal Trade Commission policies as they relate to EEO and Affirmative Action programs.

  — Provide technical, procedural and legal guidance to counselors on EEO complaint processing issues.

- <u>Program Development and Implementation</u>: Conduct research, program development, program implementation, and training activities.

  — Appointed to coordinate the development of the agency's upward mobility program. Developed comprehensive program package, including format, procedures, and policy objectives. Designed recruitment strategies to increase the participation of women and minorities in career development programs. This key effort has been advanced substantially during this period.

  — Developed Auxiliary Orientation Program for New Employees on career development, EEO, and related issues.

  — Prepare and deliver briefings and presentations to man-

49

agers, employees and labor unions on Affirmative Action Program requirements and progress.

— Consult with managers in goal-setting and implementation of Affirmative Action Program objectives.

— Conduct statistical analyses of workforce data and prepare a variety of reports.

• <u>Casework</u>: Oversee and analyze work of EEO Counselors.

— Review all reports from EEO Counselors for timeliness, quality and accuracy of information, and clarity; edit and correct reports as necessary.

  Brief supervisors on issues addressed in reports; develop suggestions and effect settlements as appropriate.

— Analyze Reports of Investigation and official records. Write Proposed Dispositions and draft Final Agency Decisions (which are normally upheld), and support findings with appropriate documentation.

New Federal Resume

EEO Specialist GS-260-9   *11/94 to present*

FEDERAL TRADE COMMISSION, Washington, DC

Manage agency-wide EEO effort. Train and supervise eleven EEO counselors in serving a 2,700-person staff. Extensive responsibility in training, program development and implementation, budget, and reporting.

- Analyze and interpret laws, regulations and policies impacting the EEO work environment. Identify new issues and developments in EEO, personnel and labor law. Consult with key agency managers.

- Interpret policies and provide technical, procedural and legal guidance to counselors on EEO complaint processing issues. Conduct research, program development, program implementation, and training activities.

- Brief and advise managers, employers, and labor unions on EEO and Affirmative Action issues. Deliver numerous presentations agency-wide. Research and author statistical and compliance reports.

- Analyze Reports of Investigation and official records. Write Proposed Dispositions and draft Final Agency Decisions (which are normally upheld), and support findings with appropriate documentation.

Key Accomplishments

- Developed agency upward mobility program. Developed comprehensive program package; designed recruitment strategies; achieved measurable results. Developed orientation for new employees on career development, EEO, and related issues.

Logistics Management Specialist GS-346-12. Target, Logistics or Contracting Position, GS-13

OLD SF-171 COPY

SCOPE OF RESPONSIBILITY

Manage and administer a $28 million logistics support contract for telecommunications equipment, serving as Contracting Officer's Technical Representative (COTR), with broad responsibility for developing logistics support strategies, concepts and schedules for overall Integrated Logistics Support (ILS) considerations. Review and analyze pricing data for peculiar support equipment to render technical opinions on cost and necessity. Provide technical support to contract modifications with large potential dollar impact. Chair conferences and meetings; prepare and deliver briefings; interface with contractor management; ensure quality and contract performance.

SPECIFIC DUTIES AND RESPONSIBILITIES

- Conduct complex and advanced logistics planning, which involves a multidisciplinary approach impacting on supply, procurement, contracting, accounting, and other activities. Coordinate and integrate these diverse program elements to ensure that full ILS support is provided.

- Manage and coordinate government and contractor efforts for this $28 million program to provide ILS for field telecommunications equipment. Serving as COTR, interface directly with contractors and government officials in all the functional activities impacted by the program. Ensure that program meets system maintenance, technical data, support equipment, supply support, and related goals and objectives.

- Hold a leadership role in all activities related to the contract. Participate in program management reviews, source selections, maintenance demonstrations and technical reviews. Chair logistics guidance conferences, provisioning conferences, and logistics support record reviews.

- Conduct financial analysis and review of pricing data for support equipment. Develop and render technical opinions on man-hours and other cost elements. Provide technical support and research in complex contract modification negotiations involving significant dollar-cost increases and changes to scope of work.

ACCOMPLISHMENTS

- Developed and presented reports and briefings to higher management, including a Logistics Management Review, Program Management Responsibility Transfer (PMRT) document to transfer program logistics responsibilities, and other materials.

- Wrote the logistics section of a production statement of work. Wrote the ILS Support Plan for telecommunications equipment. Expedited the response to requests and inquiries from contractors and government activities. Analyzed LSA documents as part of an LSAR review concerning maintenance tasking, identification of parts and support equipment, and achievement of contractual logistics objectives.

- Reviewed Support Equipment Documents (SED) to ensure test equipment capabilities met support requirements without incurring increased life-cycle cost or special procedures. Validated the accuracy of technical manuals by field observation of technical performance. Updated the Air Force Logistics Management Information System (ALMIS) database.

- On very short notice, organized a conference at a contractor facility that resulted in the identification of problems and development of remedies, thus ensuring smooth transition from development to production of telecommunications equipment.

New Federal Resume

Logistics Management Specialist GS-346-12   *8/92 to present*
DEFENSE MAPPING AGENCY, Washington, DC

Manage and administer a $28 million logistics support contract for
telecommunications equipment.

- Conduct complex and advanced logistics planning, which involves a
  multidisciplinary approach impacting on supply, procurement,
  contracting, accounting, and other activities.

- Manage and coordinate government and contractor efforts for this
  $28 million program to provide for field telecommunications
  equipment, serving as COTR.

- Chair or facilitate management reviews, source selections,
  maintenance demonstrations, technical reviews, and logistics
  support meetings.

- Conduct financial analysis and review of pricing data for support
  equipment. Render technical opinions. Advise in complex contract
  negotiations involving significant cost increases and changes to
  scope.

ACCOMPLISHMENTS

- Ensured test equipment capabilities met support requirements
  without incurring increased life-cycle cost. Validated the accuracy of
  technical manuals. Updated the Air Force ALMIS database.
  Organized a contractor conference on short notice to ensure smooth
  transition from development to production.

Supervisory Communications Specialist GM-393-14. Target, GM-15 or SES

<u>OLD SF-171 COPY</u>

SCOPE OF RESPONSIBILITY

Appointed <u>Acting Director, U. S. FTS2000 Service Oversight Center</u> (SOC-B), with direct management responsibility for creating this office and associated policies and programs in the management of the FTS2000 Federal telecommunications network contract, covering the total aspect of all telecommunications services provided by GSA to all Federal agencies on a nationwide basis, described by GSA officials as *"unprecedented in the Federal government in terms of scope and responsibility."* Received <u>outstanding performance ratings and bonus</u> for each rating period.

Specific Duties and Responsibilities

<u>Transition Management/Creation of the Center</u>

- Administered the development, staffing, organization and creation of the entire SOC, involving over 70 employees in grades ranging from GS-2 through GS/GM-14, through an organizational structure of subordinate divisions and branches, with an annual budget of $20 million and responsibility for a contract totalling $300 million.

- Coordinated the transition from the existing FTS network to the new range of FTS2000 services, including switched voice service, switched data service, switched digital integrated service, packet switched data, video transmission service and dedicated transmission service.

- Conducted extensive study and analysis of policy and program issues, needs and alternatives relating to the organizational and administrative requirements to accomplish a smooth transition and to implement FTS2000 management and oversight functions.

- Managed and directed the staffing of the center, including review, evaluation, interviewing, and selection of personnel. Initiated training for all personnel to ensure ability to perform their assigned technical, administrative, and contract management functions.

- Developed a network of agency agreements, designated agency representative (DAR) officials, and service ordering and acceptance programs for FTS2000. Developed and implemented billing management interfaces and procedures to ensure accurate information for verification of contractor invoices.

- Managed the technical implementation and conversion from FTS to FTS2000 to ensure conversion completion accuracy and schedule adherence. Verified and accepted transitioned service delivery points after each cutover phase.

- Serve as <u>Contracting Officer's Technical Representative</u> (COTR) for the FTS2000 contract. Managed and directed facilities test and acceptance activities; ensured accurate technical procedures and full compliance of Center Support Systems with the FTS2000 contract.

- Conduct extensive liaison with senior officials of all Federal agencies and programs in the implementation of FTS2000; regularly coordinate with senior GSA program officials at SES and political appointee levels. Prepare and deliver reports, briefings, and other support materials.

<u>Technical/Contract Management</u>

- Provide executive technical direction and oversight to a system of unprecedented scope, complexity and responsibility, involving the full range of voice and data communications services for all Federal agencies.

- As COTR (previously, Alternate Contracting Officer's Technical Representative), oversee and monitor the performance of contractor's network management, system control, and customer service system. Train subordinates in the techniques of oversight management and contract compliance.

- Review and approve technical data, plans, and activaties submitted by the contractor, and examine their performance through independent sampling as well as through contractor-supplied data.

- Resolve complex agency/contractor problems impacting millions of dollars as well as the Federal government's ability to ensure continuity of critical telecommunications activities, involving a high level of technical insight as well as full knowledge of contract issues, regulations, and objectives.

- Conduct highly sophisticated, in-depth analysis of operational data (*i.e.,* customer service orders, troubles, complaints, emergency situations, historical and real-time technical performance measurements, transition and implementation progress, traffic reports) and administrative data (*i.e.,* service and feature pricing using an automated cast system, billing data by user/agency/service per call, classified and sensitive material protection compliance).

- Prepare reports, briefings and recommendations relating to contract performance, contract continuation, and contract changes; initiate decisions for change and improvement.

Administration/Operations Management

- Develop and implement objectives, policies and procedures for the administration of a 70+ person organization impacting the entire Federal telecommunications network and $3 billion.

- Initiate and develop operating budgets for the activity; ensure adherence to budget authority.

- Manage, supervise, and appraise subordinate staff, including senior executives, consisting of a variety of occupations including Computer and Communications Specialists, Electronics Engineers, and a variety of support personnel in grades GS-2 through GS/GM-14. Ensure compliance with EEO and affirmative action program goals and objectives.

- Direct the resolution of agency/contractor problems on both a technical and administrative basis, involving both the implementation of new services as well as continuity of currently-provided service; personally manage the most sensitive and difficult problems.

Accomplishments and Achievements

- Received <u>Outstanding Performance Appraisal</u> and <u>Cash Bonus</u> for *"exceptional managerial capability and knowledge of the FTS2000 program to accomplish his assigned tasks in an outstanding manner."*

- Successfully built center from the ground up into a functioning and effective organization.

- Achieved implementation of FTS2000 throughout the federal government.

New Federal Resume

Acting Director, FTS-2000 Center GM-14   *8/90 to present*
GENERAL SERVICES ADMINISTRATION, Washington, DC

Created this office, covering the total aspect of all telecommunications services provided by GSA to all federal agencies on a nationwide basis. Described by GSA officials as *"unprecedented in the federal government in terms of scope and responsibility."* Received **outstanding performance ratings and bonus** for each rating period. Commended for *"exceptional managerial capability and knowledge of the FTS-2000 program to accomplish his assigned tasks in an outstanding manner."*

- Administered the development, staffing, organization and creation of the center, involving over 70 employees, an annual budget of $20 million, and a contract totalling $300 million.

- Coordinated the transition from the existing FTS network to the new range of FTS-2000 services, with comprehensive responsibility for state-of-the-art technical issues of unprecedented scope, complexity, and responsibility. Managed all contract issues, verification, and acceptance, serving as Contracting Officer's Technical Representative (COTR).

- Conducted extensive liaison with senior officials of all federal agencies and programs on the most complex technical issues of communications and management.

- Resolved complex agency/contractor problems impacting millions of dollars as well as the federal government's telecommunications capabilities.

CHAPTER 3

WRITING AND FORMATTING THE IDEAL SCANNABLE RESUME

- Key Words
- Scannable Formats
- Areas of Expertise
- Qualifications & Skills
- Maximizing "Hits"

Writing and Formatting the Ideal Scannable Resume

Maximizing the computer's ability to "read" your resume

The latest technology in Federal Human Resources Management is the optical resume scanner. Here is how it works. Your resume is scanned into the computer as an image. Then OCR (optical character recognition) software looks at the image to distinguish every letter and number (character) and creates a text file (ASCII). Then artificial intelligence "reads" the text and extracts important information about you such as your name, address, phone number, work history, years of experience, education, and skills.

> **A scannable resume:**
>
> - Maximizes the computer's ability to "read" your resume.
> - Maximizes your ability to get "hits" (a hit is when one of your skills matches the computer search).

At the Naval Submarine Base Bangor in Silverdale, Wash., the personnel staff stack 50 applications in the scanner bin each night and return in the morning to the extracted data in five-page boxed-set format for each application. During the pilot program, the personnel staff spend the day verifying data and reviewing the performance of the scanner. Debbie Lee, Head of the Compensation & Recruitment Branch, is the director of this test site and she is amazed at how well the scanning system can pick up the skills (up to 80 skills can be notated in the data) and qualifications.

Jan Burchard, Project Director for the Project to Automate Staffing for Department of Defense, is directing four application scanning test sites at this time. Burchard is seeing successes and problems (mostly with applications) with the new process. Based on what is being received at the test sites, Burchard gives the following important tips for preparing a successful scannable application: 1) do not submit third or fourth generation copies; 2) make sure the type is straight on the page; 3) try not to fax your applications. When asked what happens if the application is not prepared with the right information, is poorly copied, is twisted or turned or has small type, Burchard simply says that the package is returned to the applicant (without human eyes reading the document) and the deadline is missed. Burchard is impressed with the software and when an applicant provides a well-written, clean, straight, targeted application presenting clear qualifications, the translation works and the applicant soars to the top of the database list.

Format

To maximize the computer's ability to read your resume, provide the cleanest original and use a standard style resume.

The computer will extract skills from many styles of resumes such as chronological (list and describe up to six jobs in order by date); achievement (describe achievements rather than job titles; functional (organize by skills rather than job titles); and combinations of resume types.

Tips for maximizing scannability:

- Use white or light colored 8-1/2 x 11 paper printed on one side only.

- Provide a laser printer original if possible, or high quality photocopy.

- Use standard typefaces such as Helvetica, Futura, Optima, Univers, Palatino, New Century Schoolbook, Times. Use 10 to 14 point type fonts except Times 10, which is too small to be easily read by the scanner.

- Use boldface and all capital letters for section headings.

- Avoid treatments such as italics, underline, shadows, and reverses.

- Avoid vertical and horizontal lines, graphics and boxes.

- Place your name at the top of the page on its own line. Also, place your name at the top of each continuing page.

- Use standard address format below your name.

- List each phone number on its own line.

> - Do not fold or staple.
> - Do not type on lines of the OF-612

Tips for maximizing "hits":

- Use enough key words to define your skills, experience, education, professional affiliations.

- Describe your experience with concrete words rather than vague descriptions.

- Use more than one page if necessary. The computer can easily handle multiple-page resumes and uses all of the information it extracts from your resume.

- Use jargon and acronyms specific to your industry (spell out the acronyms for human readers).

- Increase your list of key words by including specifics.

- Use common headings such as those outlined in Chapter 2 of this book.

- If you have extra space, describe your interpersonal traits and aptitudes. Key words could include: skilled in time management, organized, efficient, dependable, high energy, personable, leadership ability, sense of responsibility, good memory, handles pressure well, quality-oriented, responsive, dedicated, etc.

Tips:

- Some people may want to have two versions of their resume:

  One for the computer to read with a scannable format and detailed information.

  One for people to read - possibly with a creative layout, enhanced typography, and summarized information. Carry this one to the interview.

- When faxing, set the fax to "fine mode;" the recipient will receive a better quality copy.

"I see the software as a positive feature for continuing high quality service to the customer. Applications are being translated successfully and the software will be the salvation for both the applicants and the personnel staff."

Debbie Lee, Head, Scanning Project and Head of the Compensation & Recruitment Branch, Naval Submarine Base Bangor, Silverdale, WA.

This information was provided by Resumix Educational Services, developer of optical scanning software used in the federal government and corporate America.

Resumix Internet Address:
Http://www.resumix.com

Scannable Federal Resume

Michelle T. Ehrlich 222-22-2222   Page 2

Quality Control Reviewer/Health Claims Adjustor   Postmaster's Benefit Plan
1019 North Royal Street
Alexandria, Virginia 22314   September, 1981 - May, 1986
Supervisor: T. Michaelson (703) 676-7878
Starting Salary: 10,500 per year   Ending Salary: $18,500 per year

Analysis and Research of Medical Claims
Reviewed claims for medical, dental, and pharmaceutical expenses submitted by members of a major health insurance plan.
Analyzed forms for comp
fy claims. Conducted ad
Training of New Hires /
Conducted training progr
effective techniques for r
staff.

Previous experience includes co

HONORS AND AWARDS

Office Administration Aw
Citation and Monetary Av
Certificates of Commend
Nine consecutive annual

EDUCATION AND PROFESS

BA   No
          Ma

Recent Professio

Prince Georges C
University of the
Southeastern Univ
U.S.D.A. Graduat

Crestwood High

COMPUTER SKILLS

Financial Management System -
Data Base: Fo
Spreadsheets: Lo
Word Processing: We

LANGUAGE SKILLS   Sp

MICHELLE T. EHRLICH

7867 Thompson Street
Chevy Chase, Maryland 20785
(301) 778-8989

Social Security Number:	222-22-2222
Citizenship:	United States
Veteran's Status:	N/A
Federal Civilian Status:	Budget Analyst, GS-09/04
	Department of Consumer and Reulatory Affairs
	District of Columbia Government

PROFILE

Budget analyst with 8 yeas experience and an effective record for detecting deficiencies in program operations and devising strategies to recover costs. Meticulous attention to detail and thorough understanding of both Federal and District financial regulations and procedures. Effective developing and delivering training to enhance team approach to financial operations.

CURRENT EMPLOYMENT

Budget Analyst (DS-09/04)   Department of Consumer and Regulatory Affairs
District of Columbia government
614 H Street, NW, Room 1103, Washington, DC 20001   May, 1986 - Present
Current Supervisor: Mr. Michael Smith (202) 737-6868
Starting Salary: $17,000 per year   Current Salary: $29,616
This supervisor should not be contacted before an interview.

Budget Development
Collect, coordinate, and consolidate financial and accounting data to develop and administer the District of Columbia's consumer and regulatory programs and policies. Analyze operating programs' budget plans and estimates and evaluate changes to ensure consistency with legal requirements and program priorities. Develop projections and estimates from program records, and review programs' submissions for accuracy and sufficiency of justifications. Conduct cost-benefit analyses, assess program trade-offs, and propose alternative methods of funding to develop the agency's budget.

Budget Compliance
Receive, analyze, and recommend approval of modifications of budget execution documents on the basis of availability of funds and compliance with regulatory requirements. Review personnel actions authorized through appropriated, private, Federal, and other non-District revenue sources to ensure compliance with spending plans. Recommend disapproval or develop alternative proposals to ensure personnel actions comply with legal requirements. Train staff to ensure knowledge of procedures.

Establish and Monitor Financial Controls
Establish and monitor financial management controls and documentary procedures to maintain thorough and accurate records of apportionments and obligations. Monitor obligations and expenditures to ensure timely disbursment of funds and report variations in excess of funding expeditiously.
Significant Accomplishments:
- Documented deficient payments from the Insurance Fund Bureau to the Department of Consumer and Regulatory Affairs, recovering a $6 million payment.
- Conducted audit of the Uninsured Motorist Fund; results: $150,000 reimbursement.
- Established a system for collecting on bad checks and developed a profile of bad check writers for use within the Department.
- Proposed and secured implementation of a method for the Real Estate Commission to operate on interest generated by payments to the License Fund, reducing related District obligations.

CHAPTER 4

THE
FEDERAL
EMPLOYMENT
PROCESS

SEARCH

APPLICATION

RATING

SELECTION

HIRING

65

Tips from Federal Personnelists

In researching this book, we talked with numerous federal personnelists and staffing specialists. Their core advice was amazingly consistent. Here is their advice:

- Do not expect to apply for and get a job and move around as people often did formerly in federal service; with downsizing by attrition, many agencies are not hiring into vacant positions and people in good jobs are tending to stay in them longer.

- Honesty is the best policy — if you stretch the truth and get a job you are not really qualified for — or worse, don't really want — you may be stuck. Much better to wait longer for the right job.

- Do not be demoralized if you are finding your applications do not result in rapid hiring. Remember that federal jobs are scarce and will remain so for the foreseeable future. You may be perfectly well qualified in today's market and still not get hired. Think of alternative strategies.

- While the resume may be written in somewhat general terms, your factors should be tailored and specific. Even the resume must show your exact experience.

- If you are working your way up the career ladder, you can follow several strategies: (1) indicate on your resume your new objective; (2) talk with your senior person (manager, team leader, etc.) in the area of your interest about your goals, and ask ways to build toward them; and (3) talk on projects, volunteer responsibilities, and education that equip you for advancement. And be patient, but be persistent!

CHAPTER FOUR

The New Federal Employment Process
Search • Application • Rating • Selection • Hiring

With the NPR recommendations have come a wide variety of efforts to make the entire federal process more applicant-oriented. However, we are aware that the resultant "user-friendly" approaches emerging throughout the federal government can seem as bewildering as previous policies. Here we hope to simplify the information so you can find the entry-point that is appropriate for you, and, in addition, know how your application will be handled once it leaves your hands.

Soup to Nuts:
How to Find, Apply for, and be Competitive for Federal Jobs

This chapter will walk you as a job-seeker through the entire job search process. From the time you think about applying for a federal position through rating and review of your application, selection, and final requirements prior to actual hiring, there are clear steps in the process. In each step, we will identify "how-to's" so that you can confidently complete the application process.

Step 1:
Find federal positions of interest to you.

Step 2:
Determine whether you may apply for a position (based on whether the position is government-only, agency-only, or "all sources").

Step 3:
Apply for the position(s) you select.

Step 4:
The Review, Rating, and Selection Processes

67

Step 1:
Find Federal Positions of Interest to You

The federal position search is different from its private-sector counterpart. Although federal employers must guard against favoritism and lack of openness, federal position information is readily available if you know where to look. Locating positions appropriate to your background can be accomplished in a number of ways:

1. The "Career-America Connection" (also referred to as the "Federal Employment Information Highway"). OPM has information on virtually all current vacancies (the only exceptions could be highly specialized or secure positions with very specific position requirements). Career America is a seven-day-a-week/24-hours-per-day system that includes information on current vacancies, student employment opportunities, and other job topics. Phone (912) 757-3000.

2. The "Federal Job Opportunities Bulletin Board," an electronic bulletin board containing "electronic want ads" for the federal government "and much more," according to OPM publicity. Available seven-days-a-week/24-hours-per-day, the system scans nationwide announcements online. **Phone (912) 757-3100** or reach through **Internet (TELNET only)** at **FJOB.MAIL-OPM.GOV or 198.78.46.10.**

3. Agency Announcements. Through individual agency personnel offices, agency bulletin boards, agency inhouse employee newsletters, and increasingly through agency online information systems (some with "touchscreens"), you can find public announcements of job openings.

4. Newspaper Ads. In the Washington area, the *Washington Post* lists federal positions almost every Sunday. Major metropolitan papers in other areas of dense federal employment will too.

5. Professional Journals. While recruitment has diminished for "generalist" positions due to the flood of applications for such positions, jobs requiring highly specialized skills, for example, nursing, banking, data processing, writer/editors with scientific backgrounds may be found in association publications.

6. Job Fairs. Though much less common than they used to be — "we already get more applicants than we can manage for many jobs, especially those in the administrative and clerical classifications," said one federal personnelist — there are still opportunities for some through job fairs. Be sure you are ready to stand out from other applicants with a good federal resume written according to the guidelines in this book.

7. Other Recruitment/Outreach Activities. As mentioned under professional journals, recruiting continues for scarce capabilities. Nurses are recruited for federal positions with such agencies as Department of Veterans Affairs; border guards are recruited by Immigration and Naturalization Service; air traffic controllers are recruited by FAA; FBI and Secret Service still recruit because their standards are so high; Federal Highway Administration recruits due to its insistence on hiring the top graduating engineers from across the country.

It is worth finding out what areas are in demand in the federal sector and thinking through your own future career plans accordingly.

8. The Grapevine. People inside agencies themselves will also tell you that the "informal grapevine" should not be overlooked as a job source. Think long-range. Listen for new programs and initiatives, especially those that will require specialized technical skills. Watch news sources for federal offices and agencies that are moving (such as the new FBI center in West Virginia) or building satellites (such as the Air and Space Museum has been considering in Northern Virginia). While employees are often given an opportunity to move to the new agency or program site, many choose not to. Also, even with cutbacks, high-demand jobs will still need to be filled. When an imminent relocation or new program is announced, you may find that you have time to master or expand technical skills of interest to that potential employer. You may have as much as six months or a year before the change. Find out what skills will be needed. Enroll in a course or technical training to make yourself more attractive. Then, when the job openings are announced, you will be ready!

Step 2:
Determine Whether You May Apply for a Position

Federal positions are available to different groups of people depending on the amount of federally-related background necessary for each job. This requirement is noted somewhere at the top of each vacancy announcement under the headings "Area of Consideration," or "Who May Apply." The position announcement will then identify whether the position is:

• **Department-wide or Agencywide:** Many agencies are advancing a policy of promoting from within. Particularly agencies in the process of downsizing are giving preference to keeping experienced agency employees. This policy, long advocated by federal employees themselves, does exclude most from outside the agency.

Possible Exceptions: There may still be some very specialized positions that will require outside "sourcing." Taking a temporary or other short-term position can sometimes (though rarely) lead to conversion to full-time status.

• **Government-wide or Federal Government Only:** Many positions require experience in the federal sector. Sometimes the term "Government-Wide" will be followed by the phrase (Status Candidates Only). This means that only those at the grade level(s) indicated will be considered. Occasionally the notation will be "Local Commuting Area Only" or "Metro Area." These are self-explanatory and usually indicate some local knowledge needed by the position (as needed, for example, with some law enforcement officials).

> In any case, the most important data you **must** include on **every** application is **the Vacancy Announcement Number** (for example, "OSPM-95-11") and the Position Title and Series (for example, "Building Management Specialist, GS-1176-7/9"). Post this **on the top corner** of the **first page of your application,** whatever form you choose.

Possible Exceptions: Some job-seekers who have in the past worked in the federal sector but now work in the private sector may qualify for these positions; if you have such a background, it is worth checking. Occasionally those from outside the federal government are considered and even selected for federal-only positions, due, again, to a specialized background or a persuasive approach. This takes some research but may be worth a try if you are determined. For example, someone with an outstanding corporate track record in marketing may be attractive to an agency that is stepping up its public affairs program. Also, state government employees can sometimes make a strong case for their usefulness in the federal sector.

• **All Sources or All Qualified Persons:** These positions are truly open. The terms do in some cases, indicate a desire on the part of the hiring authority to bring in some non-governmental experience. Particularly in upper-level positions (GS-13 and above), in recent years the federal government has become increasingly open (where new hires were possible) to gain the "cross-fertilization" and "bridge-building" made possible by "new blood" from outside the federal sector.

Step 3:
APPLY FOR THE POSITION(S) YOU SELECT

Ways to Apply for Federal Positions

With the new National Performance Review emphasis on federal accessibility, even while jobs are relatively scarce, methods to apply are proliferating and becoming increasingly computerized.

At this writing — depending on the specific area of consideration, whether the position is an OPM-administered or agency-administered position, and whether software programs are being used in the application process — you can apply for a federal position in a number of different ways:

1. Through Specific Federal Agencies

Job announcements are available from personnel offices of specific federal agencies. If you have selected a particular department, agency or office which may be able to utilize your skills, find the telephone number and address of that agency. Since the federal government has become newly "customer-oriented," telephone conversations with personnelists should be more available than previously.

2. Through OPM.

OPM has a nationwide listing of virtually all positions available throughout the federal government. **While OPM does not provide rating and review for most federal positions,** they do adminster a large number of positions agencywide and nationwide. Many of these positions require both a federal resume (or other acceptable application), plus a written Supplemental Qualifications Statement.

Info: Office of Personnel Management - **Room 1416**
Federal Employment Information Center
1900 E Street N.W.
Washington, DC 20044

Call: OPM Automated Telephone Service
(202) 606-2700

Mail to: Office of Personnel Management
Office of Washington Examining Services
Attn: Vacancy Announcement # _____
[insert specific number here]
P.O. Box 14080
Washington, DC 20044

Deliver to: OPM - **Room 2469**
1900 E Street N.W.
Washington, DC 20415-0001

Using OPM's new "MARS" System (Micro-Computer Assisted Rating System) optical scanner and automatic rating system. Only available for some position openings — and only for those reviewed and rated by OPM — the MARS system helps expedite processing of applications by OPM.

3. On-Line Federal Listings:
If you have a computer, modem, and service with Internet, American On-Line or other service bureau, you can research job listings through a number of on-line job listings. This list was found through AOL, Job-Search Resources and Services compiled by D. Spearing of Stanford University.

General Job Listings:
- Department of the Interior Automated Vacancy Announcement System (AVADS) - job announcements for the Interior Department.

- Federal Jobs - Lists thousands of federal government job openings taken from a variety of Office of Personnel Management computer bulletin boards. Maintained by Dartmouth. gopher://dartsms1. dartmouth.edu

- FedWorld Information Network - a huge listing of federal jobs, updated daily. Also available via telnet://fedworld.doc.gov.

- FEDIX/MOLIS - Federal Job Opportunities for Women and Minorities.

Step 4:
THE REVIEW, RATING, AND SELECTION PROCESSES

The basic federal personnelist's review process remains very much the same as before. That is — while many agencies instituted merit promotion plans in the early 1990s, and all agencies are now working to be responsive to National Performance Review (NPR) guidelines — as mentioned in Chapter 5, review processes still operate with goals of equity, fairness, access to all qualified applicants, and provision to the federal sector of the best possible workforce. This last goal, the best possible workforce, naturally is becoming even more crucial as agencies downsize or "rightsize."

Where and How Are Applications Reviewed?

OPM now performs reviewing and rating for only a minority percentage of all positions, and contracts with other agencies (notably personnel selection for Headquarters offices of the U.S. Department of Interior, and nationwide for the U.S. Department of Energy) to do a small percentage more.

Upon application, most federal positions are reviewed directly by the agencies themselves.

Eligibility

Basic **eligibility** is based on issues such as:

- **Area of consideration:** government only, agency only, or all sources.

- Your **current grade level** and whether you are thereby eligible to apply for the specific position grade level. For a position at the next higher grade level, you usually need to have at least one year at the next lower grade level.

- Areas of **responsibility** and **level of autonomy** in those responsibilities. Is there a matchup between the tasks you have mastered and the tasks being sought? Have you directed, coordinated, or implemented a program? Does your current position provide experiences of team leadership or independent judgment?

Federal personnelists often make determinations of such basic eligibility. Based on NPR recommendations, many agencies now "put to a panel" only those positions with more than five eligible candidates. Fewer than five are often given directly to the position manager or team leader for selections to interview, and then hire.

Launched in 1992, MARS can be used for all positions available through OPM, including, at the time of this writing, positions with the headquarters offices of U.S. Department of Interior and nationwide positions with the U.S. Department of Energy. You can verify positions available through OPM by contacting their offices through their address and phone number below.

Even with use of the MARS form, you will still need to include your federal resume,

MARS Application Packages may be obtained from and delivered to the same contact points identified above, or

For some applications, through OPM's Telephone Application System. Once you have completed the MARS Form C Supplemental Qualifications Statement, call the system at 1-800-409-6527. Answer questions as requested. The calls take about 20 minutes.

A Special Word to Veterans

For active duty service before October 15, 1976, and separation under honorable conditions, you may be eligible for veterans' preference, an additional number of points automatically added to your application. For service beginning after Oct. 15, 1976, you will need a campaign badge, expeditionary medal, or a service-connected disability to receive veterans' preference.

For further information about veterans' preference and federal employment of former military personnel in general:

• **Call OPM at (912) 757-3000:** Select **"Federal Employment Topics"** then **"Veterans"** or

• Dial the OPM electronic bulletin board at **(912) 757-3100**.

Ten-point preference is given for active duty service-connected disability. To claim this preference, attach to your position application **SF 15, Application for 10-Point Veterans' Preference.**

Five-point preference is given for honorably separated veterans within the timeframe guidelines. To claim this preference, attach to your application DD-214, **Certificate of Release or Discharge from Active Duty,** or other proof of eligibility.

Note: Veterans' preference is not in any case a factor for Senior Executive Service (SES) positions, or for positions restricted to status candidates (current or former federal career or career-conditional employees).

The Rating Panel

In all cases where there are more than five eligible candidates, the applications go to a **rating panel.** These panels are **separated from the selection chain.** That is, they have responsibility **only** to determine the most-qualified candidates, but do not at this time interview or hire. This is to provide a "detached process," according to federal personnelists.

Even if you are fully qualified for a position, your federal resume, KSAs and application material must be complete in order to become "best qualified" through the rating panel.

Rating panels are **peer groups** that are usually comprised of "subject matter experts" of the position being sought. These panel members may be from the office where the position is located, or they may be from elsewhere in the agency. In rare cases of interagency positions, they may be drawn from several agencies. To ensure fairness, panels are required to have Equal Employment Opportunity (EEO) specialists as observers to the process. Some agencies which are unionized have union observers as well.

Because some panelists are experts in their fields, they have very busy schedules as team leaders, advisors to special projects, or serving on details elsewhere. Convening a panel, therefore, takes time, and is one reason why the federal review process may seem slow.

Once convened, according to federal personnelists, the panels tend to look first at the KSAs, then the resume and other materials. A typical way that panels rate candidates is with three benchmark scores for each quality and selective ranking factor: (5) for "superior" qualifications; (3) for "satisfactory" qualifications; and (1) for "minimally acceptable" qualifications. The panels total these scores for each candidate, and the top-rated four or five candidates then enter the selection process.

The Selection Process

The Selection Process

Once top-rated, these candidates enter the "managerial chain," for interviewing and selection. While many interviews are conducted by the departmental manager alone, federal interviews are not uncommonly performed by several people. These groups may be comprised of the manager or team leader, that person's supervisor, leader(s) from interdependent offices, and again, an EEO officer.

When the manager or group has decided on the preferred candidate, the job offer is made. Before hiring, determination of final suitability may be requested to verify baseline requirements such as citizenship status, military background, and other relevant matters.

Delivering Your Application

Agencies are usually comfortable with various methods of delivery. Many candidates like the security of hand-delivery themselves. In-town messenger services, Federal Express, Express Mail, and other forms of delivery are all fine, as long as they arrive on time. In virtually all cases, agencies are prohibited from accepting applications after the closing date and time.

CHAPTER 5

ANALYZING THE VACANCY ANNOUNCEMENT

- Recognizing the "Key Words and Phrases"

- Understanding the Application Directions

- Reading the Fine Print

- Preparing the Selective and Quality Ranking Factors

77

Analyzing the Vacancy Announcement

There are now efforts underway to streamline all personnel processes, based on National Performance Review (NPR) recommendations. Nonetheless, guidelines for federal vacancy announcements still aim to achieve access, equity, clarity, accuracy, and sufficient depth to attract qualified candidates.

Reading the Vacancy Announcement

In reading through a vacancy announcement, be sure to note the following:

Job Level. This indicates the position's grade level. If you are not "status-eligible" (e.g,. if the position is GS-13 and you are currently GS-12), then you will generally be expected to exhibit job-related experience at the next lower level. To verify job-related experience, check the X-118 for position groupings.

> Carefully read the Vacancy Announcement, especially the Duties and the Quality Ranking Factors. See the "Key Words."

Area of Consideration. This can be agency-only, government only; or all sources. The latter may be advertised in area newspapers and, in the case of scarce skills (such as nursing or banking), in professional journals.

Closing Date and Time. Closing dates are rarely, though occasionally, extended, especially if the original search did not attract sufficient qualified candidates. Close-of-business times in agency personnel offices vary as much as two hours, so it is a good idea to call well before the closing date to verify the exact time an application must be deliverd by.

Position Description. The specific duties and qualifications of the job are described in the opening text of the vacancy announcement, usually in very specific language.

Selective Placement Factors. These must be addressed to prevent disqualification of the application.

Quality Ranking Factors. These must also be addressed to ensure consideration of the application. While you can apply for most federal positions in one of three ways (with the SF-171, OF-610, or a federal resume), you must in any case address all necessary factors on separate sheets.

Although the type is small and difficult to read, it is important that you strain your eyes to read and analyze this information.

Vacancy Announcement

U.S. DEPARTMENT OF JUSTICE
OFFICE OF THE U.S. TRUSTEES
PERSONNEL MANAGEMENT BRANCH

ANN. NO. 95-09-D

AREA OF CONSIDERATION: ALL SOURCES
CLOSING DATE: 03/17/95
PROMOTION POTENTIAL (IF ANY) TO: GS-09
CONTACT: Valerie Rice (202) 616-1013
TTD: None

This position is in the Excepted Service.
Paralegal Specialist, GS-950-7/9, (1 position), Office of the United States Trustee, Atlanta, Georgia. **DUTIES:** The incumbent is responsible for performing a variety of analytical and investigative duties in support of the United States Trustee. Duties include: reviewing chapter 7 or 11 bankruptcy petitions and schedules for legal and procedural compliance with Bankruptcy Code, related state statutes, etc. In instance of debtor noncompliance legal requirements, makes recommendations regarding U.S. Trustee action and drafts motions commensurate with recommendations; reviews applications for retention of professionals ensuring qualifications and their necessity; where necessary, drafts motions regarding applications for payment of professionals' fees and expenses; conducts analysis of disclosure statements for legal sufficiency and advises attorney or analyst; analyzes facts and technical questions on case administration received by phone or correspondence, answering those that have been settled by interpretations of applicable legal provisions and researching those which present legal issues; as necessary performs research to assist attorneys and draft pleadings. **QUALIFICATIONS:** Applicants must have one year of specialized experience equivalent to the next lower grade in the Federal service. **Specialized Experience:** Experience which demonstrates knowledge of bankruptcy law, rules, regulations, policies, and precedents, and skill in interpreting and applying them to varying situations; skill in analyzing case issues, summarizing pertinent data on the issues involved, developing and/or evaluating evidence, resolving conflicting data, clarifying factual and legal issues, and recommending appropriate action. **SELECTIVE PLACEMENT FACTOR:** Knowledge of bankruptcy regulations and procedures, at least 6 months experience minimum. **QUALITY RANKING FACTORS:** 1) Ability to communicate effectively in writing and orally. 2) Knowledge of computerized systems. **Applicants are encouraged to submit a separate narrative addressing all factors. EVALUATION METHODS:** Applicants will be evaluated on the basis of quantity and quality of experience, education and training, job-related awards, and performance appraisals. **HOW TO APPLY:** Applicants must submit one of the following to U.S. Department of Justice, Office of the U.S. Trustees, Personnel Management Branch, Suite 770, Washington, D.C. 20530, Attn. Valerie Rice: a **Resume** or other written format; an **OF-612** (Optional Application for Federal Employment); or an **SF-171** (Application for Federal Employment). If you choose to send a resume or other written format, it **must include** the information outlined in the U.S. Office of Personnel Management's (OPM) flyer, "Applying for Federal Job," (OF-510). The OF-510 and the OF-612 may be obtained from: the UST office listed above; your local OPM Employment Information Office or by calling OPM's automated telephone system at (912)744-3000: or, by TDD at (912)744-2299. In addition, a performance appraisal issued within the last 12 months is required. **NOTE: APPLICANTS MUST MEET THE QUALIFICATIONS AND TIME-IN-GRADE REQUIREMENTS BY THE CLOSING DATE OF THIS ANNOUNCEMENT. IF POST MARKED BY THE CLOSING DATE, APPLICATIONS WILL BE ACCEPTED FOR UP TO THREE WORK DAYS, AFTER CLOSING DATE. RELOCATION EXPENSES ARE NOT AUTHORIZED. SELECTEES WHO ARE NOT CURRENTLY EMPLOYED BY THE OFFICES, BOARDS AND DIVISIONS OF THE U.S. DEPARTMENT OF JUSTICE WILL BE REQUIRED TO SUBMIT TO URINALYSIS TO SCREEN FOR ILLEGAL DRUG USE PRIOR TO APPOINTMENT. THE U.S. TRUSTEE PROGRAM IS AN EQUAL OPPORTUNITY EMPLOYER.**

Vacancy Announcement Analysis

Department of Justice, Office of the U.S. Trustees
Personnel Management Branch

ANN. NO. 95-09-D - must be listed on the first page of your application.

AREA OF CONSIDERATION: ALL SOURCES - open to outside applicants.

CLOSING DATE: 03/17/95
The last paragraph of the announcement states that the application can be post-marked by this date and will be accepted three days following that date.

PROMOTION POTENTIAL: GS-09
No promotion potential in this position.

CONTACT: Valerie Rice (202) 616-1013
This person can provide information about close times, clarify the meaning of any obscure position qualifications, provide a job description if time allows.

This position is in the excepted service.
This means that an applicant with proof of disability may be hired without competition, despite other requirements at the agency to give preference to qualified and available candidates who may have been separated from the agency by reduction-in-force.

TITLE: Paralegal Specialist, GS-950-7/9, (1 position), Office of the United States Trustee, Atlanta, Ga.
This is the position title, the grade level (and administrative tracking code), and indicates that only one person is being sought at this time.

DUTIES: See underlined key words, phrases, skills, knowledge and experience:

The incumbent is responsible for performing a variety of <u>analytical and investigative</u> duties in support of the <u>United States Trustee</u>. Duties include:

•

   Reviews <u>Chapter 7 or 11 bankruptcy petitions and schedules </u>for legal and <u>procedural compliance with the Bankruptcy Code</u>, related state statutes, etc. *(critical requirement - key words)*

•   In instance of <u>debtor noncompliance legal requirements</u>, makes <u>recommendations</u> regarding <u>U.S. Trustee action</u> and <u>draft motions</u>

81

commensurate with recommendations. *Clearly the position requires paralegal expertise that includes the ability to conduct independent research, formulate ideas for recommendations, and drafting legal motions.*

- Reviews <u>applications</u> for payment of professionals' <u>fees and expenses</u>.

- Conducts analysis of <u>disclosure statements</u> for legal sufficiency and advises attorney or analyst.

- Analyzes facts and technical questions on <u>case administration</u> received by phone or correspondence.

- <u>Answers questions </u>that have been settled by <u>interpretations of applicable legal provisions</u> and researching those which present legal issues. *This calls for the ability to serve as public spokesperson and representative of the office on certain matters, to locate relevant statutes, and to conduct responsible legal research.*

- Performs <u>research to assist attorneys and draft pleadings</u>.

Your federal resume and KSAs should use these key words and phrases as many times as possible.

QUALIFICATIONS:

Applicants must have one year of specialized experience equivalent to the next lower grade in the federal service.

Since the area of consideration is "all sources," this experience may have been obtained outside the government; indeed, law firm or law research experience would likely be seriously considered.

Specialized Experience:

Experience which demonstrates knowledge of <u>bankruptcy law, rules, regulations, policies, and precedents,</u> and skill in <u>interpreting and applying</u> them to varying situations;

Your application should show specific relevant proof of this knowledge, identifying by title and number those you know are most appropriate. You also need to cite specific instances when you have applied them. Especially good are examples where you have addressed a variety of needs through astute applications.

Skill in <u>analyzing case issues</u>, summarizing pertinent data on the issues involved, developing and/or <u>evaluating evidence, resolving conflicting data, clarifying factual and legal issues,</u>and <u>recommending appropriate action</u>.

Indicate exactly to whom you reported and provided recommendations, the level of autonomy you exercised, and favorable results of your recommendations.

SELECTIVE PLACEMENT FACTOR:

Knowledge of bankruptcy regulations and procedures, at least six months' experience minimum.

The Selective Placement Factor can be written on a separate page or covered in your federal resume. The instructions do not require you to write a separate statement.

QUALITY RANKING FACTORS:

1) Ability to communicate effectively in writing and orally.
2) Knowledge of computerized systems.

Applicants are encouraged to submit a separate narrative addressing all factors.

The word "encouraged" implies that it is your choice if these ranking factors are addressed. Most vacancy announcement will state that the factors are "mandatory." If you do not write the factor statements, candidates who DO write the statements will rank higher than you.

Preparing the Selective and Quality Ranking Factors

Some preparatory work based on the vacancy announcement can launch an effective response to the Selective and Quality Ranking Factors. Here is a step-by-step process:

Step 1:
Build Your Portfolio for the Specific Position.

Think through and bear in mind the following aspects of your own portfolio of marketable qualifications:

- Your employment background.

- Your volunteer, civic, church, neighborhood, sports leadership, or government experience (in addition to that of your federal positions).

83

- Knowledge and skills you have developed as a result of both your paid and unpaid experience.

- All of the training and education you have received.

- All training and education you have taught others.

- Special assignments, details, team responsibilities, "acting" positions — and all capabilities you exercised in performance of these.

- Any publications, products, prototypes, or research experiments to which you may have contributed (especially as team member or junior subordinate), as well as those you created independently.

- Presentations and briefings you have made, whether inhouse to key people, to other agencies, to conferences, and other forums.

- New systems, procedures, plans, or processes you have conceived and/or instituted.

Step 2:
Determine the Specific Position Qualifications.

Read through the "job description" section of the vacancy announcement, highlighting or underlining specific requirements, perhaps using two different colors — one color for those qualifications you are sure you have, and another color for those qualifications you are not sure about.

The next chapter will examine in detail how to write a narrative statement that includes Selective Placement Factors and Quality Ranking Factors. To prepare for writing that comprehensive narrative statement, we recommend you develop the worksheets described below.

Step 3:
Determine Specific Requirements that Are Met by Your Portfolio.

On a separate sheet of paper, list on the left side of the sheet each of these requirements. Then make a list of specific examples where you have, in your "portfolio," exhibited at least minimal competence at each task and technical area, or have received academic or certified training.

Step 4:
Pay Special Attention to the Selective Placement Factor(s).

You must address this one fully and clearly if you want to be considered for the specific position. While you want to present your background concisely, for this factor you will also want to present your portfolio fully. Prepare by listing all related experience and education from your portfolio.

Step 5:
Assess the Quality Ranking Factors (KSAs).

The Quality Ranking Factors (also referred to as "KSAs," or "Knowledge, Skills, and Abilities") also must be addressed fully and with enough specific detail to enable reviewers to assess you fairly. Again, prepare a list of all items in your portfolio that relate to each of these factors. For each factor, list supporting experience and education ranging from the most sophisticated, expanded skill level back to the first, earliest stages of development.

CHAPTER 6

WRITING NARRATIVE STATEMENTS KSAS

- Guidelines for the Effective Narrative

- Story-telling Techniques

- Outstanding Accomplishments

- Action Verbs

87

THE PENSION BENEFIT GUARANTY CORPORATION IS AN EQUAL OPPORTUNITY EMPLOYER

NOTICE OF POSITION VACANCY

Announcement No. 95-92	**Opening Date: 2-7-95 **Closing Date: 2-23-95**
_____ **Bargaining Unit**	_____ **Non-Bargaining Unit**

POSITION: Accountant - GS-0510-7/9/11/12

PROMOTION POTENTIAL: If selected at GS-7, 9 or 11 level, may be noncompetitively promoted to GS-12.

ORGANIZATIONAL LOCATION: Financial Operations Department, Controller Operations Division General Accounting Branch

AREA OF CONSIDERATION: All Sources	**NUMBER OF POSITIONS: One (1)**

TRAVEL REQUIREMENTS: None

DUTIES:

1. Processes a full range of accounting transactions for assigned departments and programs within PBGC.
2. Serves as an accounting liaison, providing accounting assistance and technical expertise in resolving problems and questions from budget liaisons, COTRs, and commercial vendors.
3. Prepares a variety of special reports and analyses relating to assigned areas of responsibility.
4. Provides assistance in fiscal and calendar year-end reporting.

EVALUATION METHOD: Qualification determinations will be based upon information submitted in accordance with the instructions in this vacancy announcement. These applicants may be awarded up to 40 points based on the performance appraisal, up to 10 points for awards, and up to 100 points based on experience and training/education/self development. The Office of Personnel Management is responsible for determining the best qualified from amongst the non-status applicants. Applications from status candidates will be measured against the following Quality Ranking Factors. Attach a narrative describing how your experience and/or education relates to each Quality Ranking Factor.

1. Knowledge of general accounting principles and procedures.
2. Knowledge of Treasury, GAO, and OMB regulations governing accounting for revolving funds.
3. Ability to analyze and review financial data and accounts data to identify discrepancies and variances.
4. Ability to plan, organize and schedule workloads and unplanned priorities to meet established deadlines.
5. Ability to communicate effectively both orally and in writing with all levels of personnel both within and outside the organization.

PROBATIONARY PERIOD REQUIREMENTS:

No supervisory/managerial probationary period required.

PERFORMANCE REQUIREMENTS:

May be reviewed in the Personnel Office, Suite 120.

MINIMUM QUALIFICATION REQUIREMENTS:
U.S. citizenship required for this position

Candidates must have a full four (4) year course of study in an accredited college of university which meets all of that institution's requirements for a bachelor's degree with an accounting major; or a full four (4) year course of study in an accredited college of university that meets all requirements for a bachelors and that included or was supplemented by at least twenty-four (24) semester hours in accounting; or four (4) years experience in accounting, or equivalent combination of accounting experience, college-level education, and training that provided professional accounting knowledge equivalent in type, scope and thoroughness to that acquired through successful completion of a four (4) year college curriculum in accounting which included at least fifteen (15) semester hours, but which does not fully satisfy the twenty-four (24) semester hours requirement, provided that applicant has successfully performed work at or equivalent to the next lower grade level in accounting, auditing or a related field..

Writing Narrative Statements / KSAs

Referred to by a variety of names — "narrative statements," "KSAs," "factor statements," and, more formally, the "Supplemental Qualification Statement" — this is the strategic and critical part of your application process. If you can get past anxiety and other troubling reactions to the process, it can (perhaps unbelievably at this point) also be fun!

First, a word on the over-arching importance of the narrative statements: The federal resume (like the SF-171 and optional new OF-612, and in contrast to private sector resumes) can actually be considered the **"first interview."** In that light, the narrative statements are the hard-hitting **interview questions** to be sure that you and the job are a good fit. In your resume you want to be sure to include enough factual information in a generic way so that you can apply for a variety of jobs relevant to your background and skills. In your narrative statements, you will want to hone and refine that information to make a convincing case that you are the very person for the specific job.

In preparing to write your narrative statement for a specific position, be sure first to read through **Chapter 5, Analyzing Vacancy Announcements**. Your narrative must reflect the needs of the position as well as how you meet those needs — with great specificity.

However, remember that the narrative statement, above all, is a strategic document. This is where you tell your unique, individual story. The balance you want to strike is somewhere between Jack Webb's "Just the facts, ma'am," and journalistic creativity. A formula for building your strategic document is boxed at right:

The Position Requirements
+
Your Accomplishments
+
Apparent Obstacles =
The Successful Narrative Statement

You may find the "Apparent Obstacles" part of the equation above puzzling. The reason it is important is that you must address questions you can guess will be in the minds of your reviewers. These questions can range from (1) "Why is this gap of time here?" (2) "How sophisticated was the competence developed by this person for this particular skill — the position title was 'Program Manager,' and yet we see described interagency liaison. How did this more advanced responsibility come about?" (3) "He has a Ph.D. in linguistics — how does this relate to the position requirement of effective writing?"

You may find real "pay-dirt" in thinking through how your background may give pause to potential readers of your application. In answering these possible questions, you can give a fuller picture of who you are. For example, in addressing each of the above sample questions, you might write:

(1) "Due to my mother's prolonged illness, I was her sole primary caretaker, which required my taking a leave of absence from my position. During this time, I gained extensive knowledge of victims of stroke and worked closely with a variety of social workers. Through reading medical journals, I also gained familiarity with a wide range of related long-term disabilities. This experience has equipped me with skills that I believe would be useful in this position of Board of Medical Examiners staff member."

(2) "Though my current position is formally titled Program Manager, due to performance as team leader during a period of agency-wide change and reinvention, where I was rated on my most recent evaluation as "Outstanding," my supervisor and his supervisor selected me personally for service as interagency liaison on a task force to export change skills to other agencies."

(3) "My Ph.D. in linguistics, which I undertook through my interest in globally widespread language patterns, focused in part on how to communicate widely with readers from diverse fields reading information unfamiliar to them. As a result, my writing has been improved. I am much more sensitive to the ambiguity possible from the vague use of words. Furthermore, I have several publications on this subject that were printed in lay journals, including: [*here you would list specific titles of publication or titles upon request.*]"

Several additional tips you may find useful:

- Keep your mother out of the room! This may sound harsh but is addressed to the reality that many of us were told, "If you don't brag about yourself, nobody else will." The truth is the opposite: In the narrative statement, if you don't announce your own strengths and accomplishments clearly, no one else will know what they are.

- Think about each position you held. How did you make a difference? What innovations, process improvements, new systems, or better ways of doing things did you introduce? What happened that only happened because you, with your unique background and strengths, were there?

- Pull out everything in all those boxes in the basement or back of the closet.

Get together **all** the files and project records and training certificates and publications that may be relevant to the position you are seeking.

• Set aside **at least** one entire weekend to write the narrative statements. Write in full and then redraft and hone. Add things, move things around, see how the whole statement flows. Clearly, some items can substantiate different factors. Where are they most needed? Where are they strongest?

• **Always** indicate in which position and during what timeframe a given accomplishment occurred. **Make it easy, not hard,** for your reader to figure out when you completed a certain project or mastered a specific skill. **Show how you have grown** over time in your competence.

• Avoid adjectives as much as you can. Use Jack Webb's advice: use the facts. But use them fully. For example, avoid such vague sentences as "Contributed significantly to the final outcome of the project, which was considered a noteworthy addition to the agency."

Rather, use specific, actual information to decribe the same thing: for example, "Commended by supervisor on performance evaluation for 'Outstanding Accomplishment' for providing contract oversight of this project, accomplished under the $50,000 budget and within constraints of an eighteen-week deadline. Due to effective agency/contractor partnership established as a result of my early negotiations with the contractor, preserved effective working relationship while reaching deadlines. In establishing this agency's first formal joint agency/contractor goals, achieved breakthrough for contract management, resulting in a model for partnership now used as a model throughout the agency."

Who is Speaking in Your Narrative?

The understood subject in each sentence of all narrative statements should be "I." All factors should be written from this first-person. You may use the actual word "I" in the text, especially if you prefer to write in a colloquial, conversational style; for example:

> *"I directed a pioneer project to establish a new facilities management systems of productivity."*

Or you may have the subject unsaid but understood, especially if you prefer a terse, businesslike style. For example:

> *"Led reduced staff in achieving record performance goals."*

- Be specific: Show you meet the requested qualifications — work experience, training, awards, certificates, publications, volunteer experience (especially if technical abilities have developed, such as budgets or contract management). Include time periods. No generalities. Be sure to address the specific position requirements: unrelated Ph.D.'s will be disqualified **faster** than someone obviously working toward a particular job (for example, data processing).

- Be creative: Do not be afraid to make it interesting! You need to identify and reveal your strengths to show most benefit to your future employer. Here is an example: "Integrated my background in budget management with my recent program oversight expertise to achieve the department's strategic alliance with our sister agency in regulatory reform, the attention of National Performance Review leadership."

- Let the details work for you: Use dollar figures (e.g., "managed budget of over $1.5 million"); mention exact disciplines on your team ("integrated the best ideas of a diverse group of engineers, computer technicians, personnel specialists, and several customer representatives"); identify publications you produced (e.g., "gathered information from across the agency and edited the annual **Report on Wildlife Areas,** Pub. No. 425, 1994"). These details add credibility and keep your readers alert and interested.

- Claim credit for all significant accomplishments — even if a paper is unpublished, or a fact-finding or assessment project did not result in a full-blown follow-on project. If you have a publication or a project report or some other product to show, or someone to vouch for the quality of your work, you can claim these as substantiating your competence. You may have saved the government money by evaluating a project that was not continued due to your cost/benefit analysis. This is an important achievement too.

- Also remember to sell what you have, who you really are, and what **you** want to do: If you are ingenious and like startup operations but are impatient with detail, be honest. If your forte is bringing order to complexity and disarray, emphasize that rather than maintaining that you "like to be flexible." If your strength is understanding and facilitating people, focus on situations in which you will work in teams rather than "lone-wolf" positions. The work world of the 21st Century is going to need **true diversity** - all types of people - and being forthright about your natural preferences and areas of competence will help, not hinder, your placement in the job of your choice in which you will then be most productive.

How to Put Liveliness in Your Life Story

Tell the story — like a newspaper reporter. Think about "headlines." Show development and growth over time. Here is a "before and after picture" example for a GS 7 Teacher/Supervisor in Child Development Services, applying for a GS/GM 9 position as a Child Development Specialist. The factor being described is, "The ability to develop, implement, and manage child development programs, including child care centers, family day care programs, etc." The "before" picture is her original draft. The "after" picture shows her results after following instructions in this chapter.

The "Before" Picture

As a teacher, I worked with preschool student in a summer headstart program. As an Education Specialist, I had two years experience working in a child care center. My college courses included several in early childhood education. I worked in a childcare lab in college with preschoolers. I trained caregivers, providers, and staff on early childhood education principles and skills.

The "After" Picture

Teacher-Supervisor, Child Development Services (CDS) 7/94 to present

For the past seven years, I have regularly applied professional knowledge of child development principles to develop, implement and recommend curriculum and age-appropriate activities to meet the needs and interests of assigned children. I plan materials for varying age groups, various learning levels and abilities. I participate in reviewing the quality of development programs utilized at the child development center. I observe and evaluate child development levels and make adjustments to programs as needed.

As member of team involved in preparing the center for receiving the National Association for the Education of Young Children (NAEYC) Accreditation, I work to implement policies and procedures within accreditation guidelines.

Education Program Specialist for Child Development Services   2/91 - 6/93

During the entire period, I served as both Developmental Program Specialist and as Trainer for CDS Staff and Family Child Care (FCC) Providers. I monitored developmental programming quality through observation and role modeling in child activity areas. I demonstrated the appropriate use of space, time, equipment, materials, and activities to support developmental programming. Serving as major departmental contributor to annual assessment of $300,000 departmental program budget, I recommended cost-saving strategies. I worked closely with direct service personnel, child interaction specialists, and support staff to develop curriculum based on child development principles.

93

Notice that the factor above is not addressed by positions in chronological order. This is usually the case: you may select those positions that are directly relevant to a specific factor and need not find something in every single position to meet the qualifications.

For several fully-developed examples of Narrative Statements, See Appendix B.

Working Your Way Up

A good definition of a "career" is **"a time-extended working out of purposeful life pattern."** While you cannot expect the federal government or any other employer to hand you your "dream job," by making yourself useful to each employer and by building your competencies toward your preferred goals, you can realize your dream job — and possibly even surpass that attainment!

If you are working your way up your own career ladder, you do not need to wait to be selected for advancement opportunities. You can help create them by seeking out informal mentors and other supporters. Talk with supervisors and others in leadership about your long-range goals. Use your Individual Development Plan to position yourself for advancement. Think of your entire life as a "learning ground" for future advancement: many has gained valuable skills through serving as classroom aides, Little League coaches, Scout leadership, civic leadership, volunteer church service, and other opportunities. And volunteer on the job for projects, teams, special details, and publications! Even if you are working with others, you may claim credit for the accomplishments of a working group through such language as, for example:

> Think about how you can align your goals and your employer's goals to achieve a win/win outcome over time. You never know how an immediate job can lead to other things, so always offer quality in everything you do, and then negotiate advancement.

> "I collaborated with an inter-disciplinary team to design the agency's first software program aimed at streamlining the customer response process. My contributions included guidance on how to attain a user-friendly system by providing data on the customer patterns of our agency over the past two years."

Using Lively (and Accurate) Language to Describe Accomplishments: Action Verbs

You may already know about the use of action verbs to create interest in your writing and accurately target the level of competency required. To use action verbs when writing narrative statements, you will want to think through how well developed each of your skills is, your proficiency level.

A scale that may be helpful to you in deciding the level of each of your proficiencies is drawn from the field of education. Designed by Benjamin Bloom, this scale describes mastery of knowledge or skill from the simplest (#1) at the left, to the most complex (#6) at the right:

1	2	3	4	5	6
Grasp	Recognize	Explain	Practice	Perform	Innovate

Level #1, "Grasp" indicates a very early stage of understanding or development; **#2**, "Recognize" indicates an ability to know how a skill or knowledge is used; **#3**, "Explain" indicates being able to discuss the matter with some degree of knowledge; **#4**, "Practice" implies being able to show how a technique or skill is applied accurately; **#5**, "Perform" indicates consistent, safe, accurate, quality performance; and **#6**, "Innovate" implies an ability to use the specific knowledge and skill to create, design, or institute something new.

Please note: This scale is not a depiction of official federal personnel rankings, and **should be used as a guideline only** to analyze your portfolio in terms of:

- The position(s) you are considering and its overall required KSAs;
- The levels of proficiency required in each area of the position, and
- The levels of proficiency both overall and in each area which you have attained.

Perhaps even more importantly, the scale can provide direction on appropriate action verbs to describe your experience in the narrative statement.

Ordinarily, you will want to use examples for each factor, your most highly developed proficiency for that factor (the exception would be where you are applying for a position that is less advanced than your highest skill level in one factor, in order to fit yourself for a position that has other attractive features for you).

CHAPTER 7

SENIOR EXECUTIVE SERVICE

Five Executive Core Qualifications

Critical factors:

- Strategic Vision

- Human Resource Management

- Program Development

- Resource Management and Planning

- Organizational Representation and Liaison

Pay Schedules
Senior Executive Service
January - 1995

ES-1	$92,900
ES-2	$97,400
ES-3	$101,800
ES-4	$107,300
ES-5	$111,800
ES-6	$115,700

OPM publishes SES Vacancy Accouncements bi-weekly.
SES vacancy announcements are also online, including six OPM
electronic bulletin boards:

Atlanta, GA	(404) 730-2370
Detroit, MI	(313) 226-4423
Los Angeles, CA	(818) 575-6521
Philadelphia, PA	(215) 580-2216

Washington, DC "PayPerNet," (202) 606-2675 or 1876

Washington, DC "OPM Mainstreet" (202) 606-5800

See Appendix D for excerpt of SES Qualifications publication by OPM.

Senior Executive Service
The Five Executive Core Qualifications

The Civil Service Reform Act of 1978 created the Senior Executive Service (SES) in an effort to develop a corps of highly-qualified federal managers who would be able to perform a range of functions at the highest levels of government. Rather than follow traditional career paths through single agencies, the idea behind the SES was that well-trained managers should be able to move between agencies, and that a broad background on the part of federal managers would counteract some of the inbreeding associated with people spending entire careers in a single agency. Also managerial service within government would not be the primary criteria for gaining a senior position in federal agencies.

> The U.S. Federal Service, unlike nearly all professional government officials around the world, remains open to the possibility of people entering on the basis of experience gained outside of government service.

Applications for positions among the more than 7,500 positions in the SES require—in addition to a strong resume—statements addressing three sets of qualifying factors for each position. Each agency defines sets of both **mandatory** and **desirable** technical qualifications for any SES position advertised. These vary according to the requirements that the agency defines as appropriate to the position. An applicant, for example, for a position as an assistant administrator of the Federal Aviation Administration for airway facilities must be able to demonstrate professional knowledge of the design and engineering of radionavigational systems. It might be desirable for that applicant to have first-hand flying experience in the air navigational system, but that would be a desirable, rather than a mandatory, technical requirement.

First and foremost, entry into the Senior Executive Service requires the establishment of "Executive Core Qualifications;" i.e., the combination of managerial skills that are the precondition for entry into the SES. Unless the resume and the statements demonstrate possession of the Executive Core Qualifications, even exceptional technical qualifications will not be enough to develop a successful SES application.

> The 1993 National Performance Review recommended that the Senior Executive Service develop a "corporate perspective" that supports government-wide cultural change.

More than managerial responsibilities, SES core qualifications require a demonstration of leadership potential. Most importantly, these descriptions of executive abilities cannot stand in isolation. As one personnel officer responsible for SES positions commented, "I want to know not merely what the applicant claims to have done; I need to know when and where it was done to make the case credible." This personnelist reported receiving as many as 60 applications for each advertised SES announcement. Nearly one-third of these will be rejected for not meeting fully the advertised qualifications for the position. Of the rest, effective statements of ranking factors can make the difference between being grouped among the "well-qualified" who gain interviews for the position and the "qualified," who do not get to the interview stage.

There is no substitute for substantial experience in gaining an SES position. Most SES members have worked at least ten years in the federal service before gaining consideration for such high rank—and many have 25 to 30 years of experience. As is the case with most federal positions, the important dimension of an application responds to the question, "What have you done lately?" Federal personnel officers and selecting officials are most interested in the development of progressively responsible performance at or near the level for which one is applying. Typically, the SES announcement will specify at least one year of experience at the GM-15 level. A strong record of accomplishment will devote attention to demonstrating achievement that approaches the complexity of the anticipated position. If an applicant is dwelling on accomplishments at the GM-13 level, the description will be less favorably received than comparable accomplishments at the GM-15 level.

> Effective statements of the Executive Core Qualifications will combine breadth of accomplishments, clear indications of exceptional professional training, and a record of supervising other people in the successful completion of substantial tasks.

At any agency, advertisement of an SES opening indicates some change in the organization—whether it is merely the retirement of an experienced executive, or the creation of a new position to address some weakness identified by agency leaders. Knowing the agency is important, and any SES statement will be strengthened if the applicant knows what the agency leadership perceives as the needs of the position. The knowledge need not be gained from inside the agency, but the applicant bears the burden of demonstrating—to a panel of reviewers within the agency—that experience and knowledge gained elsewhere provide enough background to perform effectively once a selection is made. Under these conditions, any candidacy is strengthened if the rating officials reviewing the applications—usually made up of other senior executives at or above the level being considered—know the individuals and the application is a reaffirmation of accomplishments that are already well-known within the agency. Whether the applicant is known or unknown, <u>the successful application must demonstrate an ability to think at least two bureaucratic levels above the position.</u> An SES appointment will usually require the approval of an agency head, so a senior executive applicant must be able to speak that executive's language.

Writing Executive Core Qualifications is no different from any other writing challenge: well-written material that keeps the reader's interest will get attention faster than sleeper prose. Still, the challenge of isolating twenty years of accomplishments into five pages (one page per factor is what reviewing officials say they like to see) is significant—especially if there are too many successes to fit in the allotted space.

Make selections. Consider the following examples:

> Nothing can substitute for reviewing the core qualifications as a group, sorting through your resume and supporting notes, and making hard choices about where your achievements fit into the factors.

- As a senior investigator in an FBI District Office, an agent assembled a team to address a major smuggling operation. He conceived the investigative strategy, coordinated participation from other federal enforcement agencies as well as state and local law enforcement agencies, and directed operations that resulted in 15 arrests, twelve convictions, and the seizure of more than $3 million in assets for the agencies involved. Should that story be related as "Strategic Vision," "Program Development and Evaluation," or "Organizational Representation and Liaison?"

- As a senior financial manager at an agency operating both with appropriated funds and fee receipts, the applicant identified a substantial source of new revenue that did not quite fit into statutory categories that yield fee revenues—resulting in a major portion of agency services being provided for a limited populace that might have been charged a fee with a small change in the law. This manager developed the proposed statutory change, then worked with senior management to gain support for the legislation at the department, OMB, and congressional levels—yielding additional revenues from user fee accounts. Does the achievement count as "Resource Planning and Management," or "Organizational Representation and Liaison?"

- Congress enacts a major new program, requiring a shift in the agency's mission — at least in the eyes of many agency managers. A program analyst within the policy office develops and articulates a rationale—consistent with the legislative history—and organizes a policy planning team to give the new legitimacy within the agency. He then provides effective support in the development of budgets, personnel classifications, and an operational strategy to get the organization running within months of the deadline established in legislation. Does this get listed under "Strategic Vision," "Program Development and Evaluation," or "Resource Planning and Management?"

> For most credible SES candidates, there is no one easy answer for any of these questions.

In each case, a candidate with genuine likelihood of success will have numerous achievements in each of the categories, and have to make selections based upon which factors most need elaboration in order to achieve the best possible presentation for the advertised position. For a technical professional in a low-visibility program, experience speaking for the agency before congressional committees and staff could be rare—so any credible claim should be mentioned in that category. For an attorney who has been managing development of congressional testimony during his entire career, the same experiences could be written with an emphasis on program accomplishment or evaluation aspects of the same event.

Three critical factors that must be considered in developing statements of Executive Core Qualifications

First, Know Yourself.

Or, to paraphrase Robert Burns, "See yourself as others see you." Claims advanced in the Executive Core Qualifications must be consistent with the portrayal made at other points in the application, and supportable by the people listed as supervisors and references.

Second, Know the Position.

Here, the important point is to understand what selecting officials believe they need in the position. To some extent, recent reports of congressional investigations, oversight hearings, identification of high risk factors in OMB reports, or news events will help to portray the problems facing the agency—and its leading selecting officials. As in any successful job search, the critical challenge is to ensure that the people doing the selecting believe that your skills match their needs.

Third, Strive for Consistency.

In the case of Executive Core Qualifications, consistency is best demonstrated by a focus on interrelated achievements in each previous position to demonstrate a logical development of skills. If, for example, an attorney was winner of moot court competitions in law school, the claim to be an articulate and forceful representative before congressional committees is more credible than if the same attorney were an insightful scholar with numerous publications, but no record of having appeared in court during his career.

In short, successful presentations of Executive Core Qualifications must be made consistent continuations of other elements of the federal application package. They should summarize—concisely—a record that demonstrates readiness for the responsibilities that the successful applicant will fulfill.

Competition for Senior Executive Service positions will become more intense in the next 10 years. Not only are numerous "Baby Boomers" seeking the promotions that will cap careers that began in the late 1960s, but the Clinton administration has promised to reduce the number of SES positions as part of its **National Performance Review.** At the end of the Bush administration, there were approximately 7,500 SES positions filled out of 8,200 SES positions authorized. As a result of an executive order issued early in his term, President Clinton plans to eliminate most of the unfilled positions, and will probably not fill many of those affected by "buy-outs" of current SES members.

> There is no substitute for the research that would be involved in doing the job when it comes to getting the job.

The following pages contain samples of core qualifications statements developed to reflect the kinds of skills sought in different kinds of positions. Some of them are composites of real people—all of the positions are variations on positions that exist in different agencies of the federal government.

Richard A. Long
456-78-1234

Vacancy NASA-95-343-1
Assistant Administrator for Satellite Operations

1. **Strategic Vision — The ability to ensure that key national and organizational goals, priorities, values, and other issues are considered in making program decisions and exercising leadership to implement and to ensure that the organization's mission and strategic vision are reflected in the management of its people.**

My career in the federal service now spans 23 years providing leadership in the development of satellite applications, most recently as Director of the Office of Commercial Space Transportation within the Department of Transportation. I have supported the development of private sector initiatives to offset the reduction in Federal resources, and gained support from associations and corporations in the aerospace industries for research and development programs that make effective use of the satellite capacity for communications, navigation, and other innovative applications.

While pursuing a master's degree in aerospace engineering, I became familiar with opportunities for using satellites for navigational precision that was not feasible with a ground-based system. In reviewing design proposals and research strategies, I also came to understand that development of commercial applications of space-based communications and navigational applications required new applications of U.S. and international commercial and property law. I completed both the engineering and the legal education to prepare for a professional career in this emerging area.

My initial federal employment was with the Defense Applied Research Projects Agency, where I advanced to manage a $350 million series of research projects exploring national technical means of gathering intelligence. I coordinated system planners to design options that could be expanded. In the course of this work, I participated in interagency research and development projects—often with the Office of Science and Technology Policy, the National Science Foundation, the National Academies of Sciences and Engineering, and the National Aeronautics and Space Administration. Proposals researched through these committees included the National Airspace Plane, use of satellites for global telecommunications (voice and data) purposes, and the Global Positioning System—now proving adaptable for air traffic control.

This experience combined with my technical and legal education to provide a sound foundation for leadership when the Office of Commercial Space Transportation opportunity opened. For the past seven years, I have revitalized an office that seemed unsure of its mission within a department dominated by commercial and regulatory concerns—primarily service oriented. I concentrated upon the linkage of satellite operations—within NASA, the Department of Defense, and the private sector—to build support for the program at other agencies and to enhance morale within the organization. As a result of these team development efforts, the office absorbed the Department's Research and Special Projects Administration—combining research agencies under a unified leadership, and our team won a Secretary's award for advancing a leadership position among government agencies on behalf of the Department.

This combination of education and experience includes the achievements essential to understand the long-term implications of current technical developments, to demonstrate the ability to lead increasingly large and complex organizations, and to build the team morale necessary to accomplish the agency's mission in a challenging environment. From my experience dealing with the agency within the government, I believe that I have demonstrated a familiarity with the agency's responsibilities and opportunities that will enable me to chart an effective direction for its future development of satellite programs.

MARVIN A. MANAGER
987-65-1234

Vacancy Announcement Department of Energy-95-SES-301-AE
Associate Administrator for Nuclear Programs

2. **Human Resources Management — The ability to design human resources strategies to meet the organization's mission, strategic vision, and goals and to achieve maximum potential of all employees in a fair and equitable manner.**

During a 22 year federal career, I have participated in organizational development at three agencies, all with major responsibilities in the initiation of innovative programs to address technically-complex responsibilities. I have—consistent with agency practices—participated in human resource management programs that foster the advancement of a culturally diversified workforce while sustaining engineering and scientific programs required of nuclear development and environmental clean up of hazardous materials resulting from Department of Defense development programs.

I approached my responsibilities using methods that enhance the development of a quality workforce, recognizing the interrelated activities of agencies responsible for nuclear development while addressing critical environmental concerns. The reduced tensions resulting from the termination of the Cold War necessitated a shift in the nation's priorities with regard to management of fissionable materials. Having developed teams responsible for the production and regulation of such materials with the Atomic Energy Commission, I readily understood conversions to nuclear energy regulation when I transferred to the Nuclear Regulatory Commission. Both agencies required development of technically complex teams, and I recruited heavily at prominent universities to identify the people who had both the technical skills and the commitment to public service essential to regulatory agencies. I increased my understanding of special recruitment programs—such as the Administrative Careers With America—as well as temporary hiring authorities and specialized knowledge authorities (Schedules A and B) to ensure the skills necessary for effective organizations.

For the past five years, I have directed the Environmental Protection Agency's office responsible for monitoring federal facilities' compliance with environmental clean-up regulations issued under the Comprehensive Emergency Response, Clean-Up, and Liability Act (Superfund). In this capacity, I have managed attorneys, scientists, technicians, and engineers responsible for evaluating the hazards posed at numerous federal facilities used to produce and store nuclear materials and designing appropriate responses for federal agencies. I have frequently developed interagency working groups to assess the technical and legal responsibilities, and worked with the Executive Office of the President to coordinate interagency responses. Usually, this requires an ability to influence assignment of key personnel within other agencies for missions that, however important nationally—differ from their agency's primary mission. Again, I have worked within the interagency environment to ensure the selection of vital personnel and to create a working environment that sustains strong staff morale. In spite of the technical requirements of the functions, I have been able to identify and secure promotion of talented women and minority professionals in several agencies, a factor that was cited in my team's winning an EPA Administrator's Gold Medal for resolving three federal hazardous waste sites in FY-1993. That team was nominated for a Presidential Rank citation in FY-1994.

105

This record of successful development of effective teams in diverse operational settings demonstrates the ability to develop and sustain interagency teams at a highly-technical level that will be required to fulfill the responsibilities of this position.

MARJORY A. ATHERTON
543-78-9123

Department of the Interior Announcement 95-0546-354
Assistant Administrator for Finance
Bureau of Indian Affairs

3. **Program Development and Evaluation — The ability to establish program/policy goals and the structures and processes necessary to implement the organization's mission and strategic vision. Inherent in this process is ensuring the programs and policies are being implemented and adjusted as necessary, that the appropriate results are being achieved, and that a process for continually examining the quality of program activities is in place.**

My 17-year career in the federal service has been dedicated to advancing the sound financial management practices enacted into law through the Chief Financial Officers Act of 1990, and I believe that I have developed the breadth of institutional experience essential to provide the leadership needed in this financially-troubled agency.

I have not underestimated the severity of the challenge. I have been involved in the development of Department of Interior budgets for the past seven years and recognize that the Bureau of Indian Affairs has long been identified as a high-risk agency. Before joining the federal service, I earned a bachelor's degree in economics at Columbia and a master's in business administration at Yale, earning academic honors at each institution. In each of those degree programs, my course work and research required financial analyses of large organizations—usually completed in a team environment. During my career in government, I have attained significant professional honors, including two terms as President of the Washington chapter of the Association of Government Financial Officers. This academic preparation and professional affiliation with other senior financial managers has provided the strategic vision essential to evaluate the scope of the challenge and work with senior officials to resolve major issues of concern to the Secretary and the Congress.

I have the ability to organize work logically and to define parameters of systems to resolve major agency problems. As an assistant to the controller of the Minerals Management Service during the institution of a substantial program for leasing off-shore drilling sites, I participated in development of financial management systems to account for fee receipts distinct from appropriated revenues. For the five subsequent years, I supervised an account that yielded the Treasury in excess of $12 billion annually, and exercised sufficient control that the fund was the first in the Department to develop an auditable financial statement.

In exercising that control, I initiated the development of automated information systems, and guided three teams of auditors from the General Accounting Office and the Inspector General through major reviews of the program. These audits resolved critical congressional questions—earning my team recognition for outstanding financial management systems development.

My experience within the Department of the Interior has familiarized me with the special requirements of the Bureau of Indian Affairs, above and beyond the financial successes that I have achieved. I understand the treaties under which the Bureau operates, and have worked with the Office of the Secretary and key oversight committees to the extent that I understand the shift in thinking—from preservation of an honorable heritage to preparation for a challenging future—that must guide the Bureau in the future. I believe that my combination of education and experience—and eagerness to take a substantial challenge with a major program—demonstrate the strategic vision and program management skills envisioned under this core qualification.

HENRY M. ROBERTSON
411-55-6789

Department of Defense Announcement 95-21172-301
Director, Office of Executive Personnel

4. **Resource Planning and Management — The ability to acquire and administer financial, material, and information resources. It involves the ability to accomplish the organization's mission, support program policy objectives, and promote strategic vision.**

My professional career spans 24 years, during which time I have supervised the development of substantial human resource management initiatives for three branches of the uniformed services. I have repeatedly demonstrated abilities to identify the financial and human resources necessary to accomplish critical agency objectives and—working within the constraints of appropriated funding— secured support for major initiatives of agency heads.

During the past three years, I have supervised the development of a Total Quality Management program for the U.S. Coast Guard. This measure was instituted by the Commandant at the request of the Secretary of Transportation, who wanted a model emulating the Department of the Navy's program. I was selected for this position because of my role as deputy personnel officer during the Navy's adoption of TQM. In that capacity, I developed and defended budgets through Department clearance processes and wrote key justification documents that were approved by the Office of Management and Budget and the appropriations committees. The TQM approach, contrary to the long-term orientation promised in most textbooks, proved especially successful in transforming depot maintenance and executive correspondence—resulting in Secretary of Transportation Gold Awards for management improvement during my second and third years.

The TQM initiative at the Navy built upon my experiences directing a "management-by-objectives" program for the U.S. Air Force. In that capacity, I devised and implemented systems of outcomes-based performance measures that were adopted by the Secretary of the Air Force as a replacement for the "Unit Readiness Report" format that had been the Service standard for 23 years. The new standard incorporated team oriented results, and began the effort to assess results of executive training programs within the Air Force.

These experiences built upon professional training at the undergraduate and graduate levels. I earned a bachelor's degree in post-secondary education from the University of Maryland, with an emphasis on adult education programs used by many companies for executive training. I then gained a Ph.D. in Business and Public Administration at the George Washington University, with my doctoral dissertation analyzing the measurement differences between the Total Quality Management approaches of Deming and Juran.

This combination of education and experience refined written and oral presentation skills that have enabled me to develop and present exceptionally strong budget documents. I have frequently been consulted by other units in preparation for their presentations, and am often requested to participate in panels sponsored by the National Academy of Public Administration and the General Accounting Office's professional training programs. I believe that this combination of successes gaining management support for executive development programs and record of professional training for several agencies provides the combination of experience and education necessary to fulfill the responsibilities of the senior human resources management executive in the department.

PENELOPE T. MEYERS
654-32-1987

INTERNAL REVENUE SERVICE
ANNOUNCEMENT 95-1040-4U
Deputy Chief Counsel-Enforcement

5. **Organizational Representation and Liaison — The ability to explain, advocate, and negotiate with individuals and groups internally and externally. It also involves the ability to develop an expansive professional network with other organizations and organizational units.**

Since completing my J.D. degree at the William and Mary University College of Law in 1977, I have provided consistent support to the Internal Revenue Service's enforcement program at different levels. In the course of representing the Service in state and federal courts—at both trial and appellate levels—I have developed the ability to represent an organization in the deliberative procedures in all three branches of government. I believe that the range of my experiences and ability to gain cooperation in investigations, enforcement coordination, budget development, and legislation have familiarized me with the full range of responsibilities associated with this position and prepared me to provide the leadership needed by the enforcement division at this time.

My initial position with the IRS was as an assistant counsel in the Richmond District Office. After one year of reviewing audits of routine filings, I teamed with a fraud investigation unit of the Virginia State Police to document inconsistencies in state and federal filings. The project resulted in the conviction of seven leaders of a group that coordinated false filings of claims for dependents (before this risk was reduced by the requirement for Social Security numbers with taxpayers).

My promotion to the deputy counsel in the Philadelphia regional office in 1983 coincided with one of the Service's worst automated data processing failures. As a result of these shortcomings, I was responsible for defending the Service in a series of civil cases alleging failure to meet processing standards in class action litigation. My successful defense of that suit won the Secretary of the Treasury's award for litigation, and contributed to my selection as assistant counsel for legislation.

During congressional deliberations of the Tax Reform Act of 1986, I directed the drafting and editing of all Department of the Treasury testimony on the legislation and coordinated the Service's responses to technical questions. In addition to supervising a team of five attorneys and three auditors, I was in regular contact with House and Senate subcommittee chairs and their staffs to ensure that major points under dispute in the legislation were clarified.

After adoption of the tax reform, I monitored development of the Service's regulations to ensure publication in time for the 1987 tax filing season. This required swift coordination with the Office of Management and Budget through the interagency regulatory clearance process, balanced by informational discussions with congressional staff to ensure that the regulations faithfully implemented the intent of Congress in this major overhaul. After publication of the final regulations, I provided technical assistance to the litigation team that defended them against challenges in the U.S. Court of Appeals for the District of Columbia.

This experience has enabled me to provide recurrent representation of the agency before other executive agencies and with the other branches of government. I have developed teams to support successful enforcement litigation, and have exercised the leadership for major regulatory programs under tight deadlines. This combination of leadership experiences demonstrates the skills essential to the responsibilities associated with the position.

108

C H A P T E R   8

INTRODUCTION TO T.A.P.E.S.

Federal Resumes & Performance Evaluation Systems

- Career Management

- Performance Rating

- Self - Direction

- Proven Structure for Success

CHAPTER EIGHT

Introduction to T.A.P.E.S.

The Connection Between Federal Resumes and Evaluation Systems

The National Performance Review (NPR) has caused many federal employees and their supervisors to take another look at their personal performance histories. In the past, job descriptions did not truly reflect one's duties and responsibilities clearly, nor show how one had progressed by increased responsibility, authority, or scope of duties during one's career. Federal employees saw that the documentation of their careers was lackluster, incomplete, or so "generic" as not to fully differentiate their personal career development against anyone else doing the same job in a functionally disparate arena. The yearly performance appraisal degenerated to a "paper exercise" for the supervisor and employee to muddle through and left both feeling little sense of accomplishment or pride in the effort. The process of rating performance took on a negative rather than positive aspect, which employees and supervisors or managers dreaded. A better way had to be found that could accurately describe jobs, individual performance, personal goals, and employees' achievements against challenges to the mission.

- NPR impact

- Performance ratings as a positive force

- Federal resume and career development

- Communicating with your supervisor

Your federal resume can show your role, either as employee, supervisor, or senior rater, in an evaluation system which is designed to encourage good performers and surpass mission requirements or customer expectations. In the Army Civilian Personnel system, the advent of the Total Army Performance Evaluation System (T.A.P.E.S.) was a breath of fresh air that cleared away the staleness of reporting and accountability of the previous system. The format shows the job responsibilities and duties, authority and scope of work performed, the quality of that work, and the individual efforts that accomplished that work. The supervisor is more mentor and guide in the new role. The old idea of supervision being more a punishment than a help is an idea long dead, and rightly so. The enlightened employee and manager work together to build a relationship for the greater good, which will enhance the environment and the individuals accomplishing the mission in the federal workforce. Your federal resume can reflect your commitment to change and sense of personal accomplishment through the revitalized evaluation system.

What is T.A.P.E.S.?

T.A.P.E.S. is based on the military model used in Officer Efficiency Reports and Enlisted Efficiency Reports and provides a better structure for the individual to show duties/responsibilities, challenges and accomplishment, aspirations and outcomes. For the supervisors, it aids performance counseling and evaluation; for employees, it is a clearer representation of what they have attained over a year. The civilian personnel offices have disks of the format for employees to fill in, and copies of the Department of the Army Pamphlet 690-400, Chapter 4302, explains the step-by-step completion process for supervisors and employees for the Base System Evaluation and Senior System Evaluation Reports.

The Base System Evaluation Report

The document is common-sense, user-friendly and simple, while being personal to the employee as a tool to show actual development, growth, and achievement. The **Base System Evaluation Report** is designed for Wage Grade and General Schedule (WG, GS) employees to level 8. **Part I** of the T.A.P.E.S. **Base System Evaluation Report** is administrative, identifying the ratee by position, type of rating, and the rating period. **Part II** is the authentication of the rating chain: rater, intermediate rater, senior rater, and ratee. **Part III** is for awards nomination or quality step increase and approval based on the performance and can vary widely depending on funding availability. **Part IV** asks the employee to define and review the Official Position Description and to show whether the description is an accurate one of those duties/responsibilities the employee has been performing. This section asks the employee to clarify areas of special emphasis, changes in scope or authority, and to show those training or developmental assignments over the past year which have enhanced the position. The supervisor uses this section to define counseling dates with the employee. **Part Va** is a new section for the supervisor to rate employees on VALUES, which can provide insight to an employee's expressed dedication and commitment to the overall mission and can be a definite enhancement for the employee by having the supervisor show examples of adherence. It is not used in the formula to derive Overall Performance Ratings, but as a tool to better show an employee's understanding of Army values, shown in acts or words. As Army employees, this section reflects back on the Oath of Office we take when we enter federal service. **Part Vb** defines the responsibilities the employee has undertaken and reminds the supervisor or rater of the specific results the employee has accomplished. The employee can list personal goals and objectives for the next year

- Understanding T.A.P.E.S.

- The Base System Evaluation Report Explained

against specific duties, which allows the employee to outline his personal agenda for growth, diversification, and self-enhancement. The rater marks EXCELLENCE, SUCCESS, NEEDS IMPROVEMENT, or FAILS against the areas of *technical competence, adaptability/initiative, working relationships/communications, responsibility/dependability.* **Part VI** is for overall performance rating using the Responsibilities criteria SUCCESSFUL LEVEL 1, LEVEL 2, or LEVEL 3 (compared against EXCELLENCE and SUCCESS measures), FAIR (NEEDS IMPROVEMENT or FAILS criteria), and UNSUCCESSFUL (if ratee FAILS in one or more of the Responsibilities).

- Base System Ratings

- Senior System Evaluation Report

- Importance to Federal Resumes

The Senior System Evaluation Report

The Senior System for T.A.P.E.S. is applicable to SES, WS, GM/GS over the grade of 9, superintendents, and career interns. The format is basically the same as the Base System, except for the objectives in **Part Vb**, which can more fully explain career development for each employee. The Senior System has a section **Part Vc** where detailed significant contributions are highlighted to show singular accomplishments or team participation for business process improvement/re-engineering efforts. **Part VI** is the Performance Evaluation with the rater assigning objectives ratings and showing specific contributions by the employee. Many activities or tasks first outlined or explained by the employee to the supervisor may have been changed by events, but other enhancements to duties or significant tasks or challenges overcome are noted here. Supervisors are accountable for Equal Employment Opportunity/ Affirmative Action goals and objectives in their performance appraisals, as well, and are rated on their achievement or influence in this critical element of performance.

Why is Performance Evaluation Important to Federal Resumes?

Why is the Total Army Performance Evaluation System (T.A.P.E.S.) a part of the *Federal Resume Guidebook?*

The National Performance Review (NPR) has called for change in the most structured, stilted, and, sometimes, oppressive arena of personnel management — the evaluation of performance and the job application process. T.A.P.E.S. was the Army's answer to the need for change and began to evolve before the NPR was published.

Already Federally Employed . . .

If you have been using T.A.P.E.S. or something similar in a military environment, you have a clear, concise history of your career since 1993. Your resume can be built easily by using your past performance ratings to show both professional and personal development and accomplishments or achievements along your path to your career goals. Your T.A.P.E.S. can help you define priorities for yourself in the impact your work has had, show accomplishments in objectives attained, and provide targets for future growth. Raters have given you measures of success, rewarded your efforts, and set career goals for you to attain in order to be more competitive in your career field. The progress can be communicated precisely and accurately by you in your federal resume.

- T.A.P.E.S. material as Federal Resume guide

- Job seekers using performance systems to write KSAs

Newly Employed or Seeking Employment . . .

If you have not used this system previously, but are entering into federal service, you now have a blueprint for success. The performance rating systems in the future will be standardized; that doesn't mean "one size fits all" — it means you will be rated by the same standards, but you will have an opportunity to show creatively your uniqueness and individual contributions to your organization's mission.

As a new federal employee, you will want to look at the career field you have entered and study high achievers in your field. When you design your performance criteria, look to those achievements, personal and professional, which by your accomplishing them will make you stand out from the crowd. These criteria for performance should be in line with your career field, but also highlight a broader base of knowledge, skills, and abilities necessary to the next level of performance and the next. You should know what the basic standards of performance are for your level and your supervisors' levels. You should be asking for developmental assignments, mentoring opportunities (for you and by you), showing your leaders you are capable of meaningful and constructive work, meeting with your supervisors twice a year to discuss your progress, and capturing a record of performance that is reported yearly in T.A.P.E.S. You have a greater ability to meet expectations for your supervisor and yourself with the structure used in this performance measurement plan. You can share your career goals and ideas for improvement with the individual who will be making the determination on your successful achievement of those goals and who can offer you pointers on what that success should look like.

This is quite a challenge — however, any federal employee will tell you that we are each responsible for our careers. There is not always someone looking out for you or your best interests — you are accountable for that. If you are serious about getting the best out of yourself and applying the best to your career, you have an excellent opportunity with a system such as T.A.P.E.S. In the past, most supervisors went through this paper drill, remembering only where their employees had erred or failed, usually with memories of events just a few weeks back, and not truly remembering the positive contributions their employees had made over an entire year's work. This was not anybody's fault, just the way it was, and it was not fair to either employees or supervisors.

Performance management using a tool like T.A.P.E.S. is liberating and self-empowering for an employee. You are in control of the goals, objectives, tasks, or opportunities you wish and can define for your supervisor as growth to the mission and you, professionally and personally. For the supervisor, it offers a scheduled meeting procedure to better evaluate performance, give guidance for improvement or fine-tuning of goals, and provide that personal career counseling not often planned on or granted by the pressures of the work day. The supervisor has a detailed list of requirements to bounce achievements against rather than a vague job description, which may or may not be accurate, to say whether an employee has been successful in attaining agreed upon goals. As an additional help, the supervisor has a third party (senior rater) who routinely reviews and concurs or disagrees with the evaluation to provide input on individual employee development. The process builds a relationship of understanding and fulfillment of expectations for success which was absent in previous evaluation systems.

Use the performance management or standards of performance or evaluation system within your federal agency or organization as a tool for professional growth and continuously improve on detailing your career in the federal arena. It should be the foundation of your federal resume.

> Performance Management:
> - Challenges
> - Benefits
> - Tool for career development

115

SENIOR SYSTEM CIVILIAN EVALUATION REPORT SUPPORT FORM

For use of this form, see AR 690-400; the proponent agency is ODCSPER

PART I - RATEE IDENTIFICATION

a. NAME OF RATEE (Last, First, Middle Initial) Jones, Suzie Q.	b. PAY PLAN, SERIES/GRADE GM 301 13	c. ORGANIZATION US Army Training Cmd

PART II - RATING CHAIN - YOUR RATING CHAIN FOR THE EVALUATION PERIOD IS:

RATER	NAME Sam E. Johnson	POSITION Chief, US Army Trng Cmd Operations Branch
INTERMEDIATE RATER (Optional)	NAME	POSITION
SENIOR RATER	NAME Betty Lee Johanson	POSITION Director, US Army Training Cmd

DRAFT

PART III - VERIFICATION OF FACE-TO-FACE DISCUSSION

The following face-to-face discussions of duties, responsibilities, performance objectives, standards, and accomplishments for the rating period 6 June 94 to 6 June 1995 took place.

	DATES	RATEE INITIALS	RATER INITIALS	INTERMEDIATE RATER INITIALS	SENIOR RATER INITIALS	DATE
INITIAL	6 June 94				BLJ	9 June 94
MIDPOINT	13 December 94				BLJ	15 Dec 94

PART IV - RATEE (Complete a, b, c below for this rating period)

a. STATE YOUR SIGNIFICANT DUTIES AND RESPONSIBILITIES. DUTY TITLE IS: Quality Operations Officer

Direct program areas to include standardizing field operations, evaluating facilities and materials for training, and promoting improvements, overseeing contract administration for services and protecting government interests in negotiations. Monitor and evaluate performance measures through survey, on-site inspection, and interviews with staff and students. Direct and design improvements in curriculum, contracted services, and student evaluation instrumentation. Provide guidance and instruction on computer-assisted student tracking system for enrollment, entry into Total Army Academic Development System, and formulate reports to Training Directorates, Army-wide, and for Civilian Personnel Offices across the Army. Chair the Quality Training Board with staff from Operations Branch, HQs Training Command, Support Services, and Administrative Branch.

b. INDICATE YOUR MAJOR PERFORMANCE OBJECTIVES/INDIVIDUAL PERFORMANCE STANDARDS

o Initiate re-design of computer program and network across Army personnel offices and military training centers.
o Establish standardized programs of instruction with better performance measures for evaluating instructor performance and contracted services delivery.
o Complete monthly reports within 3 working days after last day of the month for timely delivery to customers.
o Visit 5 classrooms per week to evaluate learning, materials, facilities, and get input from students and staff.
o Travel to 3 field offices per month in Command, conducting surveys and evaluations.
o Expand the sphere of influence of the Quality Training Board to include representation from field offices and their Commanders.
o Set the example for Quality Operations for customer satisfaction for soldiers and civilians for training.

116

DA FORM 7222-1, MAY 93   Replaces DA Form 5397, DEC 86, which is obsolete on 31 DEC 94   USAPPC V1 00

c. LIST YOUR SIGNIFICANT CONTRIBUTIONS

+ Enhanced computer tracking system, re-designing information solicited from students and staff, contracted computer assistance to increase network capabilities and allow access to field offices and major Commands. (August-November 1994)

+ Invited major Command representatives and field office representatives to participate in Quality Training Board. 12 staff and professionals and 5 military commanders work together to enhance training for soldiers and civilians, reporting to each MACOM Director. This has had a powerful effect on visibility and the contributions have been significant.
Honorable Mention: Army Communities of Excellence Award (October 1994)

+ Conducted 38 inspections of field operating activities, 160 classroom visits and reported to each instructor and class on their survey input used to redesign standards of measurement. (June 1 1995)

+ With input from instructors, contractors, students, and curriculum designers re-designed survey process, survey instruments, standardized performance measures and reporting system. (February 1995)
Letters of Appreciation: L&L Learners, Inc. (contractor)
BGWill B. Brighter, MACOM Director, Training IPSCOM
Ms. Wilma Flintstone, Instructor

DRAFT

+ Masters Degree in Education awarded 14 December 1994.

+ Position expanded to supervise/manage 2 specific programs; supervise 3 curriculum designers/instructors (GS11/12); 1 administrative assistant (GS9). (January 1995)

Virgil L. Jones   9 June '95
SIGNATURE AND DATE

PART V - PERFORMANCE STANDARDS - SENIOR SYSTEM CIVILIAN POSITIONS

To derive Objectives ratings, apply the applicable performance standards below; the standards are written at the SUCCESS level, e.g., Ratee, in most cases:

TECHNICAL COMPETENCE. Exhibits technical knowledge, skills, and abilities to get desired results within established time frames and with the appropriate level of supervision. Sets and meets realistic milestones. Establishes priorities that reflect mission and organizational needs. Plans so that adequate resources are available. Makes prompt and sound decisions.

INNOVATION/INITIATIVE. Develops and implements or suggests better ways of doing business--methods, equipment, processes, resources. Seeks/accepts developmental opportunities. Serves on professional/technical committees, writes technical papers, joins professional societies to enhance personal knowledge and advance state-of-the-art of profession.

RESPONSIBILITY/ACCOUNTABILITY. Uses resources prudently and for intended purposes. Complies with DA emphasis programs; e.g., EEO/AA, safety/security, internal control, inventory management, quality assurance, personnel management, contract awards to small business concerns. Supports and encourages Total Army Quality (TAQ) approaches, e.g., team effort, continuous process/product improvement and customer satisfaction. Takes responsibility for personal errors, takes or proposes timely/adequate corrective measures. Establishes personal performance objectives that are challenging and reflect mission needs.

WORKING RELATIONSHIPS. Is an effective team player. Works well with group and others to get the job done. Exhibits a customer care attitude; e.g., shows respect to others; is courteous and seeks acceptable compromise in areas of difference.

COMMUNICATION. Provides or exchanges accurate/complete oral and written ideas and information in a timely manner. Listens effectively so that resultant actions show understanding of what was said. Coordinates so that all relevant individuals and functions are included in/informed of decisions and actions.

FOR SUPERVISORY POSITIONS ONLY:

ORGANIZATIONAL MANAGEMENT AND LEADERSHIP. Provides vision and communicates mission and organizational goals to all subordinates. Sets standard/leads by example. Implements/complies with appropriate DA emphasis programs. Secures/allocates/manages resources for effectiveness and efficiency. Takes timely and appropriate personnel actions. Develops subordinates through mentoring, counseling, providing challenging training and work assignments and timely performance evaluations. Recruits and retains high quality people by creating a positive environment that offers challenge and growth.

EQUAL EMPLOYMENT OPPORTUNITY/AFFIRMATIVE ACTION (EEO/AA). Applies EEO principles to all aspects of personnel management (e.g., hiring, training, work assignments/schedules, discipline, counseling and awards). As appropriate, takes immediate corrective action if sexual harassment or other discriminatory/unfair treatment is observed, reported or suspected. Provides leadership and emphasis to the execution of the Affirmative Employment Plan. Participates in EEO/AA activities and encourages subordinates to do so.

SENIOR SYSTEM CIVILIAN EVALUATION REPORT
For use of this form, see AR 690-400; the proponent agency is ODCSPER

PART I - ADMINISTRATIVE DATA

a. NAME (Last, First, Middle Initial) Jones, Suzie Q.	b. SSN 222-22-0001	c. POSITION TITLE, PAY PLAN, SERIES AND GRADE Quality Operations Officer, GM 301-13

d. ORGANIZATION US Army Training Command	e. REASON FOR SUBMISSION [X] ANNUAL [ ] SPECIAL [ ] INTERN

f. PERIOD COVERED (YYMMDD) FROM 940606 THRU 950606	g. RATED MOS. 12 [X] GIVEN TO RATEE	h. RATEE COPY (Check one and date) [ ] FORWARDED TO RATEE

PART II - AUTHENTICATION

a. NAME OF RATER (Last, First, Middle initial) Johnson, Sam E.	SIGNATURE *Sam E. Johnson*	DATE *13 Dec 95*
GRADE/RANK, ORGANIZATION, DUTY ASSIGNMENT Chief, US Army Trng Cmd Operations Branch		
b. NAME OF INTERMEDIATE RATER (Optional)(Last, First, MI)	SIGNATURE	DATE
GRADE/RANK, ORGANIZATION, DUTY ASSIGNMENT		
c. NAME OF SENIOR RATER (Last, First, Middle Initial) Johanson, Betty Lee	SIGNATURE *Betty L Johanson*	DATE *16 Dec '95*
GRADE/RANK, ORGANIZATION, DUTY ASSIGNMENT Director, US Army Training Command		
d. RATEE: I understand my signature does not constitute agreement or disagreement with the evaluations of the Rater and Senior Rater, and merely verifies Part I and Part IV data.	SIGNATURE OF RATEE *Suzie Q. Jones*	DATE *17 Dec 1995*

DRAFT

PART III - PERFORMANCE AWARD/QUALITY STEP INCREASE

a SES - AWARD, BONUS/ SALARY INCREASE	RECOMMENDATIONS			b. ST, SL, GM, GS, WS - PERFORMANCE AWARD/QSI		
	RATING (1)	SALARY (2)	PERFORMANCE AWARD - BONUS (3)	PERFORMANCE AWARD		
				PERCENT OF SALARY 1.5	AMOUNT	$735.0
RECOMMENDING OFFICIALS		YES	NO	YES	NO	QSI (GS with Successful Level 1 Rating Only) TO (Grade/Step):
RATER						AWARD APPROVED BY
INTERMEDIATE RATER						*TRNG OFFICER*
PERFORMANCE REVIEW BOARD						DATE (YYMMDD) 950704
SENIOR RATER	ES	$				FUND CITE TRNCD-04002311

PART IV - DUTY DESCRIPTION (Rater)

DAILY DUTIES AND SCOPE (To include as appropriate: people, equipment, facilities, and dollars). Position Description (DA Form 374) is correct: [ ] YES [X] NO

o Duties expanded to include supervision of 3 civilian and contracted instructors working specifically in curriculum re-design on computer-assisted programs.

o Two new programs added to management scope: New Trainer Professional Development
Performance Measurement Standardization & Improvement

PART V - VALUES (Rater)

V A L U E S

PERSONAL
Commitment
Competence
Candor
Courage

ARMY ETHIC
Loyalty
Duty
Selfless Service
Integrity

BULLET COMMENTS

o Consistently puts mission ahead of self, hard charger

o Never tells customers, internal or external, NO; always manages to explain capabilities and responsibilities of organization without disappointing customers.

o Completed Masters Program on own time, asking only for sufficient compensatory time on Fridays to complete last quarter during morning classes.

DA FORM 7222, MAY 93   Replaces DA Form 5398, DEC 86, which is obsolete on 30 JUN 95   USAPPC V1

PERIOD COVERED *(YYMMDD)* 940606 - 950606	RATEE'S NAME Jones, Suzie Q.	SSN 222-22-0001

PART VI - PERFORMANCE EVALUATION *(Rater)*

a. PERFORMANCE DURING THIS RATING PERIOD

Comparison of individual objectives against accomplishments and DA-established performance standards resulted in the following objectives ratings:

[X] Excellence Over 50% Obj   [ ] Excellence 25-50% Obj   [ ] Success All or Excellence 1-24% Obj   [ ] Needs Improvement 1 or More Obj   [ ] Fails 1 or More Obj

Includes Excellence in Org/Mgt/Ldshp **OR** EEO/AA Obj for supv/mgr   [✓] Yes   [ ] No

b. BULLET EXAMPLES

o Completed enhanced computer tracking system two months before expected. This was high-intensity project with high-visibility from MACOM HQs. It's completion was significant event in Training Command. Exceeded customer requirements and MACOM expectations.

o Quality Training Board has been successful catalyst for change and improvement.

o All planned visits, inspections, and inventories of facilities, classrooms, and evaluation of materials for curriculum and service delivery were conducted and exceeded in most cases. This was critical to providing information on survey re-designs and service delivery capability. A tremendous effort leading directly to re-design of survey processes and performance measures. Highest level recognition and appreciation from all parties involved.

o Suzie completed her Masters Degree in Education, which she has been pursuing evenings and weekends over the last four years. She should be proud of her accomplishment, our organization has benefitted by her commitment to personal excellence and education.

DRAFT

PART VII - INTERMEDIATE RATER *(Optional)*

BULLET COMMENTS

PART VIII - SENIOR RATER

a. OVERALL PERFORMANCE RATING	SR PROFILE	b. BULLET COMMENTS *(Performance/Potential)*
[X] 2 } SUCCESSFUL 3	x	o Leadership potential is great
4 FAIR		o Should be recommended for ARMY Management Staff College
5 UNSUCCESSFUL		o Makes a positive impact on each activity or task given

A completed DA Form 7222-1 was received with this report and considered in my evaluation and review:

[✓] YES   [ ] NO *(Explain NO in Part VIII b)*

Good Work!

BASE SYSTEM CIVILIAN EVALUATION REPORT
For use of this form, see AR 690-400; the proponent agency is ODCSPER

PART I - ADMINISTRATIVE DATA

a. NAME (Last, First, Middle Initial)	b. SSN	c. POSITION TITLE, PAY PLAN, SERIES AND GRADE
Williams, Will W.	001-01-0001	Files Clerk, GS-204-06

d. ORGANIZATION TAGD, Records Administration Branch Disposal and Storage	e. REASON FOR SUBMISSION
	☒ ANNUAL ☐ SPECIAL

f. PERIOD COVERED (YYMMDD) FROM 931104 THRU 941106	g. RATED MOS. 12	h. RATEE COPY (Check one and date)
	☒ GIVEN TO RATEE	☐ FORWARDED TO RATEE

PART II - AUTHENTICATION

a. NAME OF RATER (Last, First, Middle Initial) James, Jim J.	SIGNATURE	DATE NOV 15-94
GRADE/RANK, ORGANIZATION, DUTY ASSIGNMENT GS9, Chief, Records Administration Branch, Disposal and Storage		
b. NAME OF INTERMEDIATE RATER (Optional)(Last, First, MI) Franklin, Frank F.	SIGNATURE Frank F. Franklin	DATE 11-20-94
GRADE/RANK, ORGANIZATION, DUTY ASSIGNMENT GS11, TAGD Chief, Disposal and Storage		
c. NAME OF SENIOR RATER (Last, First, Middle Initial) Samuel, Sam S.	SIGNATURE	DATE 11-21-94
GRADE/RANK, ORGANIZATION, DUTY ASSIGNMENT MAJ, USA, Chief, TAGD Support		
d. RATEE: I understand my signature does not constitute agreement with the evaluations of the Rater and Senior Rater, and merely verifies Part I and Part IV data.	SIGNATURE OF RATEE Will W Williams	DATE Nov 22, 94

DRAFT

PART III - PERFORMANCE AWARD/QUALITY STEP INCREASE

PERFORMANCE AWARD		AWARD APPROVED BY
PERCENT OF SALARY 2%	AMOUNT $484.00	Elvira Jones, LTC USA Dir TAGD
QSI (GS with Successful Level 1 Rating Only) TO (Grade/Step):	DATE (YYMMDD) 941123	FUND CITE 00-TAGD-01-111

PART IV - DUTY DESCRIPTION (Rater)

a. DAILY DUTIES AND SCOPE (To include as appropriate: people, equipment, facilities, and dollars). Position Description (DA Form 374) is correct: ☐ YES ☒ NO

Work as Files Clerk, Records Administration Branch, Disposal and Storage, supervising 5 GS Files Clerks who review military personnel records, documentation, and conduct evaluations of files in accordance with MARKS regulations and policies of TAGD support. Responsible for training, management, and career development for clerks keeping the employees current on new regulations, changes to policy, and career field expansions. Distribute and blance workload, instruct subordinates on task related issues/priorities, and monitor work to insure files are timely, reviewed, and purged. Responsible for the disposal of materials in approved methods, purging computer documents, preparing materials for disposal in appropriate burn bags. Maintain current knowledge of operations and answer questions from customers and staff on procedures, policies, directives, and military guidance. Adjust work as needs dictate. Initiate formal requests for personnel actions. Maintain environment for maximum performance.

b. AREAS OF SPECIAL EMPHASIS 100% evaluation on MARKS inspection expected June 94.
All File Clerks attend career development training in Filing Records Management, Ft. Ben Harrison, by October 94.
Zero defects reported on quarterly sweep of computer records.

c. COUNSELING DATES FROM CHECKLIST/RECORD	INITIAL	LATER (Optional)	MIDPOINT May 3 '94	LATER (Optional)

PART V - VALUES (Rater)

PERSONAL Commitment Competence Candor Courage ARMY ETHIC Loyalty Duty Selfless Service Integrity	a. BULLET COMMENTS
V A L U E S	o Sets high personal standards o Always willing to help others grow and develop in career o Great rapport with customers, military and civilian

DA FORM 7223, MAY 93   Replaces DA Form 5398, DEC 86, which is obsolete on 30 JUN 95   USAPPC V1

RATEE'S NAME *(Last, First, Middle Initial)* Williams, Will W.	SOCIAL SECURITY NUMBER 001-01-0001	THRU DATE 931104 - 941106

b. RESPONSIBILITIES	Specific bullet examples of other than "SUCCESS," are mandatory. Specific bullet examples of "SUCCESS" are optional but encouraged.

1. TECHNICAL COMPETENCE
  Technical knowledges, skills, abilities
  Doing work right/on time
  Sound judgement
 	
EXCELLENCE   SUCCESS   NEEDS   FAILS
(Exceeds std)   *(Meets std)*   IMPROVEMENT
[X]
	- Designed in-house training program for clerks
	- Conducts reviews of work with employees to insure correctness and has established "Zero Defect" program with staff
	- Customer-focus on correct data, notification of documentation gaps or scheduled disposal

2. ADAPTABILITY AND INITIATIVE
  Adjusting to change - situations/people
  Trying new things
  Seeking self-development
 	
EXCELLENCE   SUCCESS   NEEDS   FAILS
(Exceeds std)   *(Meets std)*   IMPROVEMENT
[X]
	- Maintained standard
	- Should consider using computer more and better in adapting to new filing system
	- Should enter training and development courses

3. WORKING RELATIONSHIPS & COMMUNICATIONS
  Supporting team
  Respecting others
  Expressing ideas clearly
  Listening/understanding
 	
EXCELLENCE   SUCCESS   NEEDS   FAILS
(Exceeds std)   *(Meets std)*   IMPROVEMENT
[X]
	- Highest rate of attendance and job satisfaction in this unit
	- Employees respect and admire supervisory style and support
	- Well-running organization, communicating with one another well

4. RESPONSIBILITY AND DEPENDABILITY
  Dependable/reliable
  Maintaining facilities/equipment
  Conserving supplies/time
  People/equipment safety
 	
EXCELLENCE   SUCCESS   NEEDS   FAILS
(Exceeds std)   *(Meets std)*   IMPROVEMENT
[X]
	- Good attendance records, no safety violations on IG inspection
	- Maintenance contract on computers andcopy machines expired resulting breakdowns in equipment, three week delay in work output

DRAFT

Numbers 5 and 6 apply to positions with some supervisory duties

5. SUPERVISION AND LEADERSHIP
  Mission focused/performance oriented
  Sets standard/Leads by example
  Motivating/developing others
  Implementing DA emphasis programs/managing resources
 	
EXCELLENCE   SUCCESS   NEEDS   FAILS
(Exceeds std)   *(Meets std)*   IMPROVEMENT
[X]
	- All employees have attended professional development career training
	- Has excellent staff rapport and reputation for being supportive
	- Established goal of "Zero Defects" and has encouraged staff without alienating them
	- Good TEAM effort

6. EEO AND AFFIRMATIVE ACTION
  Respecting dignity
  Achieving planned actions
  Providing opportunity
  Solving problems
 	
EXCELLENCE   SUCCESS   NEEDS   FAILS
(Exceeds std)   *(Meets std)*   IMPROVEMENT
[X]
	- Sent each employee to sensitivity and awareness classes offered by OPM on EEO/Affirmative Action
	- Attended Supervisors/Managers course on EEO
	- Bulletin boards have special section for EEO-related publications from Army, DOD, and articles from private sector

PART VI - OVERALL PERFORMANCE *(Senior Rater)*

a. OVERALL PERFORMANCE	b. BULLET COMMENTS *(Performance/Potential)*
[1] [2] [X 3] [4] [5] 1 2 3 4 5 SUCCESSFUL FAIR UNSUCCESSFUL A completed DA Form 7223-1 was received with this report and considered in my evaluation and review: [Y] YES [ ] NO *(Explain NO in Part VI b)*	o Needs to attend further development classes in career field o Should consider participating in Total Army Quality classes o Share knowledge more openly with professional counterparts

REVERSE, DA FORM 7223, MAY 93

USAPPC V1

121

CHAPTER 9

WRITING AN EFFECTIVE COVER LETTER

Organizing Your Presentation to Guide the Reader.

Boosting Your Resume to the Top.

Johnson Q. McKittrick
354 Hyattstown Boulevard
St. Louis, MO 63105
(314) 655-5578

February 27, 1995

Director of Personnel
United States Secret Service
Law Enforcement Training Academy
Quantico, VA 22594

Dear Personnel Director:

This letter transmits my completed federal resume in response to your recent announcement of law enforcement officer positions, TREA/SS/1811-7/9, 95-345X. In addition to the descriptions of my employment, I have included for your evaluation:

- a copy of my DD-214, indicating completion of service with the U.S. Air Force, and an honorable discharge, effective July 27, 1994. This supports my claim for a five point veteran's preference;

- a copy of the completion certificate from the Air Police Academy, indicating previous training related to the position advertised; and

- five one-page statements responding to the knowledge, skills, and ability factors identified on the job announcement.

Thank you for your consideration. I look forward to hearing from you.

Sincerely,

Johnson Q. McKittrick

Writing an Effective Cover Letter

To Send or Not To Send?

Both the SF-171 and the OF-612 have the advantage of being self-explanatory job applications. In preparing a federal resume, a job announcement will appear where an "objective" would be found on a private sector resume. No one should be able to confuse your application with the mountains of other mail that pile into a personnel office every day.

On the other hand, because every other applicant is responding to the same vacancy announcement, even a minimal cover letter can provide an opportunity to reaffirm information contained on the first page of the application and help to distinguish your application from every other one in the pile. Even a simple letter can begin to make the distinctions that ease the transition from application to employment. The most basic cover letter should guide reviewers through the material requested of all applicants. Before signing this letter, review your completed application and make sure that all enclosures are ready for insertion into the envelope — **in the order described in the cover letter!**

> Even a minimal cover letter can provide an opportunity to distinguish your application.

A good cover letter does more than outline an application to the officials reviewing personnel files. In responding to federal employment announcements, an applicant wants to make sure that the strongest credentials are emphasized and that reviewers have reason to focus on the critical information that separates your presentation from the others in the pile. A strong cover letter will focus the reviewer's attention upon the most important parts of your file, and help to place your application among the "most qualified."

In writing your cover letter, pay careful attention to the structure of the vacancy announcement, and describe your strengths in terms that, within the limits of accuracy, meet or exceed the expectations described in the announcement. If your best falls short of the minimum required in the position announcement, and you believe that you can provide equivalent alternative experience, the cover letter can be structured to incorporate your claim. The cover letter is your best advertisement to enable the most favorable consideration of your application.

MARISUE M. SWEETWATER

776 Horizon Terrace
Lincoln, NE 67798

Federal Emergency Management Agency
500 C Street, SW, Room 1125
Washington, DC 20909
ATTN: Marie Antoinette Jones

May 22, 1995

Dear Ms. Jones:

I am submitting this application for the position as a program specialist advertised in your announcement, FEMA-95-47326-MAJ. This announcement indicates that several positions will be filled in the GS-11-12-13 range. I would appreciate your consideration, and believe that my education and experience make me qualified at the highest level.

This packet contains all information requested in the position announcement. I have included a complete federal resume in lieu of the SF-171 and the OF-612 options included in the announcement. Allow me to elaborate upon the knowledge, skills, and abilities identified there.

- My knowledge of federal, state, and local government operations has developed through both my college education (a political science minor) and seven years of progressively-responsible work for both state and federal agencies with interwoven responsibilities.
- My knowledge of program analysis and evaluation also developed through college courses in business and economic analysis, policy evaluation, and mathematics. These skills were required in previous experiences at the GS-7 and GS-9 levels.
- My ability to conduct research and develop reports is reflected in both a senior thesis, "The Legacy of Failure in Educational Policy," and in several reports prepared in junior positions at the Department of Housing and Urban Development. One of these is mentioned in my current supervisor's evaluation.
- My recent responsibilities included service on an interagency task force that required evaluation of national security contingency plans. Members of the working group included representatives of state and local governments. My college studies included courses in American history, constitutional politics and law, and American politics (including a section on national security policy).
- I have prepared briefing materials for senior officials in two agencies, including responses to congressional correspondence that required a Cabinet Secretary's signature. I have included a copy of a recent memo that provides evidence of my writing abilities. My routine responsibilities include reporting to other members of the staff as requested by my current office director.

I have requested that my current supervisor, Mr. William N. Smith, forward the supervisor's appraisal under separate cover. My performance ratings for the past four years have consistently exceeded "fully successful." This supervisor may be contacted at your convenience.

I have included a copy of my most recent Form 50, affirming my current status as a federal employee.

As requested, I have also submitted Standard Form 181, Race and National Origin Identification, with appropriate responses.

Thank you for your consideration, and I am eager to provide any additional information that you might need to evaluate this application.

Sincerely,

Marisue M. Sweetwater

Responses to SES announcements require abundant supporting material—especially if applications are being considered from outside the current federal workforce. OPM data indicate that SES members typically have at least 10 years' federal experience prior to the first SES position, and many SES positions require a level of background that is not available to younger professionals. Moreover, an SES position will commonly require a unique combination of experiences that few applicants will satisfy.

An effective SES cover letter will ensure the reviewer of the level of experience requisite to the SES (including a cursory summation of the executive core qualifications), then direct attention to the particular strengths that the candidate brings to the position. The critical challenge in writing the SES cover letter is to emphasize that one's strongest qualifications are most vital to the position advertised, while convincing the reader that other factors can be strengthened to exceed the hiring agency's requirements. Again, the letter must be concise and targetted to the position advertised.

> An effective cover letter should not duplicate the plethora of material that is already in the file, but it should help personnel reviewers to identify the salient qualifications in the experience.

JOSEPH T. JOHNSON

147 Seven Locks Court
Raleigh, North Carolina 28509
(919) 549-9876

Office of Executive and Technical Resources
U.S. Department of Energy
ATTN: Janice W. Paiges
1000 Independence Avenue, SW
Washington, DC   20585

April 10, 1994

Dear Ms. Paiges:

Enclosed is my application responding to your announcement #ERD-95-79, Associate Director for Research, Applied Sciences (ES-1301). This application contains:

(1) A federal resume highlighting my accomplishments in a federal career that now spans more than 22 years. My current position, Director of Waste Disposal Technology Research for the Environmental Protection Agency's Air and Radiation Research Laboratory demonstrates my ability to design and manage a program of the scope and complexity of the one envisioned in your announcement. In addition, my third previous position—as Deputy Director of EPA's Office of Federal Facility Compliance—required regular review of waste disposal plans developed by Department of Energy personnel. In that capacity, I assisted the approval process for several Environmental Impact Statements that would be relevant to the advertised position.

(2) A summary of additional professional training relevant to this position. Although I do not have the Ph.D. in physics that is normally associated with directing major engineering research and development programs, these records document the presentation of more than 50 technical papers at professional conferences—including the American Physical Society, the American Academy for the Advancement of Science, and the Association of State and Territorial Air Pollution Control Officials. Moreover, the topics covered in these papers include critical evaluations of current research and technology in the pollution control field that is especially relevant to the Department of Energy's current disposal requirements.

(3) Responses to the Executive Core Qualifications required for all members of the Senior Executive Service. As reflected on the enclosed federal resume, my three most recent positions have involved increased complexity, supervisory responsibility, and budget authority, even though all have been graded at the GM-15 level. I am scheduled to complete the course of study at the Federal Executive Institute in May, which would provide additional demonstration of my SES capabilities prior to the anticipated starting date of this position.

(4) Detailed statements addressing both the mandatory and optional qualifications announced in the advertisement. In all cases, my extensive experience is especially suited to the engineering and physical science technical requirements identified as vital to this position.

(5) I have requested that Mr. Robert Quinones, who served as my supervisor in my immediate previous position, complete the required supervisory appraisal. He will forward the form under separate cover. As indicated on this federal resume, I have not informed my current supervisor of my employment search, and she should not be contacted at present.

(6) A completed SF-181, Racial and National Origin Identification, as requested.

(7) A copy of my DD-214, confirming three years of active duty in the United States Army and qualifying me for a five-point veteran's preference.

Thank you for your consideration. I will call your office in two weeks to confirm receipt of this material and to ascertain your procedures for evaluating applications and filling this position.

Sincerely,

Joseph T. Johnson

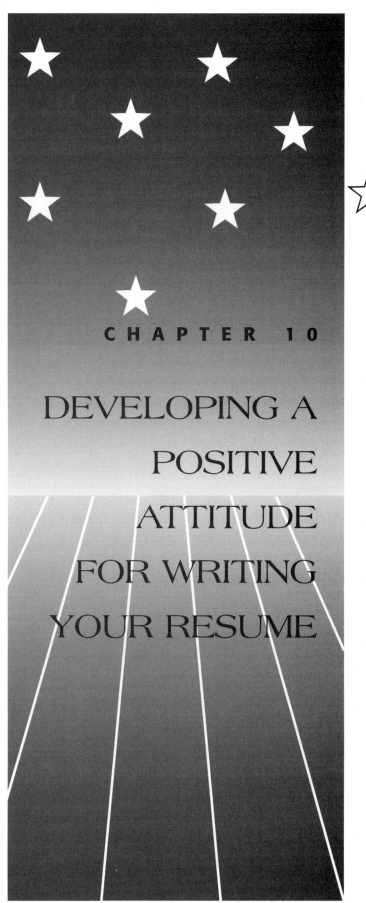

CHAPTER 10

DEVELOPING A
POSITIVE
ATTITUDE
FOR WRITING
YOUR RESUME

Step 1: Shock

Step 2: Depression

Step 3: Anger

Step 4: Limbo

Step 5: Restructuring

> This chapter is dedicated
> to the 660,000 employees
> who will face job change
> in 1995-1996.

Excerpt from the Status Report of the National Performance Review,
September 1994

Workforce Reduction

In order to reinvent government and increase performance, NPR has
sought to reduce the command-and-control structures that stifle
innovation and evoke fear in workers. Perhaps NPR's most controversial
recommendation was to reduce the federal workforce by 252,000
positions by 1999. No NPR recommendation has caused more confusion,
if not hostility.

By reducing control structures, and the number of individuals at the
controls, NPR seeks greater legibility for workers. Unfortunately, some
federal workers have interpreted this recommendation as an assault on all
government employees. In fact, front-line workers are not the prime
candidates for this 13 percent reduction. Rather, it is the 660,000 in
positions of overcontrol and micro management.

Workforce reductions were inevitable - with or without NPR and last
year's report; the budget deficit continues to squeeze all federal spending.
The question, then, was not whether to reduce the federal workforce, but
how.

Supporting the reduction - and acknowledging the difficulty of
achieving it fairly - Congress overwhelmingly approved the
Administration's request for legislation to allow agencies to offer buyouts
of up to $25,000 per employee. Generally offered through next March 31,
1996, 60,000 to 100,000 employees are expected to sign up.

**"For the first time, an administration will have an alternative to hiring
freeches and layoffs."** *The Washington Post.*

Developing A Positive Attitude for Writing Your Resume

Great performers always warm up before a performance. The best theaters have the "green room" where actors and musicians can calm themselves, energize, focus, concentrate, and prepare their "instrument" to perform. This is their preparation to express themselves fully and clearly.

Your preparation is essentially the same. You want to approach your resume writing with high positive energy. Meanwhile, your work and personal history would best surface from within a calm, centered and well-contained personal presence. This is you at your best, about to present yourself in one of several best lights. You want to be at your best as you begin, indeed, all through your resume writing.

> "People are always blaming their circumstances for what they are. I don't believe in circumstances. The people who get on in this world are the people who get up and look for the circumstances they want, and, if they can't find them, make them."
>
> ***George Bernard Shaw***

Your state of mind can powerfully impact the basic strength which you extend to your resume, your choice of words, your framing of your experience, the meaning which is conveyed. If your frame of mind is unsettled; if you are rushed or unclear; if you feel weak and out of sorts; you are better off waiting for a turn of mind before you begin. For, whatever you feel will in some way come out on your resume.

Clear the Decks

There are a great number of professional and hourly staffers who have been laid off through no fault of their own. Their performance may well have been superior to those who continue to work in their former organization. That is a sign of the times. There are a lot of well-qualified individuals who have been severed. If that is your reality, you may want to consider whether you need to go through the essential stages of grief to be able to begin the resume writing process.

Step 1. Shock

The first step of grief and loss may be a "state of shock," if indeed your separation was quickly executed and a surprise. We tend to go on overload and check out mentally when we are met with circumstances which seem to be too much at the time. Our eyes glaze over. We adopt a blank stare. But not everyone begins the loss and grieving steps here. Many begin with depression.

Step 2. Depression

This is not the depression for which many take Prozac. This is a natural part of the human condition. We lose capabilities, relationships, possessions. Even choosing what we want may require giving up some circumstances that we wanted to hold onto. When someone hands us our fate, we may feel powerless and out of control over our own destiny. This brings about a true sadness, reduced sense of energy, interest, and involvement. And it requires time to work through it. It may help to know that this is a necessary and natural part of living. If you have always met loss or change with a quick replacement, recent events may have gotten your attention. You may have to give it time.

> Even when we have a choice, we can not always have all of what we want.

In the meantime, your old employer may have you on an outplacement operation and you feel the hot breath of a jobless future egging you on to get a resume together. Your reality may dictate that you move swiftly. However, it helps to understand what you are going through, for you will go through it one way or another.

Step 3. Anger

Everyone feels some sense of outrage at the seeming injustice of the changes we have to deal with. You may still feel out of control. Even employees who have been promoted to supervisor many get a sense of anger about moving out of a comfortable job position. And they may hold on to that anger and their resistance to the new job to the detriment of their employees and their own careers.

There are times when you may feel angry and depressed all in the same moment. Feelings are like a beach ball sometimes. You can try to hold them under water, but eventually they will pop up, hard as you try to hold them under. You have to let those angry and depressed feelings flow through you and pay attention, deal with the experience, and move on.

Being in between jobs is an easy time to become intransigent and passive. You feel it is an unjust world. All of your life experience has come to this. You feel unappreciated. Long ago you expected life to be more assured and automatic, especially once you qualified with so much experience, a certain dossier, a valued degree. You could not have known the changes that have occurred. However, you will have to deal with them.

Step 4. Limbo

This is not a Caribbean dance. This is a neutral state of mind about your circumstances. Once you quit resisting your reality through depression and anger, like many, you may feel a little gray, sluggish, punked out about your situation. This is a consolidating time - kind of a winter of your existence during which you lie fallow for a while, gathering strength, deepening your taproot - to emerge stronger and more resilient.

It is toward the end of this stage that you would be doing well to start the work of a job search. Many do not have that luxury. Once again, you may be required to go through the motions. It helps to understand why you are not sprinting quite as fast because of the normal and natural stage of loss and grieving that you are working through. So even if you are faking it till you recover, you can gather some validation from this loss process to know that you are not chronically depressed or losing your mind. You are right on target.

Step 5. Restructuring

At some point, the clouds part. There is a dawning. You being to gather interest in the moment and the future. You are no longer overcome, your mood dominated moment to moment by your wrenching inner life. You can truly take an interest in others and in your future. In this light you are ready to emerge into light and clarity about what you want and what you have to contribute. At this step you are ready to revise any resume you have already written, or begin the process for the first time.

> You effectively rise on your own inner tide.

Others may have been presenting compelling arguments about why you should get a move on. Yet, you are best ready to write when you feel an emerging, impelling impulse from within. When you do, it is time to seize that surge and rise of energy to begin in earnest. So, even if you have been compelled to write an earlier version, only when you are truly ready, will you present yourself optimally. Up until now the only interest you can cook up without the assistance of a professional writer, would be about as attractive as a healthy helping of spackling paste. Be ready to present yourself full flavor.

Retracking the Offtrack

A dentist once spoke up at a career seminar. Sitting toward the back row, he raised his hand and his voice boomed over the group. "Do you know why I am a dentist today?" he asked his fellow participants rhetorically. "I'm a dentist today because some 17-year-old kid thought it would be a neat thing to do. Now I'm 35. And I hate dentistry. I want to find something I want to do. But I don't know how."

His dilemma is so similar to many of us facing a career continuation or change. Do we stay on course? Have we leaned our career ladder and career investment up against the wrong objective? Do we now dare change direction?

We generate a resume out of ourselves. Some do not believe in actively choosing a direction or goal and then pursuing it. They would rather be blown whimsically around, only later looking in their rear view mirror to determine if they can detect any sort of a career path or pattern. This may be the time to chart out your prior journey and really consider whether you are on course.

Many of us still harbor someone else's agenda as our life script. We are afraid to explore our own true selves. We die with our best music still in us. Personal exploration is best done prior to writing the resume, sending out job applications, and interviewing.

> You may be discovering a whole new person in the process of positioning and promoting your next growth and job opportunity.

Most people approach an interview with the idea that it is a one way process. They do it to you. Wrong! That again is a passive approach. As you are preparing to write your resume, see it as part of the job search, self-expression, attraction, personal contribution quest that it is. The process is a flexible one. You may be writing your resume from a different slant for each job to which you apply. And somewhere in this process, you need to discover what you want.

Your criteria of judgment for selecting your next job may develop as you converse with recruiters and interviewers. You may take extra time simply to explore and expand your own sense of what is available. Writing the resume is a process within a process. Be easy with yourself as you do it. Allow yourself to be curious, to explore parts of your own experience that provided you with vital and alive moments. This can be a review that you truly enjoy. And rather than driving your career by your rear view mirror, you can chart it out from where you have truly been, what brought you to "peak presence" and found you seizing the moment. What brought you bounding out of bed in the morning? What would?

What follows are some suggested techniques that may assist you in preparing to apply for a federal job:

Keep a journal. In it record major memories from your life and work experiences. Pick out one major event from each three-year period of your life, beginning with 0-3, 4-6, 7-9, etc. For each event, determine some of the main ingredients, properties, characteristics, payoffs, relationships. You may detect some central thread or theme, a pattern of properties. Give yourself several weeks for this exercise. You might also include in the journal your reactions and mental state, wishes, concerns, doubts, strengths, etc.

Spend time in reflection. Sit. Meditate. Pray. Talk with friends, family, career counselors. Talk with headhunters. Interview potential employers. Create your own job position or function and present it.

Do you have the position description? If so, put it where you can see it and get to know it. Post it on the refrigerator door or the bathroom mirror. Try to imagine what they are looking for. See if you know anyone familiar with the agency, office, job.

As you consider portions of your resume, paint a comprehensive picture of interest, capability, competence regarding the job you want. Each line needs to provide a benefit in getting the job. You have never done that exact work? — You come with a fresh perspective. You are a quick study as evidenced by examples. You have a driving passion for this work. Reason through each factor in your resume in order to thread through your "criteria of judgment" about the job, and your "criteria of competence," that you will present as assurance in your resume.

APPENDICES AND GLOSSARY

Appendix A: Federal Resume Samples

Appendix B: KSA Samples

Appendix C: OF-612

Appendix D: Guide to SES Qualifications

Appendix E: OPM Qual Standards

Appendix F: OPM News Release

Appendix G: General Schedule Pay Scale, 1995

Appendix H: NPR Resources

Glossary

Appendix A

Labor Economist, GS-11

GARY L. BLANKENBURG
SS# 225-68-6975
U.S. Citizen

8 Windswept Lane
Columbia, MD 21030

Home: (410) 744-4324
Work: (410) 881-9943

Veterans Preference: 5 points

Federal Status: N/A

OBJECTIVE:

Labor Economist, GS-0110-11, U.S. Department of Labor
Announcement: NCSC/ILAB 95-046

EDUCATION:

University of Tennessee, Knoxville, TN 32408
B.Sc., Economics, 1993
GPA: Overall: 3.4   Economics: 3.5

ACADEMIC AWARDS AND HONORS:

Fulbright Grant in Stockholm Sweden, August 1993 to May 1994.
Research focused on efforts to improve the labor market in the United States by researching historical and current institutions in Sweden. Interviewed Swedish government officials, academicians, and business executives who provided volumes of data and anecdotal references. Researched, analyzed and interpreted economic data.

Utilized specialized methods such as sampling, statistics and economic forecasting to gather data. Tools of analysis included supply and demand, cost benefit, labor market, ISLM equilibrium, inter-temporal external balance methods, 1st and 2nd order condition optimization, and Lagrangian optimization techniques. Procedures for quantifying and measuring economic relationships included: game theory, econometric forecasting, regression analysis, OLS methods, etc. Utilized Mini-Tab and SAS statistical programs.

Top Economic Award (Przygoda) at University of Tennessee for Exceptional Standard of Economic Scholarship, May 1993.

International Honor Society in Economics: Omicron Delta Epsilon, April 1993.

Macro Economics Award for Excellence, University of Tennessee, May 1992.

Dean's List for Academic Excellence, University of Tennessee, May 1992.

Graduate, Oakridge High School, Oakridge, TN May 1982.
Member, National Honor Society

PAPERS & PRESENTATIONS:

Federal Tax Receipts Associated with Two U.S. Labor Market Improvements:
A Proposal. Summary proposal of Fulbright research conducted in Stockholm, Sweden. May, 1994. This work anchors itself in progressive labor economic concepts, innovative child care modeling techniques, and specialized policies and programs regarding contemporary womens issues.

Economic Systems Analysis: A Case Study Comparing the Economies of Sweden and the United States. Conference paper presented at The Society for the Advancement of Socio-Ecomonics, New School for Social Research in New York City on March 27, 1993.

PAPERS & PRESENTATIONS (continued):

Economic Systems Analysis: A Case Study Comparing the Economies of Sweden and the United States. Conference paper presented at The Society for the Advancement of Scandinavian Studies, University of Texas at Austin in Austin, Texas on April 22, 1993.

Structural and Political Analysis of European Economic and Monetary Union. Research paper. April, 1993.

Two Labor Market Ideas to Strengthen the American Family: Lessons from Sweden. Research paper. March, 1993.

Economic Systems Analysis: A Case Study Comparing the Economies of Sweden and the United States. Extensive 130-page symetrical study which critically examined areas for cross-fertilization of economic and social ideas in Sweden and the United States. Academically supervised semester course, August-December, 1992.

Papers published in **Tennessean** (university newspaper), 1992-1993.

EMPLOYMENT HISTORY

Baltimore Savings Bank
21 N. Calvert Street, Baltimore, MD 21203   July 1994-Present
Assistant Branch Manager
Salary: $25,000 annually   40 hours/week plus overtime
Supervisor: Greg Summers (410) 244-3628   Please do not contact
Assist with managing retail bank operations, including supervision of 10 tellers and customer service representatives. Train staff in policies, procedures, bank products, cash management and customer services. Provide account services, bank product sales and coordination of loan applications. Introduce consumer and mortgage loan services to customers. Assess customer financial and bank service needs and make appropriate recommendations.

Fulbright Commission
12-1855 First Avenue, Stockholm, Sweden   June 1993-June 1994
Researcher
Salary: $1000 per month grant stipend   40 hours/week
Supervisor: Carol Lundstrom 011-46-08-107-2789

Learning Resource Center at Loyola Marymount University
55 Surrey Lane, Greeneville, NC 40840   January 1992-May 1993
Senior Writing Tutor
Salary: $400 per month   20 hours/week
Supervisor: Kevin O'Connor (310) 338-7702
Provided writing support and course specific tutoring in economics, history and English to undergraduates.

United States Marine Corps Intelligence Field   January 1988-January 1992
Cryptologic Spanish Linguist
Salary: $1500 per month   40 hours/week.
Supervisor: Edward A. Hall (202) 736-3259
Top Secret Clearance. Honorable Discharge, 1992.

139

MILITARY CLEARANCE AND AWARDS:

United States Marine Corps, 1988-1992.
Cleared for Top Secret information and granted access to Sensitive Compartmented Information based on a special background investigation completed on 880802 under CCN #88132-1366.

Awards:
- National Defense Service Medal (Operation Desert Shield/Storm)
- Rifle Expert Award
- Good Conduct Medal
- Overseas Service Ribbon
- Letter of Commendation
- Letters of Appreciation

LEADERSHIP ACTIVITIES:

President of the Economics Society at University of Tennessee, 1992-1993.

Student Selection Committee, 1993.
> Special appointment by University Academic Vice President for the selection of the new Dean of Liberal Arts.

Student Advisory Council, 1993.
> Special appointment by the University Dean of Liberal Arts.

Vice President of the Sailing Club at University of Tennessee, 1986.

Vice President of the Oak Ridge High School Student Body, 1981-1982.

SUMMARY OF RELEVANT SKILLS:

Economics
- Utilize knowledge of economic relationships to advise senior researchers.
- Apply money, banking and foreign exchange principles to current research.

Econometrics
- Prepare economic and governmental forecasts.
- Provide information to support policy decision-making.

Computers
- Mini-tab and SAS statistical software.
- Data compilation, statistical analysis.
- Spreadsheet and report production.

Written Language
- Construct clear, concise, audience specific reports.
- Conduct extensive research to support team-oriented work projects.

Public Speaking
- Design and present informative, demonstrative or persuasive speeches.
- Deliver animated conference level presentations with visual aids.
- Interview specialized professionals and executives on economic research.

Student - Paralegal Specialist, GS-7

ELAINE McCARTHY

1854 Arthur Street
Washington, DC 20055

Day: (202) 812-8188
Evening: (202) 554-3372

SS#: 215-76-8066
U.S. Citizen

Veteran's Status: None
Federal Eligibility Status: None

OBJECTIVE

To obtain the position of Paralegal Specialist (Ann. #GS-90, Grade 7) with the Civil Division of the U.S. Department of Justice.

EDUCATION

Loyola College, Baltimore, MD 20230
Bachelor of Arts Degree, May 1993
Majors: French, Psychology
- Top 10% (3.6 GPA)
- University of Paris Sorbonne, Summer Program, 1992

Glenelg Country School, Glenelg, MD 21228
Graduated, May 1988
- Vassar College Summer Program for Graduating Seniors, 1987

PROFESSIONAL EXPERIENCE

Davis & Lloyd, 1725 Connecticut Ave., NW, Washington, DC 20006
Legal Assistant, June 1983 - present; Full-time, $20,000 per year
Supervisor: John Jacobson (202) 872-9217, contact may be made
- Provide support services to assist civil litigation activities of a major Washington law firm.
- Review depositions of witnesses or experts providing testimony in a variety of civil proceedings.
- Prepare written summaries highlighting key points of testimony and identifying potential issues of importance.
- Generate charts demonstrating crucial points of evidence.
- Compile material necessary to prepare witnesses for trial.

D.C. Crisis Counseling Center, P.O. Box 30987, Washington, DC 20036
Counselor, May 1994 - present, 6 hours per week, volunteer
Supervisor: Carolyn Weeks (202) 872-9711
- Assist victims of sexual assault in an active rape crisis center operating in the District of Columbia.
- Provide counselling, information and referral.
- Completed 65-hour training program regarding services, local laws, and counselling techniques.

141

ELAINE McCARTHY   Page 2

Columbia Theatre Festival, P.O. Box 772, Columbia, MD 21237
Box Office Manager, Summer of 1990 and 1991, Full-time, $250 per week
Supervisor: John Levin (410) 872-9874

- Managed box office operations during a busy three-month summer season.
- Responsible for handling as much as $700,000 in transactions each summer.
- Maintained records of more than 750 trustees and subscribers to ensure timely notification of upcoming events.

COMPUTER SKILLS

Word Processing: Microsoft Word, Wordperfect
Databases: Dbase IV, Paradox
On-Line Research: NEXIS/LEXIS and BASYS

TRAINING

- D.C. Crisis Counseling Center / May 1994 / 65 hours / training in counselling and in local laws.
- Davis & Lloyd / September 1994 / 10 hours / training in how to use on-line legal databases (LEXIS/NEXIS)

SKILLS

- Proficient with Dbase IV, Paradox, Microsoft Word and Wordperfect.
- Skilled in using legal research software: NEXIS/LEXISD and BASYS.
- Comfortable in either Macintosh or PC environment.
- Fluent in French.
- Type 30 WPM.

AWARDS

- Who's Who Among Students in American Universities and Colleges
- Red and Blue Honor Society
- Vassar College Summer Program for Graduating High School Seniors
- Nominated for Dean's Award
- Outstanding Member - Alpha Chi Sorority

Realty Specialist, GS-9

JESSICA L. HEIL

2122 Alberta Street • Greensboro, NC 90847 • (310) 456-0987

U.S. Citizen
Federal Status: Secretary, GS-4, 1968-69
Department of Transportation, FAA

SS#: 214-80-9990
Veterans Preference: N/A

PROFILE

Fourteen years experience as resident property manager of a luxury condominium in northwest Washington, D.C. Skilled in tenant relations, administration, and supervision of staff. Acted as construction liaison for a $10 million rehabilitation project that involved total post-tension reconstruction. Oversight of many capital improvement projects including corridor decoration, replacement of HVAC equipment and two roofs. Successfully managed restoration project after a $5 million fire in 1983.

Ten years experience in commercial real estate property administration, leasing administration and tenant liaison for Charles E. Smith Companies for office building and retail portfolio. Experienced with GSA leasing administration.

Experienced administrator/office manager with diversified background in supervising staff, contracting, accounting, budgeting and purchasing to manage building operations.

PROFESSIONAL EXPERIENCE

THE HAY-ADAMS
4200 Massachusetts Avenue, NW
Washington, DC 20016
Supervisor: Jan McPherson (202) 872-9712

6/80 - 11/94
50 hours/week
Salary: $27,500/year
Supervisor may be contacted

Building Manager
Responsible for the on-site management of a luxury condominium with 126 units in Northwest Washington. Responsible for the supervision of a staff of 20, acting as contract manager for renovation and service contracts, and ensuring services and security to persons and property.

PERSONNEL SUPERVISION:
- Received, reviewed and delegated job orders to mechanical engineering (unit maintenance and central plant), property, service and landscape personnel. Reviewed job performance for quality workmanship and timeliness.
- Coordinated construction with owners; resolved problems surrounding construction noise, dust and traffic flow.
- Delegated assignments and motivated employees to perform job duties responsibly, efficiently in a spirit of teamwork. Increased customer service and employee morale resulting in low turnover of employees.

MANAGEMENT REPORTING:
- Attended and provided reports for monthly board of director meetings.
- Implemented new facility programs, policies and procedures.
- Made recommendations for improvements in services, control of cost and efficiency to property owners.

FACILITIES MANAGEMENT:
- Managed the care and maintenance of entire building and landscaped gardens.
- Monitored inventory control of maintenance, janitorial and office supplies.
- Supervised mechanical engineering staff maintaining physical plant and HVAC.

143

Jessica L. Heil, SS# 214-80-9990

ACCOUNTING & OPERATIONS:
- Managed an operating budget of $1.4 million.
- Maintained accounts payable, accounts receivable, prepared payroll information and prepared workpapers for accounting and taxes.

CUSTOMER SERVICES:
- Communicated with owners concerning all types of needs and problems; attentively and responsively made recommendations and provided assistance to resolve resident problems.
- Negotiated and resolved problems surrounding construction projects.

CONTRACT MANAGEMENT:
- Acted as owner's representative for $10 million property renovation project over a term of 3 years involving a major structural project.
- Successfully restored facility after a $5 million fire in 1983.
- Reviewed contract performance, quality and authorized payments to contractors.
- Liaison between contractor, subcontractors, owners and board of directors.
- Negotiated changes in services, security and noise control during construction.

DAVID E. KELLY, INC.   1970 - 1980
Commercial Management Division   40 hours/week
1101 17th Street, NW, Washington, DC 20036   Starting salary: $24,500
Supervisor: Tom Davidson (202) 737-8637   Ending salary: $25,000

Executive Assistant, Executive Vice President, Commercial Management Division

- Hired, trained, and supervised all administrative personnel. Record-keeping responsibilities for staff included $6,000,000 per month in rental income.
- Involved in Division operations consisting of 40 office buildings and 8,500,000 square feet of shopping centers, hotels and recreation facilities.
- Served as contractor's representative in creating specifications and analyzing bids for annual contracts.
- Responsible for control and privilege of confidential information.
- Acted as Division representative for all inter-departmental coordination of day-to-day activities and special projects.
- Liaison between General Counsel, Computer Services, Leasing, Tenant Alterations and Account Payable/Receivable.
- Acted as Office Manager and Purchasing Agent for Division.
- Provided leasing and tenant support GSA-leased office space, who was a major tenant in several of the multi-use and commercial properties.
- Compiled GSA lease agreements and interacted with GSA leasing specialists and tenants.

EDUCATION

Northern Virginia Community College, Arlington, VA 22304	1968 - 1971
George Washington University, Washington, DC 20006	1971 - 1978
Institute of Real Estate Management, Completed IREM 101, 201, 301	1984
John Kennedy High School, Arlington, VA 22304	Graduated 1970

Hold Active D.C. Real Estate License

Appraiser, GS-9

JEROME V. BUSHNELL

4138 East-West Highway
Silver Spring, MD 21094

Home: (301) 737-8637   Office: (202) 872-9217

SS# 219-98-0987   U.S. Citizen

Position Desired:	Realty Appraiser, GS-9
Agency:	General Services Administration
Vacancy Ann. No.:	RA-910-GSA
Veterans Preference:	U.S. Marines, 2/69 - 2/73, Honorably Discharged; 5 points
Federal Status:	Contract Negotiator, GS-1102-12 (10/79 - 8/88) Property Utilization Specialist, GS-1101-9 (8/88 - 12/90)

RELATED EMPLOYMENT

CENTURY 21
Real Estate Agent   8/90 to present
9418 Frederick Road   Laurel, MD 20706
Supervisor: Wayne Gresham (202) 943-5176 (pager)   Hours per week: varies
Starting salary: Commission (varies)   Supervisor may be contacted

Sell and list residential homes in the Baltimore/Washington metropolitan area. Skilled in communicating with potential buyers, researching listings on the multi-list software and assisting with contract and financing arrangements.

JOHN H. WILSON REAL ESTATE CO., INC.
Real Estate Agent   1987 to 1990
4 Millersville Blvd.   Millersville, MD 20745
Supervisor: No longer in business   Hours per week: varied
Starting salary: Commission (varied)   Responsibilities same as above

ABC PROPERTY SERVICES
Real Estate Agent   1985 to 1987
4133 Washington Blvd.   Savage, MD 20003
Supervisor: No longer in business   Hours per week: varied
Starting salary: Commission (varied)   Responsibilities same as above

LICENSES / CERTIFICATION

State of Maryland Real Estate License; license currently held by Century 21, Laurel, MD
Certified Real Estate Appraiser; District of Columbia Board of Appraisers, 1/8/94
Licensed to sell life insurance; District of Columbia, 1980

PROFESSIONAL AFFILIATIONS

National Association of Realtors, 1985 to present
Washington Board of Realtors, 1985 to 1990
        Member of Commerce Leasing Committee, 1989
National Association of Appraisers, 1990 to present

PROFESSIONAL TRAINING

Computer Learning Center   Baltimore, MD
- Diploma in Computerized Business Systems, July 1994

Catonsville Community College   Catonsville, MD
- Principles of Appraisal (30 hours), 10/93 to 11/93
- Standards and Ethics (15 hours), 9/93

Johnson's Appraisal School   Fairfax, VA
- Appraisal practice, completed required 30 hours, received certificate as Certified Real Estate Appraiser, 5/7/90 to 5/11/90

Jackson Realty Co. (Real Estate academy)   Washington, DC
- Completed required 45 hours; passed DC Real Estate Exam, 5/7/85 to 5/9/85

PREVIOUS EMPLOYMENT

D.C. PUBLIC SCHOOLS
Procurement Analyst   9/90 to 6/93
415 12th Street, NW, Room 807   Washington, DC 20004
Supervisor: Mr. Hill (202) 727-2495   40 hrs./week
Starting salary: $43,179/year   Ending salary: $43,179 year

Analyzed and evaluated the procurement policies and methods within the school system and served in an advisory capacity to the Procurement Officer on matters concerning the formulation of internal procedures and the initiation, development, and recommendation of new and revised procurement policies and methods within the school system.

Reviewed federal, D.C., and School Board rules, regulations, and directives affecting procurement; recommended changes in procedure to conform to the relevant laws. Monitored and evaluated the procurement functions to ensure their compliance with a wide variety of federal, D.C., and School Board regulations.

Reviewed contracts of an unusual or complex nature requiring amendments and made recommendations to the Procurement Officer and Office of the Legal Counsel. Coordinated and conducted negotiation of contract issues between the contractor and the school system in concert with the Procurement Officer and Office of Legal Counsel.

Provided expertise in the broad spectrum of procurement related areas such as formal advertising, contacting by negotiation, special contracting methods and differing types of contracts; the development and management of socioeconomic programs and set asides; the standardization of general contracting requirements; and the fair disposition of protests, disputes and appeals.

Developed and recommended solutions to unusual and non-routine problems and situations within the procurement area.

GENERAL SERVICES ADMINISTRATION   6/73 to 12/90
FEDERAL SUPPLY SERVICE
Property Utilization Specialist, GS-1101-9   8/88 to 12/90
1941 Jefferson Davis Hwy.   Washington, DC 20406
Supervisor: William Albertson (202) 557-0807   40 hrs./week
Starting salary: $31,001/year   Ending salary: $35,000/year

Jerome V. Bushnell   SS# 219-98-0987   **Page Three**

GSA, FSS, Property Utilization Specialist (continued):
Maintained selected Utilization and Donation statistics. Assisted in returns of foreign excess. Scheduled and arranged branch conference calls and made administrative arrangements for branch meetings. Significant projects: compiled annual report of property furnished to non-federal recipients; compiled utilization and donation statistics for the annual stat book; updated the AUO address directory; reviewed and analyzed the SF-121 report input, and assisted in compiling the report; tracked state agency audits.

Contract Negotiator, GS-1102-12   10/79 to 8/88
1941 Jefferson Davis Hwy.   Washington, DC 20406
Supervisor: Alfred Hardy (703) 557-1661   40 hrs./week
Starting salary: $24,703/year   Ending salary: $40,000/year

Responsible for negotiating Multiple Awards Schedules and Definite Quantity Contracts for furniture products involving extensive correspondence with many regional offices. Reviewed all available commodities and selected those items acceptable for set-asides for the small business community under the preferential Set-Aside Program dictated and mandated under the Small Business Act. Worked closely with the SBA Procurement Center Rep to assure that preferential treatment was afforded to small businesses.

Handled a multi-million dollar contract to purchase computer furniture. Managed an FAA procurement for air traffic controller chairs for U.S.-wide distribution. Knowledgeable of FARS and GSA multi-year and negotiated bid preparation. Experienced in setting up bench-marks for contract procurements.

Previous positions held at GSA, FSS include:
Procurement Agent, GS-1102-11   5/78 to 10/79
Procurement Agent, GS-1102-09   12/75 to 5/78
Procurement Agent, GS-1102-07   4/74 to 12/75
Procurement Clerk, GS-1102-04   6/73 to 4/74

USASA (U.S. Army)
Local Purchase Officer, E-5   2/69 to 2/73
4000 Arlington Blvd.   Arlington, VA 22212
Supervisor: Jim Sheffield (703) 692-0434   40 hrs./week
Starting salary: $293/month   Ending salary: $650/month

OTHER EMPLOYMENT
Insurance Agent, Security Financial Management, Inc., Jessup, MD, 1981 to 1984
Insurance Agent, Prudential Insurance Company, Bethesda MD, 1980 - 1981

EDUCATION
Dayton High School; Graduated, June 1966   Dayton, OH 44108
Greater Dayton Community College, 9/66 to 8/68   Dayton, OH 44103
Catonsville Community College, 33 credit hours, 7/73 to 1/77   Catonsville, MD 21228

ACTIVITIES / AFFILIATIONS
Toastmasters International, 1979 to 1990
Community Christian Church: Member of Finance Committee; Member of Praise and
    Worship Team; Outreach/Prison Ministry Volunteer

147

COMPUTER SKILLS
Training and experience in: MS DOS 5.0, Word Perfect 5.1, dBase IV 4.0, Lotus 123, Accpac 6.0, PageMaker 4.0, Networking with Novell Software 3.12.

Program Assistant, GS-9

DONNA STEPHENS
9006 Mill Court
Ft. Washington, MD 20744

Home: (301) 248-8831   Work: (703) 695-1647

Social Security No.:	215-76-8066
Citizenship:	U.S.
Federal Status:	Correspondence Analyst/Expediter (GS-8)
Veterans Preference:	None

OBJECTIVE: Program Assistant, GS-301-09
                        Announcement No. C-863-F

SKILLS SUMMARY:

Fourteen years experience with the Department of the Navy in Administrative positions serving as Correspondence Analyst, Team Leader, Research Assistant and Personnel Assistant.

Skilled in assisting with program functions, supporting and communicating with senior managers, coordinating work load and projects, ensuring compliance and quality control. Effective at communicating and responsively serving customers and constituents regarding activities and information.

- Research, analyze, process and track files, documentation, correspondence and information.
- Communicate with government managers and staff.
- Maintain awareness of program and management functions in order to act as effective intermediary between managers.
- Coordinate office administrative functions.
- Troubleshoot computer system.

EMPLOYMENT HISTORY:

DEPARTMENT OF THE NAVY, Washington, DC 20350   9/80 to present
Secretary of the Navy (Administration Office)

Correspondence Analyst/Expediter (GS-8)   2/92 to present
Allan Grisolm, Supervisor (703) 744-4324   40 hours/week
Supervisor may be contacted
- Read, analyze, prioritize and forward incoming correspondence to various professional offices within the Administrative Office of the Secretary of the Navy, the Department of Defense and other agencies.
- Create abstract of the correspondence using key words, cross-references and relationships to other correspondence and programs.
- Track documents and maintain information concerning action items and deadlines.
- Retrieve and update status of documents on computer tracking system.
- Review and ensure quality control for word processed documents for the Secretary for the Navy's signature.
- Representative for an Information Systems Group. Provide information to users concerning system and application updates.
- Communicate with Congressional offices, Department of Navy Heads and other inquiries via telephone concerning the status of correspondence and documents flowing through the Administrative Office.
- Utilize WordPerfect and Lotus 1-2-3 to produce correspondence, and track and report statistics on documents and correspondence.

148

DONNA STEPHENS, page two
SS#: 215-76-8066

Additional Responsibilities:
Representative, (NSSORA) Recreation Association (1993-present)
- Represent the association with three companies providing services and products to employees of the Department of the Navy.
- Select, negotiate prices and handle logistics of receiving clothing, movie tickets and event tickets for employees.
- Communicate with senior executives concerning prices, programs and activities for the Recreation Association.
- Currently serve as Assistant Secretary.

Team Leader (GS-7)   12/86 - 2/92
Ms. U. Schlegel, Supervisor (703) 695-1648   40 hours/week
Maintained efficient operations in the Outgoing Mail Records and Reference Branch.
- Provided direct supervision to student aides and clerical employees.
- Implemented training programs to improve efficiency and accountability.
- Enhanced job-related skills by cross-training and quality reviews.
- Improved efficiency of document control and processing.
- Reviewed all final documents for procedural and format compliance with DoD guidelines.
- Provided input into staff performance reviews.

Accomplishments:
* Developed and implemented a basic internal hands-on training program for the installation of the electronic document archiving systems. Trained the staff, oversaw the archiving of all previously manually maintained files, and met project deadlines.
* Wrote job descriptions for summer hires manpower. Utilized this staff to handle the backlog workload and administrative processes.
* Improved daily operations, cutting down on duplication of efforts. Analyzed systems and improved efficiency of paper flow within the Outgoing Mail, Records and Reference Branch.

Research Assistant (GS-6)   1/85 - 12/86
Mike James, Supervisor (703) 695-1648   40 hours/week
- Reviewed and analyzed technical, policy and organizational material; applied classification number according to Standard Subject Instruction Manual.
- Maintained/integrated permanent correspondence with micrographics equipment.
- Maintained and compiled a dossier for the Secretariat and staff.
- Edited and modified data from automated correspondence control system.

Accomplishments:
* Performed job responsibilities during a time of reorganization and severe personnel and equipment shortages. Participated in quality control projects; provided special service to the executive director; and delegated activities to 10 new employees handling the administrative responsibilities of this office.
* Received a Sustained Superior Performance Award.

Assistant for Awards & Personnel Actions (GS-5)   1/84 - 1/85
Ms. B. Shephard, Supervisor (703) 695-1648   40 hours/week
- Provided administrative support for personnel actions and awards. Researched personnel actions and maintained files; retrieved data from automated system; answered personnel inquiries and requests from individuals and agencies.

149

DONNA STEPHENS, page three
SS#: 215-76-8066

Naval Military Personnel Command

Mail & File Clerk (GS3/4)   9/80 - 1/84
Ms. D. Sewell, Supervisor (703) 694-2821   40 hours/week
- Received and analyzed mail and materials to be placed into military personnel records. Verified documentation and reviewed correspondence for correctness. Researched information in the database and Bidex for personnel information. Responded to inquiries concerning personnel files and entries.

EDUCATION:

Bachelor of Arts Degree, University of Maryland, College Park, MD, 1992
Courses:
Personnel & Labor Relations (24 credit hours)
Business Management (27 hours)
Information Systems Management (12 hours)

Associate of Arts Degree, Prince George's Community College, Largo, MD, 1990

Graduated Oxon Hill Senior High School, Oxon Hill, MD, 1988

AWARDS:

Superior Scholastic Achievement Award, 1992
Quality Step Increases / Cash Awards, 1987 through 1992
Sustained Superior Performance Award, 1987
Naval Developmental Scholarship, 1982

Management Analyst, GS-343-11

MARGARET T. THOMAS
SSN # 445-78-7575

1010 Edmondson Avenue
Silver Spring, Maryland 21209

Home: (301) 343-7878
Office: (202) 333-8787

Candidate for: Management Analyst, GS-343-9/11, Office of the Secretary of Defense
Announcement Number: 140-A-94-250-LP
Federal Civilian Status: Management Analyst, GS-343-11, 11/89-present
Veterans Status: Not applicable
Citizenship: United States

SUMMARY OF RELEVANT QUALIFICATIONS:

Over seven years of progressive experience as a Management Analyst in the following areas:
- managing civilian personnel actions;
- coordinating civilian and military performance appraisals;
- providing management analysis;
- monitoring evaluations, promotions, reclassifications, grievances, and incentive awards;
- advising supervisors on personnel actions;
- identifying personnel problem areas and recommending solutions;
- developing organizational structures for human resource operations;
- providing coordination of pay awards;
- maintaining a thorough knowledge of personnel rating systems;
- researching, analyzing, and preparing data.

EMPLOYMENT HISTORY

MANAGEMENT ANALYST (GS-343-11)
BUREAU OF NAVAL PERSONNEL DETACHMENT
NAVAL OCCUPATIONAL DEVELOPMENT AND ANALYSIS CENTER (NODAC)
Building 36, Washington Navy Yard
Supervisor: Dr. F. Waters (202) 666-5656 (contact: yes)

11/89 - present, full-time
Salary: $38,551

- Manage all civilian personnel functions within the Bureau of Naval Personnel.
- Coordinate civilian and military performance appraisals.
- Advise the Technical Director and Officer-in-Charge about emerging human resource management issues and recommend solutions to any problem areas.
- Provide staff coordination of pay awards for merit pay employees.
- Develop organizational structures for human resource operations.
- Advise managers and other NODAC personnel on preparation of civilian personnel actions.
- Maintain civilian personnel library including directives, documents for routine actions.
- Coordinate preparation of NODAC instructions, notices, and directives.
- Attend operational and personnel briefings and conferences.
- Act as Administrative Officer in absence of the incumbent.

Note: other positions in this resume follow this format.

EDUCATION:

George Washington University, Washington, DC 20006 - **B.S., Human Resources, 1985**
American University, Washington, DC 20009 - Completed 39 hours in Communications, 1986-87

TRAINING & DEVELOPMENT:

Department of the Navy (45 classroom hours):
Equal Employment Opportunity, Manpower and Management Analysis, EEO and Human Awareness, Managing Accelerated Production, Work Force 2000, Elements of Management Analysis, Intro to Personnel Management, Team Leadership and EEO, Staffing Part I.
Computers: PCs, Word Perfect 5.1, 6.0, Windows 3.0, Lotus 123, dBase III; Type 65 wpm
Dale Carnegie's Course, "How to Win Friends & Influence People," 1989.

151

SPECIAL SKILLS, ACCOMPLISHMENTS & AWARDS:

- Civilian of the Quarter, Naval Military Personnel Command, 1989
- Civilian of the Quarter, Navy Occupational Development and Analysis Center, 1988
- Superior Performance Awards, 9 times in 10 years, 1983-1993
- Quality Step Increases, 1985, 1980

Computer Programmer Analyst, GS-11

HAROLD L. WALTERSON
U.S. Citizen
SS# 218-86-4321

1008 Edmondson Avenue / Baltimore, MD 21228
Home: (410) 744-0112 Work: (410) 744-4324

Highest Federal Civilian Status: Veterans Preference: N/A
Computer Programmer Analyst, GS-334-11, 11/91 to present

OBJECTIVE:

Information Technical Systems Development Programmer/Analyst

SUMMARY OF QUALIFICATIONS:

- Experienced in mainframe systems environment - Current
- IBM/MVS/ESA system architecture
- TSO, CICS/VS, COBOL/COBOL II experience
- Knowledge of A/P, A/R and accounting principles
- Ability to perform detailed system analysis
- Experienced working independently

WORK EXPERIENCE:

DEFENSE INVESTIGATIVE SERVICE   **11/83 to present**
Information Systems Management & Planning Directorate   Salary: $32,000
National Computer Center Systems Development Division
45 N. Charles Street, Baltimore, MD
Supervisor: Chris Troutman (410) 744-3762   Supervisor may be contacted

Computer Programmer Analyst, GS-334/11 (promoted 1991)

Duties & Responsibilities:
- Member of Computer Programmer Analyst team providing design, development, enhancement and maintenance services to application systems.

- Perform design activities including program specifications for development and modification tasks.

- Assist in cost and feasibility analysis to determine the best solutions that will meet immediate needs of the agency.

- Provide support to application systems including feasibility studies, cost benefit studies, resource requirement studies.

Projects:
- Developed a <u>label creation system for the mailroom.</u> System included CICS programs for: data entry, updating, deleting, selecting labels for printing System; also included batch program written in COBOL for actual printing of labels.

- <u>Member of conversion team managing system changeover from DOS to MVS.</u> Responsible for identifying differences, in establishing standards for the new environment, and running parallel to verify results.

HAROLD L. WALTERSON
SS# 218-86-4321

- <u>Member of conversion team</u> that took system in Ohio running in SAMSAM/ SAMTAM environment and adapted them to run in a <u>CICS/COBOL/VSAM</u> environment. Approximately 100 CICS programs and 125 batch COBOL programs had to be written to accomplish this task. Worked closely with the end-user development test data

- <u>Created system to upload data from PC (off-site)</u>; ran data against mainframe files; downloaded results back to PC.

U.S. CUSTOMS SERVICE   1/81 - 11/83
Financial Management Division, Computer Section
Customs House, Baltimore, MD
Supervisor: Andrew Shuster
    (U.S. Customs is the only U.S. bureau that creates profit from tarriffs, export fees, etc. The Financial Management Division was responsible for A/R, A/P, general ledger management and financial information management)

Computer Operator/Programmer Trainee, GS-334/5

Duties & Responsibilities:
- Utilized an on-line system communicating with 3 out of 7 regional offices
- Wrote programs to produce ad hoc financial reports for Comptroller
- Maintained existing A/P and A/R programs
- Performed detailed system analysis working independently
- Maintained Accounts receivable; maintained receivable data from import-export brokers
- As requested by user, designed, developed, coded and implemented an on-line Inventory Control System for regional Logistics Management Branch.
- Wrote programs in Datashare language system automated a manual system and generated reports used by both local management and HQ personnel.
- Responsible report preparation for Financial Management Branch.
- Maintained existing programs.

EDUCATION

Howard Community College, Columbia, MD
Data Processing Technology Major
Associate of Arts Degree, 1980
Major: Data Processing Technology   Minor: Accounting
Deans List: 2 semesters

TRAINING

Job Control Language & Utilities, State of Maryland, Certificate
Datashare Programming Course, Datapoint Corporation, Certificate
CICS Application & Design, Advanced Technology Systems, Inc., Certificate
Introduction to IBM-PC, Dundalk Community College, Certificate

SPECIAL SKILLS, ACCOMPLISHMENTS, AWARDS

Superior Performance Award 1992
Quality Step Increases 1992 and 1993

153

Child Development Specialist, GS-12

CAROLINE P. DAWSON

54 Rockledge Drive / Perryville, MD 21228 / (410) 744-0112

SS# 218-90-4321
U.S. Citizen

Highest Federal Civilian Status: Teacher-Supervisor,
Child Development Services, GS-1710-07-10

POSITION DESIRED:

Training & Curriculum Specialist, GS/GM 1701
Announcement #95-T&C SPEC

PROFILE:

Education program specialist for child development programs and services. Experienced teacher with pre-school, elementary and secondary levels. Skilled as supervisor and instructor of teachers and staff. Consulting background in areas of curriculum and program development; assessing program quality and effectiveness; and selection of age-appropriate toys and materials. Skilled researcher, writer and presenter. Strong administrative, budget and program management abilities.

EDUCATION:

B.S., University of North Carolina, Chapel Hill, NC 48098 Major: Dietetics
Graduate Coursework in Elementary & Early Childhood Education
St. Leo College, Ft. Lee, VA; Old Dominion University, Norfolk, VA; Longwood College, Farmville, VA; Virginia State University, Petersburg, VA (54 credits)
Harriet Tubman High School, Boone, NC 48987

CERTIFICATION:

Elementary Education Certification, 1972
Vocational Home Economics Certification, 1968

EMPLOYMENT HISTORY:

ABERDEEN PROVING GROUND, Maryland
Supervisor: Jackie Wade (410) 719-8800
Starting salary: $29,300/year

5/94 to present
Contact may be made
40 hours/week

Teacher-Supervisor - Child Development Services
- Responsible for supervising six education technicians; planning and implementing instructional activities for children, ages 18 to 36 months. Communicate with parents concerning children's progress and instructional goals.
- Program instruction responsibilities include: developing and recommending curriculum and age-appropriate activities to meet needs and interests of children.
- Responsible for administrative duties including: maintaining child records; ordering and monitoring inventory; and ensuring that sanitation, safety and emergency procedures are followed.
- Participate in the selection process of new employees by reviewing qualifications, interviewing candidates and selecting new hires. Provide Center orientation.
- Act as Child Development Center Director supervising 4 teachers, 40 staff members. Responsible for Center functions in the absence of the Director.

Caroline P. Dawson, Page 2
SS# 218-90-4321

CHILD DEVELOPMENT SERVICES 1991 - 1993
    46-56 Kinderstrassen, Bonn, Germany
    Superviser: Ingrid Dreiseen 001-34-234-0987   40 hrs./week
    Starting salary: $25,600/year   Ending salary: $26,500/year

Education Program Specialist for Child Development Services (CS)
Development Program Consultant/Trainer - CDS Staff & Family Child Care Providers
Detailed as **Center Coordinator and Director** in their absence.

Education Program Specialist:
- Cooperated with the Development Assessment Team to develop an assessment and overview of the Center.
- Consulted with teachers to select age-appropriate toys and materials.
- Assessed Center programs using environmental rating scale and the Child Abuse Risk Assessment Tool (C.A.R.A.T.).
- Monitored developmental programming through observation and role modeling in child activity areas.

Training Specialist:
- Provided technical assistance on training and availability of resources to other proponents contributing to Child Development Services training components.
- Monitored direct service personnel, child interaction and supporting staff.

Accomplishments:
- Implemented and managed an active program of parental involvement.
- Maintained professional library for staff and parents.
- Coordinated the successful relocation of a child care center.
- Conducted community-wide needs assessment survey.

Substitute Teacher - Sewell Public Schools, Sewell, NJ, and Germany   1989 - 1991
- Implemented curriculum and teaching programs.

Facilitator - U.S. Army Family Symposium, Germany
- Developed program topics, recruited speakers and panel experts. Organized, planned and chaired family programs. Organized community leaders and volunteers to assist with planning and carrying out programs.

COMMERCE MANAGEMENT ASSOCIATES 1987 - 1989
    10331 Baltimore-Washington Blvd., Baltimore, MD 20003
    Supervisor: Wade Levinson (410) 456-0987   40 hrs./week
    Starting salary: $26,500/year   Ending salary: $28,500/year

Research Assistant / Executive Assistant
- Supervised a junior research assistant. Conducted orientations for new employees. Managed and monitored state and federal contracts. Managed a budget of $750,000 for the U.S. Department of Health and Human Service. Interacted with personnel from the corporate President to project officers.

Caroline P. Dawson, Page 3
SS# 218-90-4321

CHARLOTTE SCHOOL SYSTEM   1984 - 1987
   45 Canola Circle, Charlotte, NC 54365
   Supervisor: Lettie Owens (804) 987-4329   40 hrs./week
   Starting salary: $19,489/year   Ending salary: $24,897/year

   Home Economics/Title I Reading Teacher
   • Established and implemented teaching program activities and curricula. Developed teaching strategies based on needs assessment of students and institutional requirements. Planned and arranged for home economics students to participate in local and state level of competitions.
   • Coordinated with professionals in educational programs to conduct workshops and seminars for students. Developed training plans for teacher's aide and volunteers.

ARLINGTON COUNTY PUBLIC SCHOOLS   1982 - 1984
   34 Arlington Blvd., Arlington, VA 20003
   Supervisor: John Byrd (703) 987-0987   40 hrs./week
   Starting salary: $17,897/year   Ending salary: $18,098/year

   Home Economics Teacher

HEIDELBURG ELEMENTARY SCHOOL   1977 - 1980
   50 Belmont, Heidelburg, Germany
   Supervisor: Ari Lowenstein   40 hrs./week
   Starting salary: $14,879/year   Ending salary: $16,800/year

   Elementary Education Teacher

OTHER PROFESSIONAL TRAINING:

   Civilian Personnel European Training Program
      Heidelburg, Germany, 40 hours, 1993
      Fundamentals of Writing Basic Management Techniques
   Child Development Services, Dresden, Germany, 40 hours, 1991
      Child Development Services Orientation
      CDS Coordinator Training
   ASCD's National Curriculum Institute, University of North Carolina
      Bonn, Germany, 16 hours, 1991
      Current Issues in Early Childhood Education
   Lowenstein Elementary School, Lowenstein, Germany, 1993
      In-service training in Child Sexual Abuse.

HONORS & AWARDS:

   Army Certificate of Appreciation for Patriotic Civilian Service, 1993
   Scroll of Appreciation for Volunteer Service, Zweibrucken, Germany, 1993
   Scroll of Appreciation for Outstanding Service, Belmont Community, Germany, 1993
   On-the-Spot Award for Outstanding Job Performance, Bonn, Germany, January 1992
   Exceptional Performance Ratings, 1992, 1993

Engineering Technician, WS-10

JOHN H. SMITH

U.S. Citizen
SS: 210-99-8439
Veterans' Preference: 5 points
Highest Civilian Grade Held: WS-5402-12, 4/94-present

53 Crownsville, Road
Baltimore, MD 21225
Home: 410-744-4324
Work: 301-737-8637

OBJECTIVE: Engineering Technician (Project Manager) GS-802-12
Announcement Number: N-905

SUMMARY OF QUALIFICATIONS:

- Project manager for new and renovation construction projects.
- 15 years of experience as supervisor.
- Skilled budget manager.
- 30 years of technical construction knowledge regarding equipment, materials, design specifications, and environmental considerations.
- Skilled as liaison between customers and contractors to assure proper implementation of changes.
- Extensive training in supervision, management, job skills, and EEO.
- 13 years experience as EEO counselor.

CERTIFICATIONS:

First Grade Engineer, State of Maryland, 1995

EMPLOYMENT EXPERIENCE:

Department of the Navy, Naval Surface Weapons Center
10910 New Hampshire Avenue
Silver Spring, MD 20910-5000
Supervisor: Mark Cohen (301) 744-0800

4/94 - Present
50 hours per week
$24.50 per hour
Present supervisor may be contacted

**ACTING PROJECT MANAGER, MINOR SPECIFIC CONSTRUCTION
CODE 580, WS-5402-12**

ENGINEERING TECHNICIAN, WS-5402-10
Project manager for Washington District-wide projects ranging from 1,000 to 80,000 sf and with budgets ranging from $25K to $700,000K. Manage an average of 4 to 9 projects simultaneously on an ongoing basis. Customers include the U.S. Army, Navy, Marine Corps, Washington Naval District. Supervise an average of 20 to 40 tradesmen per project. Report to a Zone manager concerning minor specifics. Responsible for all aspects of project from intake, construction analysis, planning, scheduling, managing budget, customer liaison, quality control AND COMPLETING PROJECT ON TIME AND ON BUDGET.

As Project Manager manage all active customer requests (CR-1s) for designated customers. Track customer requests from receipt into PWC through completion and close-out. Handle warranty issues; researching problems and ensuring customer satisfaction. Customer requests include the following: renovation of office space, remodeling of offices, heating, a/c, electrical power modifications, ceilings, lighting, floors, applications of flooring, painting, erection of doors, storage areas and modifications to specific construction.

DUTIES & RESPONSIBILITIES:

Construction Consultant -
Planning, Design and Management Stages:
- Technical supervisor of construction and engineering projects involving new construction design and management, repair, and modifications.
- Participate in pre-scoping and design conferences with A/E and customer representatives.
- Technical assistant and advisor analyzing construction, engineering and architectural aspects, complex technical specifications and special laws and regulations.
- Interact with designers and customers to determine the best needs to fulfill project. Review additional services for electrical, domestic and sanitation provisions to meet the needs and provide customer comfort throughout construction phases.

Project Management:
- Coordinate project schedules; ensure commitment of all parties including design, SCE, PWC related departments, supply commitments and procurement needs.
- Plan work schedule and timetables and develop plans and solutions:
  - initial and final assessment for expenditures
  - environmental and safety procedures
  - quality of equipment and material
- Manage materials and equipment for projects.
- Experience in identifying risk for asbestos, hazardous waste, removal and disposal, and recommendations for alternative needs.
- Ensure that databases are maintained.
- Utilize best methods to accomplish any type of construction project.

Public Work Center Liaison:
- Monitor changes in work flow to improve operations and increase productivity within guidelines set by the Public Work Center, Washington Naval District.
- Coordinate all actions with appropriate PWC personnel. Ensure prompt and unified efforts are provided throughout project.
- Represent and handle problems for the customer within the PWC.
- Assisted with formulation of goals, budget and manpower requirements throughout construction projects, proposed engineering/architectural designs.
- Provide technical direction to constituent areas of study. Analyze results from project scope, funding and resolving problem areas.

Customer Relations:
- Communicate with customers throughout project in order to meet budget and project schedules. Attend weekly meetings to discuss project and resolve issues.
- Perform evaluations to ensure flow of work completions, monitor workload.
- Monitor customer's funded workload for Acquisition Planning.
- Coordinate surveys, inquiries and production records in order to resolve problems.

Recent project:
- Sole responsibility for the renovation of the Naval Inter-Agency Postal Service at Building 94, Anacostia Naval Station.

John H. Smith, SS# 210-99-8439 Page Three

Naval Surface Warfare Center 1/81 to 4/94
10901 New Hampshire Avenue, Silver Spring, MD, 20903 40 hours per week
Supervisor: Carter Barnes (202) 294-1415 $12.60/hour to $16.94/hour

Acting Superintendent PW Shops (1991, 6 months)
- Served as Acting General Foreman of Public Works maintenance shops.
- Responsible for the day-to-day operation of all public works functions including carpentry, machine, paint, pipe, refrigeration, boiler plant, roads and grounds, and trouble-center repair shops.

Supervisory Foreman Boiler Plant
Acting General Foreman (1987-1988)
- Managed a main boiler plant and 35 boilers throughout facility.
- Supervised a staff of 86 tradesmen. Coordinated, scheduled manpower.
- Planned preventative maintenance programs.
- Led safety and training seminars.
- Prepared production reports on fuel consumption, cost and maintenance operations reports, equipment modifications/up-grade estimates.
- Maintained/updated instructions, regulation manuals, files, logs and equipment.
- Responsible for safe and efficient operation of all buildings/plants throughout the military complex, including: control of steam, hot water and humidity levels.
- Responsible for the electrical shop operations and served as troubleshooter during any storms or other mechanical problems.

Previous Experience:
Utility System Repairer and Operator, General Services Administration (1979-1981)
Boiler Plant Operator in Charge - Naval Surface Weapons Center (1977-1979)
Foreman, Heating Mechanics, Housing Authority, Baltimore City (1976-1977)

EDUCATION

Maryland GED Certificate, April 1975

ADDITIONAL TRAINING/EDUCATION

Community College of Baltimore, Math - 6 credits
Basic Electrical Maintenance, 96 hours, Dundalk Community College, 1974
Quality Assurance Manager, 40 hours, Washington Navy Yard, 1985

EEO training: Performance Appraisal Review, Preventive Discipline, Performance Evaluation and Appraisal Rating, Supervisor Development Program, Rights of Supervisors, Building Productive Labor-Management Relations, Prevention of Sexual Harassment, Top Quality Management Initiative Training.

Supervisor training: Practical Personnel Management, Preventive Discipline, FERS Training, Communications Skills, Internal Control, Career Planning, Legal Responsibilities, Timekeeping, Setting Goals, Supervisory Development.

Safety training: CPR, Supervisor Safety, Hearing Conservation, Protective Equipment Supervisor, Health and Safety, Confined Space and Rescue Techniques, Asbestos Removal and Protection, Hazardous Waste Handling, Elevator Safety Training, Safe Handling Compressed Gases, Ordinance Qualifications Certification.

Technical training:
Contracting Officer Technical Representative
Corrosion Control, Equipment Design and Usage, Fiberglass Facilities
Cleaver Brooks Boiler Construction
Energy Conservation
Bureau of Mines Feedwater Treatment
Fundamentals of Pneumatic Controls
Corrosion Control Underground Facilities and Equipment
Drew Feedwater Treatment and Watertowers
Mechanical Seals School
Power Principles Instructor Training
Mechanical Seal & Plumbing
Quality Assurance Evaluation

Areas of Technical Expertise:
Sheet metal, breaks, crimpers, seamers, Philia slip formers
Electrical amprobes, continuity tester, volt probes, ETC
Piping and plumbing, steamfitting, threaders, cutters, rollers, benders, light welding
Carpentry: planers, routers, joiners, skill/band saws, jug saw, lathe, all hand tools
Refrigeration: guages, sweating tools, testers, hermitic analyzers, vacuum pumps
Masonry: brick laying, concrete forming, poured concrete, block
Lagging: wet and dry insulating material, seamers, cutters
Mechanical: Lathes, planers, shapers, millers, micrometers, calipers, drill presses.

Specification Reading and Writing:
Able to write, interpret specifications from: tech manuals, manufacturer's specifications, verbal instructions, schematic drawings and blueprints, standard operating instructions, security and safety pamphlets, equipment and personnel safety regulations.

SPECIAL SKILLS, HONORS, ACHIEVEMENTS

Superior Performance Award, 1981, 1982, 1983, 1987, 1988, 1991, 1992
Special Achievement Award, 1982
Public Works EEO Award, 1990
Public Works Safety Committee Chairman, 1984
Certificate of Recognition, Adult & Community Education for Peer teaching & Basic Skills Teaching, Board of Education City of Baltimore, MD, 1987
Certificate of Appreciation for the National Committee for Employer Support of Guard & Reserve
Member, National Association of Power Engineers
Notary Public for the City of Baltimore

Program Analyst, GS-12

MICHAEL L. GENSTAR

1010 Rockville Pike, Unit 102   U.S. Citizen
Rockville, MD 20852   SS #: 338-67-7878

                    Home: (301) 530-5400   •   Work: (301) 496-9600

OBJECTIVE: **Program Analyst, National Institutes of Health, GS-12**
                   Announcement No. I-907

PROFILE:

Sixteen year Federal government career with an emphasis on financial, budget and program analysis, research and preparation of reports and statements. Extensive computer skills utilized to research data via LAN and databases; analysis of data; and preparation of statistical reports. Communication with department and program managers concerning research and outcome of budget questions, report preparation and schedules.

PROFESSIONAL EXPERIENCE

National Cancer Institute, Bethesda, MD   12/90 to present
900 Rockville Pike, Room 10A50, Rockville, MD 20205
Thomas Stillman, Supervisor; Telephone: (301) 496-9787
Salaries: $49,567 to $55,777
Yes, you may contact present employer.

Program Analyst, Division of Cancer Prevention and Control (DCPC), (GS-12/4), Administrative Management and Planning Branch

Provide administrative and management programs support for the Director and divisional programs in areas of personnel management, administration, budgeting, property management and other related administrative areas.

Personnel management responsibilities include division responsibilities for Senior Executive Service personnel recruit actions; act as executive secretary for the Qualifications Review Committees and preparing official minutes from Qualifications Review Committee meetings. Maintain performance appraisal system management for divisional employees. Prepare and review special compensations. Member, National Cancer Institute Committee, that developed standard performance elements and standard performance standards for various positions.

Advise program Administrative officers on personnel issues, including policies and procedures. Counsel employees on personnel questions and procedures. Supervise an administrative technician.

161

Grants Financial Analyst (GS 12/2)   3/89 - 12/90
National Cancer Institute, 6120 Executive Blvd., Rockville, MD
Mary Thompson, Supervisor; Tel: (301) 496-5803
Beginning Salary: $45,999

> Prepared and analyzed grant budgets involving multi-year budget projections for grant research programs: Cancer Centers, Clinical Cooperatives Group, Small Grants, Small Business Innovation Research, Instrumentation program and Scientific Review and Evaluation Programs.

> Communicate with program directors and administrative officers concerning availability of funds for grant research programs. Prepare and analyze funds financial schedules reflecting a surplus or deficit; monitor current financial information and program information within the database system; conduct analysis on grant research programs to provide financial information on direct/indirect cost trends, grant approved rates, grant award rates and balances. Reconcile and examine accounting reports of obligations and expenditures.

> Computers: Symphony, IBM PC connected through a LAN to an IBM 370 mainframe.

PENSION BENEFIT GUARANTY CORPORATION, Washington, DC   6/87 - 3/89
Corporate Budget Dept., 2020 K Street, NW, Wash., DC 20006
Henry Thompson, Supervisor; Tel: (202) 778-8809
Beginning Salary: $39,787

Budget Analyst (GS11/3)
> Prepared, evaluated and analyzed personnel services compensation and benefits execution reports, forecasts, budget estimates, budget plans for several departments within the Corporation's Revolving Fund Account. Prepared staffing plans, advancement procurement plans, schedules, exhibits and background material for several departments within the Revolving Fund Account. Evaluated and analyzed data within financial reports.

> Oversaw FARS Funds Control Data Base System for establishing, monitoring and updating allotments for all departments in the Revolving Fund Account. Responsibilities for the budget execution functions included assigning, reviewing and approving work assignments performed by a budget assistant.

FEDERAL HIGHWAY ADMINISTRATION, Washington, DC   9/84 - 6/87
Budget Division, 400 Seventh Street, SW, Wash., DC 20590
H.A. Netheny, Supervisor; Tel: (202) 366-0611
Beginning Salary: $37,666

Budget Analyst (GS 9/6)

      Prepared summaries, evaluation of fiscal plans for the Motor Carrier Safety Program. participated in the FHA's Budget Formulation process preparing budget estimates, narrative justifications, background material and program memoranda. Worked in cooperation with budget staff members and program officials to obtain information.

INTERNAL REVENUE SERVICE, Wheaton, MD   11/78 - 9/84
Examination Division, Box 1802, Wheaton, MD
Mary Finch, Supervisor; Tel: (301) 427-7409
Beginning Salary: $31,090

Tax Auditor, Examination Division

      Analyzed individual tax returns including sole proprietorships to determine tax liability; interviewed taxpayers; applied appropriate laws and procedures; explained adjustments and negotiated agreement regarding proposed adjustments. prepared detailed reports. Skilled in analyzing financial documentation and reports.

EDUCATION:

      B.S., General Business and Management, cum laude, Dean's List
      University of Maryland, College Park, MD 1977

CONTINUING EDUCATION:

National Property Management Association
      Property Management for Accountable Property Officers and
            Federal Custodians, 8 hours, 1994

USDA Graduate School
      Facilities Management, 24 hours, 1993
      Inventory Management, 16 hours, 1993
      Intro to Property Management, 16 hours, 1993
      Federal Supply Schedules and Small Purchase Procedures, 40 hours, 1993
      Intro to Federal Acquisition, 40 hours, 1993

National Cancer Institute
      Module 6: Grants, Contracts and Administration, 11 hours, 1989

National Institutes of health
      Basic Inquiry and Reporting System/IMPAC, 20 hours, 1989

REFERENCES

      List 3 here
      name, title, organization, address, telephone

Computer Systems Specialist, GS 334-13

MOSES W. JACKSON
015-30-1691
U.S. Citizen

6415 Apple Tree Court • Cabin John, Maryland 20818 • (301) 320-6718

Federal Civilian Status: Computer Systems Analyst, GM-334-15, 10/84-4/88
Veteran's Status: U.S. Army, Honorably Dischaged

PROFILE

Computer systems engineer and project manager with effective marketing experience and extensive knowledge of Federal procurement processes. Recent accomplishments include major subcontract responsibilities for development of Automated Client Eligibility Determination System (ACEDS) to improve District of Columbia benefits administration. Experience in major Federal agencies, including Departments of State, Defense, Justice, and Environmental Protection Agency.

RECENT EMPLOYMENT

Vice President, ETHAN ASSOCIATES, Inc.
3215 Martin Luther King, Jr. Avenue, SE
Washington, DC 20032
Supervisor: Nick Ethan (202) 836-7878

August, 1994 - Present
Full Time Position
Please do not contact supervisor.
Current Salary: $72,000 per year

Manage development of plans for conversion of ACEDS from an IBM ES9000 base platform to a client/server environment. Supervise systems programmers installing new systems while maintaining functionality of existing operations. Monitor time and costs of new software installation projects.

Project Manager/Senior Technical Staff
ADVANCED SYSTEMS TECHNOLOGY, Inc.
Metro Plaza 1, Suite 450, 8401 Colesville Road
Silver Spring, Maryland 20910
Supervisor: Mike Woodson (301) 588-7000

August, 1992 - July, 1994
Full Time Position

Salary for Period: $68,000 per year

Assisted consolidation of the Department of Defense's Mega-Center for the national capitol area. Directed development of a data base for inventory management. Developed operational procedures for deployment of client/server technology in overseas offices of the State Department. Developed automated systems and procedures for PC equipment and software maintenance.

Program Manager/Senior Systems Engineer
SYSTEMS ENGINEERING AND MANAGEMENT ASSOCIATES
5111 Leesburg Pike, Suite 808
Falls Church, VA 22041
Supervisor: Cynthia Millican (703) 845-1567

October, 1989 - August,1992
Full Time Position

Salary for period: $50,000 per year

Managed computer systems operational and development projects for a technical contractor supporting the work of several Federal agencies. Major projects included:

EMPLOYMENT HISTORY

- Developed innovative applications with Project Workbench to support the Defense Information Systems Agency's JOPES implementation. Calculated software costs, planned schedules, and managed tasks to ensure completion.
- Implemented a project management system using a SuperProject Expert base to tailor templates monitoring milestone costs of electronic equipment installations at Department of State overseas posts. Developed and modified workplan to support timely allocation of resources and to schedule delivery of products.
- Evaluated performance and capacity of an IBM 3090/600S, 300E national computer center. Examined performance of Real, Virtual, and Auxiliary Storage (DASD) in a loosely-coupled MVS/ESA environment under TSO and ADABAS. Designed, developed and implemented ADABAS/NATURAL and ANSI COBOL applications using CICS/VS command functions.

Senior Computer Analyst   May, 1988 - October, 1989
FOTTEN DESIGN, Inc.   Full Time Position
1400 Fenwick Lane
Silver Spring, MD   Salary for Period: $48,000 per year
Supervisor: Daisy B. Nelson (301) 431-6630

Designed and supervised implementation of teleprocessing systems using the Neview Control Program. Projects included an optimization of MVS/XA and ESA operating systems using BEST/1. Managed a team of systems analysts and programmers to accomplish timely installation of a retail teleprocessing network using an IBM 3900 host linked to a network of IBM 3270 work stations and PS/2 microcomputers. Served as a technical consultant for applications programmers using ADABAS, CICS, COBOL, IDMS, FORTRAN INFO, JCL, JES2, JOVIAL, M-204, MS/DOS, OS/VS, PRIMOS, RPG, TSO, WYLBUR, AND VSAM. Evaluated proposals to develop an integrated dial-up system enabling PCs to network with FAX and electronic mail capabilities.

Computer Systems Analyst   October, 1984 - April, 1988
FEDERAL TRADE COMMISSION   Full Time Position
600 Pennsylvania Avenue, NW   GM-334-15
Washington, DC 20580   Starting Salary: $62,429 per year
                                            Ending Salary: $68,346
Supervisor: Charles Betton (202) 653-2073

Developed concepts for the management of information resources to support the operations of a major Federal regulatory commission. Developed and implemented management reporting procedures. Served as technical advisor for the implementation of budget, planning, and management systems. Met with senior officials from other agencies and wrote agency comments on regulatory and policy proposals governing the acquisition and development of information services technologies by Federal agencies.
- Developed Asset Inventory Management Plan for the Commission
- Developed and implemented Monthly Status Report Procedure for tracking the Automated Systems Division's performance indicators.
- Developed the Commission's Internal Controls Security Plan to improve automated systems information security.

EMPLOYMENT HISTORY

Associate Director for ADP Planning   August, 1983 - July, 1984
FEDERAL TRADE COMMISSION   Full Time Position
600 Pennsylvania Avenue, NW   ES-334-001
Washington, DC 20580   Starting Salary: $56,945 per year
                             Ending Salary: $59,203
Supervisor: Commissioner Bruce Yandle

Directed development and implementation of user needs assessment procedures to support automation of a major Federal regulatory agency. Planned for use of automated data processing systems, forecasted user demand and recommended allocation of resources to support Commission operations.

Director, Data Processing and Information Services November, 1980 - July, 1983
FEDERAL TRADE COMMISSION   Full Time Position
600 Pennsylvania Avenue, NW   ES-334-001
Washington, DC 20580   Starting Salary: $50,112 per year
                             Ending Salary: $59,945
 Supervisor: Barry Kaufman

Directed the design, development, implementation, and maintenance of the Commission's national on-line terminal system's 7-day/24-hour information requirement. Managed staff of 35 ADP professionals and a $2 million contract budget. Researched user needs and provided direct support to users and agency management in the establishment of goals and long-range objectives for system progress. Initiated effective methods of motivating professional and technical employees to perform under tight deadlines. Reviewed and provided agency comments on proposed Federal procurement regulations related to information systems.

Chief, Computer Services Division   November, 1972 - November, 1980
DRUG ENFORCEMENT ADMINISTRATION   Full Time Position
1405 I Street, NW   GS-330-15/7
Washington, DC   Starting Salary: $24,156 per year
                             Ending Salary: $50,112

Managed the analysis, design, programming, implementation, operation, and maintenance of the information systems management capacity of a leading Federal law enforcement agency. Directed design and development of the Narcotics and Dangerous Drugs Information System enabling the agency to develop and manage a three million name data base using 300 IBM 370/158 and Bunker/Ramo terminals. Directed research and development to support the agency's Information Resources Management Plan. Established a cost/benefit justification for a stand-alone computer system within the agency.

166

Chief, Systems Maintenance Section   January, 1968 - December, 1970
FEDERAL DEPOSIT INSURANCE CORPORATION   Full Time Position
350 17th Street   GS-334-14
Washington, DC   Starting Salary: $14,200 per year
                        Ending Salary: $20,298

Directed analysis and resolution encountered during the operation of more than 200 computer programs. Designed and implemented periodic modifications of payroll computation and the Bank Assessments insurance billing system. Performed teleprocessing and operations analysis to improve system performance.

MILITARY SERVICE

United States Army   1957 - 1960   *Honorable Discharge*

COMPUTER SKILLS

Hardware:	IBM ES9000, 3090/300E, 600S, 4381, 370/158, 360/50
	IBM PC XT/AT, Intel 386/486
	Prime 550, 750, 955, Univac 1180
Languages:	C++, C, ALC, BASIC, Visual VBASIC, COBOL, Fortran,
CICS,	JCL, JES2, PASCAL, ADABAS/NATURAL
Operating Systems:	DOS, VAX VMS, Windows, PRIMOS
Software:	SAS, SPSS, VTAM, VSAM, TSO, EXEC 8, dBASE, Excel,
	Lotus 1-2-3, MVS, SuperProject, PowerBuilder, FoxPro,
	WordPerfect, Microsoft Word, PowerPoint, Harvard
	Graphics, FreeLance

EDUCATION

MBA	***Central Michigan University***	*Information Management*	1976
BS	***Federal City College***	*Computer Science*	1972
	Federal Executive Institute	*Executive Education*	1974

PROFESSIONAL MEMBERSHIPS

Data Processing Management Association
Association for Computing Machinery

HONORS AND AWARDS

Attorney General's Award, Department of Justice, 1979

Inspector General for Investigations, ES-1811

TIMOTHY HUTTON

13343 Triadelphia Mill Road
Woodbridge, VA 22191

Home: (703) 744-4324   Work: (202) 709-9874

Social Security No: 265-43-0987
Citizenship: U.S.A.
Federal Status: Supervisory Special Agent, GM-1811-15
                        5/87 to present
Military Status: U.S.M.C., 1967-1978
Veterans Preference: 10 Point Veteran (3 Purple Hearts and 1 Bronze Star w/ Combat V)

OBJECTIVE: Assistant Inspector General for Investigations, ES-1811
                 Department of Transportation, Office of Inspector General
                 Announcement No: I-95-30

PROFILE: Sixteen years with the General Services Administration, Office of Inspector General. Responsible for managing Inspector General investigations, developing and directing investigative programs which are comprehensive and responsive to the Inspector General and ensuring the integrity of Agency programs and personnel and/or the administration of its affairs. Skilled in managing complex investigations that involve alleged violations of Title 18, United States Code. Experienced in establishing investigative priorities, selectivity in case initiation, and performing case and office reviews. Continually strive to improve investigative techniques, quality and effectiveness of investigative programs and personnel. Represent the office in conferences and meetings with Congressional staff, Agency officials, other OIG staff and high level Governmental officials on investigative matters. Experienced manager of agents and support personnel. Effective at implementing OIG training and workforce diversity programs. Currently implementing training and development programs to implement NPR's goals of increasing workforce effectiveness and controlling cost, as well as achieve the Agency mission, vision, and goals.

EMPLOYMENT HISTORY

GENERAL SERVICES ADMINISTRATION
Office of Inspector General   **May 1979 to present**

Regional Inspector General for Investigations, GM-1811-15   9/90 to present
    Washington Field Investigations Office   55-60 hours/week
    Regional Office Building, Room 1915   Beginning Salary: $66,125/year
    7th & D Streets, SW, Washington, DC 20407   Current Salary: $83,614/year
    Supervisor: Charles Vanderbilt (202) 432-4324 Contact can be made.

        Manage a staff of professional special agents ranging in grades from GM-14 to GS-7 (FTE have ranged between 8 and 18), as well as three support personnel. Responsible for hiring, staff and career development, reassignments, personnel and program evaluations. Management of the regional investigative program in the Washington Field Investigations Office covers both regional and national GSA programs and operations. (continued)

Timothy Hutton
SS# 265-43-0987

Regional Inspector General for Investigations (continued):
> Managed the administrative (budget, personnel, office automation) and operational workload of the office and made long range investigative plans. Provide technical advice to supervisors and special agents. Promote and require the use of information technologies in the investigative program.
>
> Accept and reject highly complex and sensitive investigative work products. Work closely with OIG headquarters and regional management personnel to enhance and improve the investigative program. Conducted sensitive and complex investigations of the highest level employee in the agency.
>
> Advanced the concept of cultural diversity in the OIG by hiring both minority employees and women. Promoted the first and currently only two female special agents to Assistant RIGI positions.

Accomplishments:
- Participated in a task group with AIGI Henderson and an outside consultant resulting in the development of the Office of Investigations Strategic Plan pursuant to the Government Performance and Results Act (GPRA) which links budget requests with performance goals and measurable outcomes. It results in mission-driven accomplishments. Issued in May of 1995.
- Also in May 1995, I developed for AIGI Henderson the Office of Investigations, Executive Management Report, an automated report for the Inspector General which reports on quarterly accomplishments.
- In September 1994, following the Office of Investigations Strategic Planning Conference, where downsizing and budget reductions were announced, initiated a training program in the Washington Field Investigations Office in accordance with US Vice President Al Gore's reinvention initiatives to make the government work better and cost less. Implemented training of the staff in Total Quality Management principles to encourage the use of self-directed work teams and employee involvement and empowerment.
- In order to accomplish my training objectives, became a trainer of a 4-day course by Dr. Stephen R. Covey entitled "The Seven Habits of Highly Effective People" in order to improve staff's personal effectiveness.
- Incorporated a customized Self-Directed Work Team course into our region's staff development program taught by the Human Resources Office of the Federal Aviation Administration in order to improve team work effectiveness and better utilize available staff following downsizing of our agency.

Director, Investigative Support
Programs and Projects Division, GM-1811-15   3/24/86 - 9/16/90
> GS Building, 18th & F Streets, NW, Washington, DC   50-60 hours/week
> Supervisor: Alfred H. Henderson (202) 401-9874

> Managed the Office of Investigation's policy development, security, records maintenance, administrative and ADP technical support to field operations.
>
> Provided technical and managerial operational advice and guidance to the Assistant IG for Investigations and advised on a broad range of subjects including: budget/personnel matters, office automation/ADP support, uses of information technologies in an investigative environment.   (continued)

169

Timothy Hutton
SS# 265-43-0987

Director, Investigative Support, Programs and Projects Division (continued):

Accomplishments:

- As the manager of the ADP Division, recognized the need to improve the ADP and management information systems within the Office of Inspector General and sub-offices (Office of Investigations and Office of Audits).

- Helped develop and prototype the Office of Audit's Audit Information System at the direction of the Inspector General and was assigned as the OIG Project Director for overall development of an OIG Management Information System. This assignment resulted in my supervising not only my division, but the OIG Systems Support and Development Division.

Acting Regional Inspector General for Investigations, GM-1811-14   8/85 - 3/86
Washington Field Investigations Office   40 hours/week
Supervisor: Ralph Emery (202) 401-9874

Managed an investigative staff of 18 agents and three clerical support personnel. Supervised and conducted highly technical and complex sensitive investigations involving the programs and operations of GSA. Provided technical advice to supervisors and agents.

Managed the administrative and operational workload of the office and long range investigative plans. Developed and implemented budget and personnel actions. Evaluated office, supervisor and agent performance. Accepted and rejected work products.

Assistant Regional Inspector General for Investigations, GM-1811-14   1/85 - 8/85
Washington Field Investigations Office   40 hours/week
Supervisor: Henry Blumfeld (202) 401-9873

Supervised a group of agents and clerical staff in the accomplishment of all investigative activity including prevention.

Assisted the RIGI in managing the office and the investigative program. Analyzed Agency regulations, laws and policies affecting the investigative program. Accepted and rejected work products.

Criminal Investigator Staff Officer Assistant to DAIGI, GS-1811-13   12/83 - 1/85
Office of Investigations   40 hours/week
GS Building, 18th & F Streets, NW, Washington, DC
Supervisor: Carroll Driscoll (202) 437-0987

As the staff officer assistant to the Deputy AIGI, helped develop and coordinate nationwide Office of Investigations policies and procedures. Helped develop and prepare budgetary submissions and personnel actions. Analyzed and prepared statistical reports regarding nationwide office accomplishments.

Planned, organized and conducted sensitive and complex investigations and special projects related to enhancing and developing administrative management processes and management goals and objectives.

Timothy Hutton
SS# 265-43-0987

Criminal Investigator, GS-1811-13
Office of Policy, Plans and Management Systems
Washington, DC
Supervisor: Jack Abrams   (202) 576-9874

6/82 - 12/83
40 hours/week

Planned and evaluated functions of and for the Office of Investigations.
- Developed policy and procedures for that office by preparing the Investigations chapter of the OIG manual.
- Developed a guide for evaluating investigation headquarters and field components. Reviewed legislation, rules and regulations of the office and Agency as the OIG assistant clearance office.

Criminal Investigator, GS-1811-13
Office of Special Projects, Washington, DC
Supervisor: Louis Corsy (202) 401-0987
- Conducted sensitive and complex criminal fraud investigations.

5/79 - 6/83
40 hours/week

MILITARY EXPERIENCE:

U.S. Marine Corps (various locations throughout U.S. and Far East) 1/67 - 9/78 Conducted criminal investigations pursuant to Chapter 10 U.S. Code and other Federal laws to include investigations of fraud against the Government, homicide, rape and narcotic violations. Conducted white collar crime investigations requiring knowledge of federal laws and federal accounting systems. These investigations required that I collect and preserve both physical and testimonial evidence, take statements and depositions under oath, analyze questioned documents and prepare and review highly technical criminal investigation reports.

EDUCATION:

GEORGE WASHINGTON UNIVERSITY, Washington, DC 20006
Completed 45 credit hours in Political Science

PENSACOLA JUNIOR COLLEGE, Pensacola, FL
Associate of Arts Degree, Political Science, 1974

FEDERAL EXECUTIVE INSTITUTE, Charlottesville, VA, 6/90 - 9/90
Studied economics and Foreign Affairs Management Studies

GEORGE WASHINGTON UNIVERSITY, Washington, DC, 12/87 - 2/88
School of Government & Business, Contemporary Executive Development Program

CENTER FOR CREATIVE LEADERSHIP DEVELOPMENT PROGRAM,
Greensboro, NC, 1988
GSA Meritorious Service Award, 1989
GSA (IG) Commendable Service Awards (2), 1989, 1993
OPM Honor Graduate, Federal Personnel Management Issues, Federal Executive Management Seminar, 1988

Appendix B

Example #1: Visual Information Specialist, GS-9

Knowledge of principles and methodology of visual communication with regard to printed material.

Editor's Note: The applicant here, a GS-9 Visual Information Specialist, was seeking a position as Visual Information Specialist, GS-11, which she knew was highly competitive and sought by many. Her background made her a natural; however, she knew she had to prove the "value-added" qualities she could bring to the new position. Note how she integrates education, job performance, and awards to provide evidence of the strength and breadth of her capabilities.

TEXT:

Throughout my educational and professional career I have devoted myself to bringing excellence to visual arts in public service. I have a strong educational background that integrates a thorough knowledge of art history with advanced work in visual arts:

- B.A. *cum laude* in Art, Hawthorne College, New York
- Graduate study at London College of Printing (Certificate in Design)
- Graduate study at School of Visual Arts, New York City (Certificate in Design and Illustration)

Over the past 11 years I have served as Visual Information Specialist with the Office of Folklife Programs, Smithsonian Institution. I manage all visual arts for annual events, including exhibition signs, Festival brochures, and other special materials. I also produce annually, from start to finish, *Festival of American Folklife Program Book,* a 100-page volume with 10,000-copy print run. This effort involves:

- Coordinating with curators in five Smithsonian program areas to select annual design focus, together with appropriate articles, photos, illustrations, maps, charts, and diagrams.
- Providing creative direction for entire program book: determining design objectives; planning integration of type, illustrations, photos, and other graphic elements; and balancing design objectives with "user-friendliness."
- Supervising Design Assistant and Editor, selecting and coordinating multiple contractors to ensure coherence of design and implementation.
- Creating illustrations, both through own original artwork and from other sources.
- Selecting and developing maps, diagrams, black and white and color photography.
- Formulating production schedules and milestones involving multiple deadlines.

In addition to producing these print materials, I serve as Art Director and Production Manager for Smithsonian/Folkways Records. I design graphics for albums and associated posters and promotional materials. I also design and coordinate illustration and design consultation for Folklife Studies Film/Monograph Series, selecting stills, line art, editing, and film titles.

Awards and Honors Related to Visual Arts:
- **Award of Merit,** for Book Design, 1994.
- **Certificate of Merit** in Graphics Communication Competition, for Folklife Festival Program Book, 1993.
- **National Endowment for the Arts,** Grant for Artist Book, 1990.
- **Design Excellence Award,** The Composing Room, New York, 1988.
- Three **Andy Awards,** from Advertising Club of New York, 1980.

Example #2: Security Specialist, GS-12

Knowledge of the theories, principles, practices, regulations, and techniques of Automated Information Systems (AIS) security for U.S. government computer systems and installation.

Editor's Note: This GS-11 applicant for position of Security Specialist GS-12, had a challenge here to present a credible case, in a military supply systems operation, for security expertise. The applicant, who had significant computer background, also had substantial informal security experience but no formal position titles to that effect. Indeed, he had been tapped for several positions that involved high-level security responsibilities.

Notice how he also "paints a picture" of his ability to communicate across military services, between civilian and military bodies, and inside and outside government. Also note how his "story-teller" use of factual detail leaves absolutely no room for doubt about his competence.

TEXT:
As a result of experience in both Army and Navy operations, in overseas as well as with U.S.-wide computer systems, maintain extensive knowledge of U.S. goverment computer systems. In addition, due to widely varied experience, cultivate network of top computer experts in U.S. and abroad who regularly inform one another about latest updates and developments in sophisticated systems.

Personally served for past 10 years on installation of both hardware and software systems, promoted during that time from GS-5 Computer Operator to GS-11 Systems Analyst due to ability to grasp quickly AIS security as well as overall systems information.

Specifically, served for most recent three positions as lead computer specialist in highly secure computer environments consisting of VAX 4000, A17J, UNISYS 5000/95, VAX PDP 11/70 and 11/785 Systems under VMS, Digital RM06 Disk Drives, Digital TU77 Tape Drives, Digital Pro 350 PC, GKI K90 Degausser, CDI7000 and GD 70 Tape Cleaners. Also worked with IBM 4341 system, IBM 14303/4245 printer, and Telex 6803 and 640 drives.

Since 1992, entrusted with sensitive position to ensure optimum data flow for critical information throughout U.S. military. Holding Top Secret/SBI Clearance, manage entire computer facility operation, with 10 remote sites located in East and West Coast of U.S. Manage hardware system that supports over 1,000 security containers interfacing with over 1,000 organizations, with up to 1 million documents.

As member of AIS Operations Division, participate in strategic planning, research and development, configuration management, application implementation, training, documentation, user support, and other oversight, all requiring extensive knowledge of government security policy, procedures, and requirements.

Regularly communicate with wide range of internal and external customers in federal sector, including White House and Congress. Balance user "need-to-know" with guarantee of highest possible levels of security. Also provide government liaison and direct efforts of up to 21 private sector contractors (including major firms and small businesses), ensuring that both technical quality and security quality are maintained.

Example #3: Pharmacist, GS-12

Ability to apply the concepts, principles, and practices of pharmacy science, including monitoring drug therapy, retrieving drug information, interpreting clinical data, developing therapeutic plans, and providing pharmacokinetic consultation.

Editor's Note: The challenge for this applicant, a GS-11 seeking a GS-12 position within the same agency, was that, in a highly competitive federal environment, there are no truly "wired" positions anymore.

TEXT:

Pharmacist/Intensive Care   **10/1/92-present**
Walter Reed Medical Center

In my current position, I exercise independent judgment, with broad responsibility for administering and coordinating all pharmacy operations for this nationally-recognized medical center. Specifically, I:

- Process and fill prescriptions for all formulary therapeutic agents, with responsibility for quality assurance and risk management. Review and verify prescriptions and medical orders written by different doctors, identify potential drug interactions and other problems with medications, and bring them to the attention of appropriate medical authorities.
- Compound sterile and non-sterile medications, including IVs, IMs, specialized and non-standard preparations. Exercise professional judgment to ensure purity and safety.
- Maintain all outpatient and inpatient medication profiles. Inspect and verify records to identify potential drug interactions, problems, and medical history issues impacting the delivery of safe and quality medical care.
- Counsel patients on medication, and teach at continuing education sessions for hospital staff on drug and medication issues. Serve as recognized internal expert and consultant on professional pharmaceutical matters.

Staff Pharmacist   **4/3/88 - 9/30/92**
Dwight Eisenhower Army Medical Center, Ft. Gordon, Georgia

I supervised a staff of eight pharmacy technicians in providing comprehensive hospital pharmaceutical services, performing final check of all new prescriptions prior to dispensing. I evaluated dosage instructions using patient profiles, and identified and resolved potential problems including drug interactions. I ordered controlled substances and implemented security requirements. I consulted on drug administration and pharmacy procedures for professional staff and patients.

In a performance appraisal dated 5 April 1989, my supervisor said of my pharmaceutical skills, *"This exceptional pharmacist has an outstanding working knowledge of policies and procedures which pertain to new prescriptions and refills .... (He) demonstrated a remarkable degree of scrutiny and discernment when checking prescriptions .... and continually demonstrated fluency regarding current drug information, state and federal pharmacy laws, and Army regulations."*

Education, Certifications, and Memberships
- Bachelor of Science in Pharmacy from Howard University
- On-going professional education (as identified on my federal resume)
- Registered Pharmacist and Certified Fitter (Health Supports & Appliances).
- Maintain current industry knowledge through memberships in the National Association of Retail Druggists, National Pharmaceutical Association, American Society of Hospital Pharmacists, and *Chi Delta Mu* Medical Fraternity.

Example #4: Chief of Medical Technical Equipment, GS-12

A general knowledge of the mission, organization, and activities of a health care facility.

Editor's Note: The applicant was an X-Ray equipment technician, GS-11, seeking a supervisory GS-12 position as Chief of a Medical Techncial Equipment Division of a Veteran's Administration medical facility. His challenge was that, while he was extraordinarily well-qualified technically, he had no formal supervisory experience and little management training.

TEXT:

With 10 years and three separate positions in leading medical facility, serve as key point of contact with wide range of related medical facilities. Apply solid knowledge of mission, goals, and programs of health care delivery to interactions with medical facility leadership, medical specialists, technicians, physicians, and externally with manufacturers and technology designers. In addition, earlier career included specialty in emergency medical support systems. Specific roles that enhance my overall knowledge of medical facilities include:

- Work closely with senior-ranking medical officers, medical specialists, and project engineers to determine full range of medical facility needs, building conversance with parameters and requirements across facility to achieve comprehensive medical care.

- Selected as Acting Branch Chief (up to four months per year) in absence of Division head, who must travel frequently to represent facility during time of budgetary cutbacks. As result, established effective working relationships inside and outside hospital at leadership positions.

- As member of annual task force for ***Technical Equipment Inspection Manual,*** contributed to text that is now distributed throughout VA hospital system, due to its relevance to a wide range of missions. Personally authored section on *"High Frequency X-Ray Generators and Radiation Dose Linearity Testing and Procedures."*

- Interface regularly among VA facilities to consult on impact of technical innovations on overall hospital operations. Specially requested as technical expert on VA's Plan and Pre-Installation Equipment Inspection Meetings.

- Serve as lead corporate liaison for Veterans Administration to assess new technology in light of mission and programmatic needs of VA. Visit corporate offices to evaluate new technology, meeting with major manufacturers, top corporate officials, scientists, engineers, and other technical experts. Advise on emerging medical needs for future equipment design and development.

Education and Specialized Training

- Currently enrolled (with 42 hours earned) in dual degree Bachelor's program at Hayward College, Reading, PA, in Business Management and Computer Sciences.
- Earned well over 1,500 hours training with advanced medical technology and equipment **(Note:** See complete listing attached to federal resume).
- In earlier career, completed over 400 hours as firefighter in fire safety, prevention, and emergency medical care.

175

Example #5: Inspector General, GS-12

Skill in the analysis of complex multi-million dollar financial transactions.

Editor's Note: This applicant was a member of a local police force who sought a GS-12 position with the Federal Deposit Insurance Corporation, Office of the Inspector General (there is such an office in every federal agency). His background contained, for a local policeman, an unusual relevance to financial investigations but his challenge was to spell this out.

TEXT:

For past ten years, manage cases that involve individuals charged with economic crimes as well as local and national businesses charged with such offenses as money laundering and procurement fraud. Assess financial records including bank records, business records, loan applications, and securities transactions.

Apply investigations knowledge of accounting and law developed both through job experience and through academic education, including over seven courses in accounting, and Master's degree with concentration in Forensic Science from George Washington University.

On regular basis, serve on task force investigation in complex, multi-jurisdictional, multi-agency efforts. Frequently called on for specialty in documentary evidence and knowledge of financial procedures to assess accurately extensive and specific paper trail involved in major financial crimes ranging in recent cases from amounts of approximately $200,000 to more than $3 million in recoverable assets. Recognized for outstanding track record of success in investigations, bringing over 90% to successful prosecution resulting in convictions.

Companies investigated often have branches in local area with corporate headquarters located elsewhere in U.S. Travel major part of time across U.S., recently to California, Oregon, Arizona, Florida, New York, Massachusetts, New Jersey, Maryland, North Carolina, South Carolina, Georgia, Ohio, and Wisconsin. Cases involve extensive knowledge of multi-divisional corporate financial processes and decision-making.

In 1993, served as Primary Investigator in foreign toll fraud investigation that involved extremely complex government/corporate cooperation. Worked in conjunction with U.S. Secret Service, Federal Drug Enforcement Administration, AT&T, C&P Telephone, Bell Atlantic Security, and local police departments.

Investigated savings and loan conspiracy case that involved three individuals, two from New York State and one from Virginia. Conducted close evaluation of accounting procedures and records that involved over $180,000 in corporate checkwriting fraud with impact on four savings and loan institutions in Northern Virginia.

In addition to academic education in forensics, regularly pursue specialized training to keep competence up-to-date, including such courses as *Financial Investigative Techniques* taught at Macon County Policy Academy, Macon, GA.

176

Example #6: Vocational Rehabilitation Specialist, GS-12

Ability to promote the rehabilitation program and to negotiate contracts and agreements with prospective employers and training facilities.

This applicant was a GS-11 seeking a position as GS-12 Vocational Rehabilitation Specialist Supervisor.

TEXT:

Promotion of Rehabilitation Programs

My work in vocational rehabilitation for the department has spanned over 20 years, and, through regular positions and special assignments, I have gained a broad understanding of the department's mission, goals, and programs. As a result, for the past three years I have been selected to speak on panel presentations regarding **"Effective Client Strategies"** at the annual National Rehabilitation Hospital Conference.

To serve the wide diversity of clients in my caseload, I maintain extensive and effective working relationships with medical professionals across the agency, promoting not only the needs of my own caseload but of our department as well. As a result, I am able to discuss and quickly resolve inter-departmental coordination needed and develop integrated case plans for specific clients. In addition, I have established critical liaison with peers and experts in other agencies to coordinate efforts when necessary for complex cases, succeeding in forging positive departmental relations.

I amplify these informal networks through active membership and task force membership in the National Rehabilitation Association, Vocational Rehabilitation Association (for which I am currently regional Program Chair), and Work Adjustment Association. To further my marketing proficiency, I recently attended a 40-hour course in **Marketing for Health Professionals,** at George Washington University.

On my recent performance appraisal, my supervisor has described my skills by noting that I *"maintain good rapport with other agencies, clients, and co-workers...serving as an excellent representative of the department."*

Negotiation of Contracts and Agreements with Prospective Employers and Training Facilities

As part of my responsibility to clients, I regularly negotiate employment contracts with employers and with training programs to optimize client development. To achieve this, I make sure that employers understand both client strengths and limitations. I have lead responsibility to evaluate hard-to-place clients that have been referred to the Center because a prior rehabilitation counselor has been unable to identify any marketable skills or develop a feasible rehabilitation plan. My success in these clients has been the highest in departmental history, and results from my follow-through, observing work behavior on-the-job, ongoing communication with employers, and multiple clinical support when necessary.

I maintain knowledge of relevant law and regulations related to employment. Furthermore, I have earned 30 semester credit hours in my pursuit of a degree in Business Administration with the University of the District of Columbia, taking classes specifically emphasizing contract law and negotiation of agreements.

Example #7: Foreign Affairs Officer, GS-13

Ability to plan and direct program activities.

Editor's Note: This applicant was a GS-12 seeking a GS-13 position, often the most difficult move up the federal ladder. In addition, she was applying for a position as Foreign Affairs Officer after serving six years at a regional program desk, and six years before that working her way up from an entry-level position with the U.S. Department of State. Note how she emphasizes her international connections built through these positions and her comfort with a wide range of people in the U.S. and overseas.

TEXT:

Regional Program Officer   **January 1991-present**
U.S. Department of State, Office of Public Liaison

Respond to public and community requests for policy forums, as well as originate outreach efforts on key issues. Develop Regional Foreign Policy Conferences that are co-sponsored with local organizations in major U.S. cities. Also serve as internal liaison between Office of Public Programs with Near East and South Asian Bureau. Serve as primary coordinator and point of contact, to:

- Coordinate with as many as 20 local co-sponsors to develop meetings led by senior Department leadership and attended by up to 500 members of interested organizations and general public.
- Handle extensive advance work and local press coverage and media interviews.
- Maintain active communication with several organizations representing foreign leaders, including Brookings Institute, Carnegie Foundation, and World Affairs Council.

For these consortia and other events, manage speaking engagements for top-level officials including Secretary of State and foreign dignitaries. During previous year, managed 72 speaking trips and total of 130 public speaking engagements.

Commended on most recent Performance Review for being *"only division officer who planned and managed two town meetings, one month apart, in St. Louis and San Francisco. The results were outstanding. The St. Louis meeting drew...over 350 citizens (despite the floods) and great media coverage. The San Francisco meeting, with a record-breaking attendance of 1300, was the first such meeting in over thirteen years. Both the Secretary and the spokesman commented publicly on their tremendous success..."*

Public Affairs Specialist   **12/86-12/90**
U.S. Department of State, Near East/South Asia Office of Public Affairs

In addition to management of major regional, state, and city programs, for four years, coordinated extensive U.S. and overseas summer intern program. Recruited interns, oriented and trained, and provided leadership during wide range of assignments.

To increase effective communication and program coordination, completed specialized studies in Arabic at the Middle East Institute in Washington, D.C.

Example #8: Environmental Specialist, GS-13

Knowledge of federal hazardous materials transportation regulations.

Editor's Note: This applicant was moving from a corporate trucking job into a federal U.S. Department of Transportation position, GS-13, that regulated the industry she was leaving.

TEXT:

For past five years, worked closely with efforts for corporation of 5,000 employees to ensure compliance with environmental and hazardous chemical controls. Over this period, developed thorough working knowledge of following Federal Environmental Regulations:

- Department of Transportation regulations, *"Federal Motor Carrier Safety Regulations,"* Title 49, Parts 350-399, and *"Hazardous Material Transportation Regulations,"* Title 49, Parts 100-179.
- Occupational Safety and Health Administration, *"Work Place Standards,"* Title 29, Part 1910, Sections 1200-1500.
- Environmental Protection Agency, *"Hazardous Wastes,"* Title 40, Part 263.

In current position as Hazardous Material/Commercial Motor Vehicle Program Manager, brought into compliance with their program requirements this company with 850 drivers and 300 vehicles, which transported 14 different classes of hazardous materials in daily operations. Personally created new programs to expand and continue this compliance throughout company. Train employees immediately involved with controlling hazardous materials in safety and corrective procedures, proper regulations, and accurate and timely reporting of accidents or violations.

Oversee efforts to ensure that all 5,000 employees have full access to information concerning hazards associated with chemical products. Designed, produced, and ensured training in Right-To-Know (RTK) training for all employees.

At conclusion of recent Safety Review by Office of Motor Carriers, commended for knowledge of regulations and programs developed for company. In addition, on most recent performance evaluation, cited for having *"excelled at meeting new challenges and improving the performance of the Fleet Safety Programs."*

Recently selected to serve three-year term as member of Maryland Governor's Motor Carrier Taskforce, Light Truck/Hazardous Materials Committee.

In prior position as Hazardous Chemical Control Specialist, directed fleet program with 4,000 company drivers and 1,300 vehicles and wrote new company policy to ensure compliance with FMCSR and Hazardous Material Transportation Regulations. Designed appropriate training and quality assurance programs in order to firmly establish these policies, and also monitored all applicable state regulations to integrate these as well.

Example #9: Construction Manager, GS-13

Expert level of engineering skills and in-depth knowledge of all construction trades and work processes combined with engineering and project management and ability.

Editor's Note: This applicant was outside government working in private industry, seeking an "interdisciplinary" GS-13 position with the U.S. General Services Administration. His challenge was to show evidence that he knows about construction from concept to design to project management to erecting actual buildings.

TEXT:

Applying my extensive knowledge of all phases of construction, in my most recent positions have managed projects involving specialized architecture, structural engineering, mechanical, plumbing and electrical engineering, civil engineering, tenant space planning and interior design.

With over 14 years experience in field observation and construction administration expertise in a variety of product types, established solid experience in dealing with contractors and subcontractors. Served as project manager of a number of multi-million dollar projects, including:

Office Buildings

New design, construction project management and tenant-build-out (design and/or review of floor plan and design in conformance with architectural plans) at the following locations.
- Dun Loring Square, Baltimore, MD: 125,000 sf, 8 stories, $14.5 million
- Reston Plaza, Reston, VA: 164,144 sf, 13 stories, $18 million
- 2200 Franklin Street, Philadelphia, PA: 99,360 sf, 4 stories, $16 million

Hotel
- Crystal City Hyatt, Crystal City, VA: 213,620 sf, 18 stories, $30 million

Elderly Housing
- Episcopal Retirement Home, Minneapolis, MN: 120,000 sf, 7 stories, $6.5 million

High Rise Apartment Buildings and Condominiums
- The Reaches, Potomac, MD: 247,560 sf, 27 stories, $34 million
- Silver Spring Heights, Silver Spring, MD: 121,783 sf, 8 stories, $11 million
- Montgomery Mansion, Bethesda, MD: 237,654 sf, 12 stories, $16.5 million
- Dumbarton Haven, Washington, DC: 414,742 sf, 22 stories, $27.5 million

Example #10: Attorney, GS-14

Ability to communicate orally and in writing.

Editor's Note: This D.C. government attorney was seeking a position with the federal National Council on Disability. She knew, therefore, that communication skills would be extremely important for the position, and she treated this factor at length.

TEXT:

My communications skills have served me effectively during my legal career as well as assisting my progression through law school and early public service. My career in public service began with the Bureau of Alcohol, Tobacco & Firearms in New York City, where I assisted a radio dispatch operation monitoring criminal activities as part of an investigation. My clear voice on the radio helped to ensure the effectiveness of that operation.

My public service continued with an internship with the Small Business Administration, where I was awarded a *Certificate of Commendation* for my contribution to a counseling program that promoted the development of minority enterprises. I also earned commendations for contributions to the Bureau of Alcohol, Tobacco & Firearms' Public Affairs and Disclosure Branch while I served as a disclosure clerk in the Washington office.

These oral communications skills have served particularly well in my role as an attorney for the District of Columbia Department of Consumer and Regulatory Affairs. In any enforcement situation, many parties enter negotiations under threat of sanctions, and other parties feel threatened that their professional livelihood might be endangered by people whom they believe lack the knowledge and training to judge fairly the professional performance in question. I have an ability to focus upon the specifics of potential disputes, discern the public interest involved in sustaining quality services under conditions that comply with legal and regulatory requirements, and to focus the attention of interlocutors on the importance to all parties of developing agreeable resolutions that ensure the health, safety, and well-being of District residents. I am proud of my record for realizing sound negotiated resolution of many disputes that reach my desk.

In addition, when parties are unable to reach acceptable agreements, I have a successful record of writing statements of charges, requests for cease and desist orders, or securing the Court's assistance through other legal venues. I write and edit the work of my staff well, and am accustomed to producing, under deadline, budget justification documents and trial and appellate briefs--both of which are necessary to provide critical public services. In the course of supervising my staff, I provide clear and concise written guidelines for office operations, and can provide sound direction in either personal counseling sessions for attorneys needing guidance or motivational speeches for the office when major projects require immediate, and coordinated, staff attention. I regularly produce written legal memoranda and conduct telephone discussions and oral briefings to elicit the support of the offices of the Corporation Counsel and the U.S. Attorney for positions being taken by the Department.

Example #11: Contract Specialist, GS-13

Knowledge of laws, codes, and regulations relative to government contracting.

Editor's Note: This applicant's career background was virtually all with a private telephone company, now seeking a GS-13 position. Her challenge was to convey two things (1) her sincere interest in, and respect for, the special requirements and needs of a federal position, and (2) her substantive knowledge of government requirements for the industry. Note how she uses specific and painstaking detail to achieve both aims. Also note that, because of her careful grounding in actual specifics, she is also able to use adjectives believably in this case.

TEXT:

As **Contract Specialist** for MCI, managed government contractual operations, with broad responsibility for the process from preparation through negotiation and implementation. Specific achievements:

- Successfully negotiated contracts with Government agencies, primarily the Department of Defense (DoD), for telephone services and equipment, involving complex, sophisticated, and highly specialized procurements of significant importance to DoD and MCI. Established collaborative partnerships with Government officials with a goal of improved public service.

- Conducted extensive research and marketing analysis to identify bidding opportunities, including the Defense Administration Services (DCAS), Armed Services Procurement Regulations (ASPR), and various information sources.

- Managed qualifying functions and negotiations for pre-award and post-award government contracts. Developed and utilized knowledge of Federal Acquisition Regulations (FAR), Defense Acquisition Regulations (DAR), Federal Procurement Regulations (FPR), Delegation of Procurement Authority (DPA), Federal Information Resources Management Regulations (FIRMR), Freedom of Information Act (FOIA), and the comprehensive solicitation and bidding process, including Request for Proposal (RFP), Invitation for Bid (IFB), and Request for Information (RFI).

- Administered the bidding process, coordinating with other MCI activities to develop effective, responsive bids and proposals, with extensive responsibility for cost analysis, arranging for testing and qualification of MCI services, etc. Completed specialized training in government and military procurement. Analyzed and assessed competitive offerings, primarily in the area of AT&T services, to ensure comparativeness of MCI offerings in all areas.

- Ensured contract compliance with various Government orders, policies, and procedures, including Executive Order 11375 (Equal Employment) and relevant orders of the Secretary of Labor governing equitable minority representation in government contracts. Negotiated and ensured compliance with Walsh-Healey Act and other laws/regulations.

- Managed government contracts including fixed price (FP), fixed-price incentive (FPI), cost-plus-fixed-fee (CPFF), cost reimbursement (CR), cost plus incentive fee (CPIF), and other types.

- Controlled contract liaison with Federal counterparts on all matters of contract administration from bidding to close-out.

Example #12: Procurement/Contract Specialist, GS-13

Experience and knowledge of the federal acquisition process, including application and interpretation of regulations and legislation, development of strategies, participation in contract solicitation, review and close-out activities.

Editor's Note: This 16-year federal employee, now a GS-13 procurement/contract specialist in a non-supervisory role, was seeking a move to the position of Supervisory Procurement Analyst, GS-14. Notice how he emphasizes his management experience gained through oversight of contracts, though his "formal" supervisory experience is limited. He also portrays well his contact with a wide range of different customers and external liaisons.

As a Procurement Analyst (GS 1102-13) with the General Services Administration, Office of Procurement since 1990, I manage Public Building Service (PBS) and Central Office procurement programs, contracts and grants.

My experience and knowledge of the Federal acquisition process is utilized daily in the application and interpretation of legislation regarding contracts. I manage up to 45 contracts/grants ranging from $10,000 to $5 million for the GSA. The contractors include corporations, small business firms, educational institutions, non-profits, and state/local governments. This oversight entails close supervision, direction, and coaching, as appropriate, of contractor personnel.

With 16 years of experience in planning, organizing, documenting and executing procurements through sealed bidding and negotiated solicitations, I manage a wide range of complex and critical contracts in conformance with FARS/GSA regulations. I have extensive experience in awarding PBS Grants in accordance with applicable handbooks, GSA policies, and procedures.

Previously, as a Contract/Grants Management Specialist with the U.S. Small Business Administration, Office of Procurement & Grants Management, I managed simultaneously up to 40 contracts or grants, ranging from $10,000 to $2.2 million each, made to contractors and small business development centers.

I am skilled in all aspects of contractor communication: conducting cost/price analysis; developing agency negotiation positions; coordinating technical specifics of contract language; identifying potential problems with contracts or grants; and acting as liaison with senior management regarding complex problems in contract administration.

I received both *Certificates of Appointment, Agreement Officer,* with authority to execute Assistance Agreements obligating SBA up to and including $500,000 and $750,000.

I hold a *Certificate of Appointment as a Contracting Officer,* with authority to execute contracts and grants obligating GSA for unlimited amounts. I also received an *"Outstanding"* evaluation March 21, 1995.

I have completed all required procurement courses for the GSA Contracting Officer's Warrant Program. *(See complete training list).*

Example #13: Safety Manager, GS-13

Knowledge of principles/practices/methods involved in the development of research studies, assessing existing technologies, and translating results into implementable highway safety programs.

Editor's Note: The challenge here was to prove that on-the-job training had in fact paid off in terms of real knowledge of over-rearching principles. The applicant was a GS-13 applying for a position as GS-14. Notice the applicant's clear use of lively detail to "paint a picture" of achievements that make a real difference in the everyday lives of citizens.

TEXT:

Each of the following activities demonstrate my knowledge of principles/practices/methods involved in and the ability to develop research studies, assess existing technologies, and translate results into implementable highway safety programs.

Chief, Safety Management, Traffic Standards and Policy Branch   3/93-present
- Developed and drafted guidelines in cooperation with NHTSA Issues Interim Rule.
- Analyzed and provided recommendations on safety and traffic legislation, including 1994 Appropriations Act and the National Highway System Act.
- Provided direction into FHWA research and technology applications programs by serving on the Safety Research and Technology Working Group.

During this period, assigned as Team Leader for cross-disciplinary **Traffic Control Device Standards Project.** In this capacity, together with team of outstanding performers, accomplished the following:
- Revised and issued Final Rule for Part VI of Work Zone Rule of *Manual on Uniform Traffic Control (MUTCD)* to include latest state-of-the-art-practice, research results and FHWA policy.
- Issued Final Rule on use of metric units for traffic control device dimensions.
- Launched national program to evaluate color strong-yellow-green for pedestrian and school crossing.
- Developed rulemaking on criteria for, and subsequently instituted, All-Weather Pavement Marking Program for application to streets and highways nationwide.
- Developed and issued national evaluation of retroreflectivity guidelines for signs and markings.
- Assigned team members to serve as individual liaisons with state and local agencies to evaluate retroreflective guidelines for signs and pavements markings.
- Coordinated and integrated team, with agencywide representatives from previously unrelated actitivities, through full-team training in essential team skills and individual coaching where necessary.

Chief, Traffic Control Standards and Application Branch   12/90-2/93
Traffic Control Device Division

Directed development and coordination of national policies, standards, procedures, and guidelines including several nationally significant programs involving new technologies used to control and guide traffic. Established standards for Nationwide Uniformity in Design and Operational Elements.

Example #14: Housing Specialist, GS-15

Knowledge of housing or community development program policies, regulations, and operating procedures.

Editor's Note: The applicant in this case was outside government in a senior management position with a real estate development firm. She was seeking a GS-15 level position with her regional office of the U.S. Department of Housing and Urban Development. The challenge was to convey governmental knowledge gained as an "outsider" that would be relevant to a senior-level position inside.

TEXT:

Through eight years in my current position and two previous positions, I have developed extensive knowledge of real estate regulations, licenses, and zoning ordinances in townships, cities, counties, and states, as well as providing liaison/representation with government officials and community development programs.

In these positions -- as Senior Sales Representative at New Market Estates, and as Real Estate Sales and Property Manager with LaSalle Properties, and as Officer and Manager of the area branch of Chase Manhattan -- developed awareness of overall real estate system that has impact on community development. While serving as bank officer, assigned lead responsibility for community loans, especially addressing needs of Spanish-speaking and French-speaking customers due to extensive travel and knowledge of those cultures and ability to speak tri-lingually.

Also developed this branch bank's staff of underwriters, directing over $4 million in mortgage loan originations and refinancings, and trained all subordinate officers and staff in customer responsiveness. Applied mastery of relevant U.S. and state governmental programs to training to ensure that entire bank staff provided most customer-responsive services possible.

In addition to relevant job experience, pursued specialized training that supports and substantiates skill in analyzing and guiding community members in housing and community development projects, including:

- **Academic Education:** Earned dual major Bachelor of Science degree in Industrial Technology and Communications, providing thorough understanding of engineering principles underlying construction, as well as technical knowledge for negotiations and management of building projects.

- **Real Estate:** Licensed as Real Estate Salesperson in states of New York (45 hours specialized training, 1985); Pennsylvania (72 hours of training, 1990); and Virginia (80 hours of training, 1992). Approved by Appraisal Institute (MAI, 1994) and by Graduate Realtors Institute (GRI, 1995).

- **Legal Knowledge:** Completed 45 hours coursework at Loyola University School of Law, with an emphasis on contract law, supporting legal understanding of real estate and construction contracts. Certified in New York as Paralegal.

185

Complete Factor Package #1:
Personnel Clerk/Assistant, GS-6/7

APPLICATION TO U.S. DEPARTMENT OF AGRICULTURE
FOR THE POSITION OF PERSONNEL CLERK/ASSISTANT, GS 6/7

Editor's Note: This applicant was an employee with D.C. City Government seeking to re-enter federal service as a GS 6/7. While this position may be seen as "entry-level," and she had prior federal experience, she understood that these positions are now highly competitive, and she wisely emphasizes unusual strengths, versatility, and assets that will make her stand out as a candidate.

1.   Knowledge of federal personnel rules, regulations and procedures.

I have a total of ten years experience in working with personnel-related responsibilities as a secretary and administrative assistant in government offices. I am familiar with classification, personnel records, recruitment and testing, time and attendance records, special projects and communication with employees regarding personnel questions.

As a Secretary in the Office of Engineering Service, Department of Public Works (1987-1989), I was responsible for preparing job descriptions from vacancy announcements. I was familiar with personnel rules and procedures relating to job descriptions duties, responsibilities and specialized skills.

As an Administrative Aide with Prince George's County Central Personnel Recruitment & Examination Division (1984-1985), I typed job vacancy announcements received from various county agencies. I communicated with individuals inquiring about employment and employment requirements for the county. I provided information on testing programs, policies and procedures. I assisted the personnel analysts in scoring and ranking applicants' test results. I notified applicants and agencies regarding eligibility and rating status. I recorded the applicant's qualification data into the personnel tracking forms and updated statistics maintained on test results. I also contacted newspapers in the area concerning job openings and ensured that placement of ads and payment was handled.

As the Secretary for the Second Leader at the Department of Agriculture (1978-1982), I maintained time and attendance records for all section employees, and prepared office-wide summary reports on this data. I communicated to employees regarding available leave and vacation leave.

Factor Package #1

2.   Ability to work with others.

I have been employed in the D.C. and Federal Government since 1978 as a Secretary, Administrative Aide, Personnel Assistant to an Executive and Purchasing Agent (six years).

Each one of my positions has involved working with others in different ways:

- Currently, as a Purchasing Agent with the Department of Public Works, Water and Sewer Utility Administration, I am responsible for purchasing technical items, service and repairs. I research sources by using published data as well as communicating with vendors concerning questions. I answer questions regarding contracts and purchases being made for various departments in the District of Columbia.

- In my present part-time position as a financial services consultant for Primerica Financial Services, I talk with potential customers via telephone and in person. I obtain information from them regarding insurance, investments, savings plans. I provide information on company services and procedures.

- As a Secretary (1987-1989) with the Department of Public Works, I assisted the Division Chief and Staff within the Construction Management Division. I was a liaison between the management and the personnel performing construction within the D.C. Public Works services. I communicated information on projects, meetings, schedules and reports.

- As a Clerk Technician for Prince George's County Public Works (1985-1986), I dispatched emergency and security personnel based on telephone emergency requests. I was responsible for obtaining exact information on whereabouts and type of emergency situations so that the correct county employees could be dispatched.

- As an Administrative Aide with the PG County Central Personnel Recruitment & Examination Division (1984-1985), I communicated with job applicants who desired information about positions, testing, job requirements and hiring processes. I provided information in person and by telephone.

Factor Package #1

3. **Ability to plan, organize and coordinate work activities.**

As a Purchasing Agent with the Department of Public Works/WASUA (1989-present), I am required to plan, organize and coordinate work activities for purchasing technical items, services and repairs using informal and open market purchasing methods for formal contracting procedures. The research, preparation of contracts, decision-making for making competitive selection for contractors requires outstanding organizational and planning skills. I have performed this position and received excellent ratings for six years.

As a Secretary in a government office (1978-1989) I am continuously responsible for planning, organizing and coordinating office projects, including typing, word processing of reports and documents. I am required to meet multiple deadlines, ensuring that my products are of high quality and consistent with format required by each office. The types of offices have varied and have included:

- Purchasing
- Public Works
- Business & Economic Development
- Cooperative Extension Services (Agriculture)
- Personnel Recruitment & Examination Division
- National Outlook Analysis (Agriculture)

I am able to learn the operations, functions and primary responsibilities of an office and develop skills to support the efficient operation, as well as communicate with employees, managers and constituents in an informed and professional manner.

4. **Ability to communicate in writing.**

My experience in writing has varied based on the office and type of work I was performing. I am able to utilize Word Perfect to compose letters, memoranda, and summaries of information. I can utilize well developed grammatical skills and knowledge of GPA manual formats to create acceptable written documents. I am skilled in proofreading and ensuring consistency in presentation.

Currently as a Purchasing Agent, I write statements concerning purchases, solicitations and bids. I write summaries and recommendations of competing vendor information.

As a Secretary (1987-1989), I prepared charts, graphs and tables utilizing WordPerfect and prepared spreadsheets using Lotus 123 and Quattro Pro software. I wrote memoranda to accompany reports. I reviewed all office material for grammar, format and consistency for office procedures. I assisted in training temporary and additional staff in word processing procedures and formats.

As a Secretary Typist with the Office of Business & Economic Development (1986-1987), I finalized letters, memoranda concerning meetings and business development projects. I wrote summary statements of conferences and meetings.

188

I received my *CTM Certification* through Toastmasters International for completing 10 speeches which I wrote and presented at meetings (1990).

Complete Factor Package #2:
Program Assistant, GS-9

APPLICATION TO DEPARTMENT OF THE NAVY
OFFICE OF SMALL AND DISADVANTAGED BUSINESS UTILIZATION (SADBU)
OFFICE OF THE UNDER SECRETARY OF THE NAVY
FOR THE POSITION OF PROGRAM ASSISTANT, GS-9

Editor's Note: This applicant was a GS-8 seeking a GS-9 position as Program Assistant. For the past 14 years she had worked with the Navy and therefore knew the system well; her challenge was to prove she was ready for the higher-level responsibility of a Program Analyst from previous administrative positions. She had served as a Team Leader and Research Assistant, both of which positions strengthen her case. Showing them to advantage was the task of this effective package.

1.   Knowledge of government operations, organizations and policies of the Department of the Navy and the Department of Defense.

In my current position as Correspondence Analyst/Expediter, I demonstrate my knowledge of government operations, organizations and policies of the Department of Navy and Department of Defense (DoD) on a daily basis. I am responsible for analyzing incoming correspondence, assigning to the proper agency and determining priority and processing of each document. I am knowledgeable of the departments, programs, organizational set-up, management hierarchy and policies of the Department of Defense and other agencies.

Previously, as a Team Leader (1986-1992), I supervised a team handling the Outgoing Mail Records for the Secretary of the Navy's Administrative Office. With six years experience organizing records, communicating with department heads and external customers regarding records and reference documents, I became familiar with Navy and DoD operations.

I demonstrated my knowledge of Department of the Navy and DoD regulations and have received Quality Step Increases and cash awards for five consecutive years.

2.   Knowledge of rules and regulations governing small and disadvantaged business utilization programs.

My knowledge of the rules and regulations governing small and disadvantaged business utilization programs comes from awareness of the program as defined in the Secretary of the Navy Instruction 4380.8A, through small business vendors, contracts (existing and pending); payment questions and other inquiries that I receive, analyze and disburse as a Correspondence Analyst/Expediter.

For the past two years, I have been my office's representative to the Recreation Association. I have been responsible for managing the purchasing, communications and product selection with three businesses. I communicate on a regular basis with decision-makers and owners of three local businesses concerning clothing items, movie tickets and Air Arena shows. I select the shows, dates and prices and work out logistics of purchases. I have become aware of small business sales and planning needs.

Complete Factor Package #2

3.   Ability to research, collect and analyze data.

I can offer 14 years experience in the Department of the Navy researching, documenting, referencing and analyzing data.

As a Correspondence Analyst/Expediter, I am responsible for analyzing incoming documents; researching similar information, files and documents; prioritizing and processing; and communicating with supervisors and program managers concerning correspondence and documentation.

Previously, as a Team Leader in the Outgoing Mail Records and Reference Branch, I directed a project involving the installation of a state-of-the-art electronic document archiving system. I planned and delegated assignments to transfer a manual filing system to an automated filing system.

In my position during 1985-1986 as Research Assistant, I reviewed and analyzed tehcnical, policy, and organizational material, and regularly prepared analytical reports on this research for the Secretariat and staff.

I am organized, attentive to detail, aware of current subjects and programs, and analytical in processing program information.

4.   Ability to deal with senior members of the public and private sectors.

As a Correspondence Analyst/Expediter, I regularly communicate with representatives from a wide range of private companies and department managers regarding the status of correspondence or requests sent into the Secretary of the Navy's office. I communicate with admirals and other executive heads to respond to their requests for information and clarify matters of question.

As a Team Leader, I communicated with senior members of the public and private sectors in coordinating the operational services of Outgoing Mail, Records and Reference Branch.

For the past two years I have served as Representative for the Recreation Association (NSSORA), a position for which I was selected by the Administrative Officer of the Secretary of the Navy. I communicate with executives and treasurers of companies regarding purchases of tickets and products for employees of the Department of the Navy. Currently, I serve as Assistant Secretary of the Recreation Association.

I completed my B.A. degree with a course concentration in Personnel and Labor Relations. My courses emphasized communications, negotiation and cooperation in the business environment.

Appendix C

Form Approved
OMB No. 3206-0219

OPTIONAL APPLICATION FOR FEDERAL EMPLOYMENT - OF 612

You may apply for most jobs with a resume, this form, or other written format. If your resume or application does not provide all the information requested on this form and in the job vacancy announcement, you may lose consideration for a job.

1 Job title in announcement		**2** Grade(s) applying for	**3** Announcement number
Computer Systems Analyst		11	GS-334

4 Last name	First and middle names	**5** Social Security Number
Thomas	Gerald	333-34-4455

6 Mailing address		**7** Phone numbers (include area code)
7111 Mapleway Dr.		Daytime 202 555 3344

City	State	ZIP Code	
Silver Spring	MD	20001	Evening 301 555 3323

WORK EXPERIENCE

8 Describe your paid and nonpaid work experience related to the job for which you are applying. Do **not** attach job descriptions.

1) Job title (if Federal, include series and grade)

Computer Systems Specialist GS-334-9

From (MM/YY)	To (MM/YY)	Salary	per	Hours per week
5/92	Present	$37,000	year	40

Employer's name and address	Supervisor's name and phone number
Department of Defense	Darrel Carter
214 C Street, NW Washington, DC 30001	(202) 555-3321

Describe your duties and accomplishments

Design, implement, and administer an on-line budget system for DOD staff. Act as back-up for RAMIS databases to support budget, linguistic and planning databases. Evaluate, select and recommend purchase with subsequent delivery of very large Zenith PC with Lotus 123 and Db III. Coordinate ICS color graphics and transfer of data to DOD and Congressional users. Users interfaced with Xerox 860, IBM terminals, or Wang Alliance.

2) Job title (if Federal, include series and grade)

Computer Systems Analyst, GS-334-6

From (MM/YY)	To (MM/YY)	Salary	per	Hours per week
4/90	5/92	$33,000	year	40

Employer's name and address	Supervisor's name and phone number
U.S. Department of Labor, 121 Constitution Avenue	Dwayne Anderson
Washington, DC 20210	(202) 555-3232

Describe your duties and accomplishments

Implemented OMB Budget Status System (BSS) and Budget Preparation System (BPS) within the Department of Labor as required by OMB Circular 79-10 well ahead of schedule. Performed necessary systems analysis to establish an maintain five databases in BSS for various phases of the budget process. Maintain all regular technical liaison with contractor and Federal edp staffs.

191

ADDITIONAL WORK EXPERIENCES

Thomas, Gerald   333-34-4455
Computer Systems Analyst   GS-334   11

3) Job title (if Federal, include series and grade)

Associate Analyst

From (MM/YY)	To (MM/YY)	Salary	per	Hours per week
3/89	4/90	$28,000	year	45

Employer's name and address	Supervisor's name and phone number
Congressional Budget Office, U.S. Congress Washington DC	Terry Nickles (202) 555-0312

Describe your duties and accomplishments

Aided in conception, design and actual implementation of Congressional Scorekeeping system. Performed systems design and analysis for the Legislative Classification System for tracking appropriation accounts with supporting U.S. Code ad Statutes. Designed and personally implemented the Budget Estimate Tracking System. Initiated procurement for Wang mini-computer lease/purchase for in-house use with supporting communications.

4) Job title (if Federal, include series and grade)

Researcher

From (MM/YY)	To (MM/YY)	Salary	per	Hours per week
6/88	3/89	$25,000	year	45

Employer's name and address	Supervisor's name and phone number
Goddard Systems 727 Military Road, Arlington, VA 21211	Elliot Connell (703) 555-2233

Describe your duties and accomplishments

Programmer, task leader, ensuring document systems were up and running. Assisted in evaluating Univac peripheral gear. Converted statistical programs to IBM and optimized and documented programs for production use. Maintained and evaluated tool to drive-on displays and integrated duplexed computer systems.

9 May we contact your current supervisor?

YES [X] NO [ ] ▸ If we need to contact your current supervisor before making an offer, we will contact you first

EDUCATION

10 Mark highest level completed Some HS [ ] HS/GED [ ] Associate [X] Bachelor [ ] Master [ ] Doctoral [ ]

11 Last high school (HS) or GED school. Give the school's name, city, State, ZIP Code (if known), and year diploma or GED received.

Central High School, Pittsburgh, PA 22232 Graduated 1988

12 Colleges and universities attended. Do **not** attach a copy of your transcript unless requested.

Name			Total Credits Earned		Major(s)	Degree - Year
			Semester	Quarter		(if any) Received
1) University of Maryland					Computer Science	
City	State	ZIP Code	122			B.A. 1990
College Park	MD	33324				
2)						
3)						

OTHER QUALIFICATIONS

13 **Job-related** training courses (give title and year). **Job-related** skills (other languages, computer software/hardware, tools, machinery, typing spee **Job-related** certificates and licenses (current only). **Job-related** honors, awards, and special accomplishments (publications, memberships in professional/honor societies, leadership activities, public speaking, and performance awards). Give dates, but do **not** send documents unless req

Training Courses

Topographic Surveyor School, U.S. Engineers, 1990
Topographic Survey Equipment Repair School, 1990
Non-commissioned Officers Academy, 1990
Computer Programming School, 1991
Federal Reserve System Assistant Examiner School, 1991

Computer Skills

RAMIS database, Unix, LAN, Lotus 123, Fortran, Basic

Continued on a Separate Page

GENERAL

14 Are you a U.S. citizen? YES [X] NO [ ] ▸ Give the country of your citizenship. _____

15 Do you claim veterans' preference NO [X] YES [ ] ▸ Mark your claim of 5 or 10 points below.

5 points [ ] ▸ Attach your DD 214 or other proof **10 points** [ ] ▸ Attach an *Application for 10-Point Veterans' Preference* (SF 15) and proof re

16 Were you ever a Federal civilian employee?

		Series	Grade	From (MM/YY)	To (MM/YY)
NO [ ] YES [X] ▸ For highest civilian grade give	9	4	5/92	Present	

17 Are you eligible for reinstatement based on career or career-conditional Federal status?

NO [X] YES [ ] ▸ If requested, attach SF 50 proof.

☆
193

APPLICANT CERTIFICATION

18 **I certify** that, to the best of my knowledge and belief, all of the information on and attached to this application is true, correct, complete and mad in good faith. **I understand** that false or fraudulent information on or attached to this application may be grounds for not hiring me or for firing me after I begin work, and may be punishable by fine or imprisonment. **I understand** that any information I give may be investigated.

SIGNATURE   **DATE SIGNED**

Excerpt from the 22-page **Guide to SES Qualifications,** 1995
Written by Office of Personnel Management
Published by the Government Printing Office

Available through:
New Orders
Superintendent of Documents
P.O. Box 371954
Pittsburgh, PA 15250-7954

Stock Number: 006-000-01405-4

Price: $2.00

The following examples illustrate good and weak qualifications statements. In addition, the examples show how the five ECQ's and their corresponding LEF Competencies and Key Characteristics are reflected in QRB cases.

Candidates do not need to have experience in each LEF Competency and Key Characteristic to demonstrate possession of the ECQ. Rather, the candidate's overall record (professional and volunteer experience, education and training, accomplishments, awards, and potential) should indicate the knowledge, skills, and abilities needed to apply the ECQ in an executive capacity.

Good qualifications statements feature the activities/context/outcomes elements described on page 8. Weak statements are vague and feature broad job responsibilities without giving specifics.

These examples, from actual QRB cases, have been altered to protect the privacy of the SES candidates.

1 STRATEGIC VISION

The ability to ensure that key national and organizational goals, priorities, values, and other issues are considered in making decisions and exercising leadership to implement and to ensure that the organization's mission and strategic vision are reflected in the management of its people.

KEY CHARACTERISTICS INCLUDE:

a. Identifying and integrating key issues affecting the organization, including political, economic, social, technological, and administrative factors.

b. Understanding the roles and relationships of the components of the national policy-making and implementation process, including the President, political appointees, Congress, the judiciary, State and local governments, and interest groups.

c. Exercising leadership and motivating managers to incorporate vision, strategic planning, and elements of quality management into the full range of the organization's activities.

	LEF Competencies	
Creative Thinking	*Leadership*	*Self-Direction*
Customer Orientation	*Oral Communication*	*Team Building*
External Awareness	*Planning & Evaluating*	*Vision*

195

WEAK EXAMPLE

"I review statutes, appropriations language, congressional actions, and external agency fiscal policy to develop plans and procedures for implementing programs and projects.1 I maintain close working relationships with internal and external activity managers in developing uniform programs and policies."2

   1. *No specific examples to illustrate these assertions.*

   2. *No explanation of how these relationships were maintained in terms of integrating issues and programs . Outcomes are not described.*

GOOD EXAMPLE

"As a member of the Space Center's Strategy Committee, I directed the development of the Centerwide Strategic Plan.1 The Committee's charter was to provide a comprehensive strategic plan to ensure the Center's continued effectiveness as a national research laboratory in support of the nation's aeronautical and space goals. I ensured that the strategic planning process involved the participation of employees at all levels of the organization, and was developed to provide a base of shared values and an awareness by the staff of technical, political, and managerial considerations facing the agency.2 As a result of the plan, the committee, through my direction, made difficult cost-saving decisions to downsize ongoing programs. Subsequently, managers made major reorganizations to align the Center's structure with the agency's mission and strategic vision. The plan has been in place for five years and continues to provide a framework for program evaluation and project ideas and a focus for research and institutional activities."3

   1. *Major activity performed.*

   2. *Describes the environment in which the activity was performed.*

   3. *A major accomplishment.*

2 HUMAN RESOURCES MANAGEMENT

The ability to design human resource strategies to meet the organization's mission, strategic vision, and goals and to achieve maximum potential of all employees in a fair and equitable manner.

KEY CHARACTERISTICS INCLUDE:

a. Acquiring a diverse workforce with the necessary knowledge, skills, abilities, and/or potential through appropriate planning, recruitment/outreach and selection processes.

b. Assessing employees' unique developmental needs and providing developmental opportunities which maximize employees' capabilities and contribute to the achievement of organizational goals.

c. Fostering a working environment where people who are culturally diverse can work together cooperatively and effectively in achieving organizational goals.

d. Providing leadership in setting the workforce's expected performance levels commensurate with the organization's strategic plan objectives.

e. Promoting quality through effective use of the organization's performance management system (e.g., establishing performance standards, appraising staff accomplishments using the developed standards, and taking action to reward, counsel, or remove employees, as appropriate).

f. Dealing effectively with employee/labor management relations matters, including resolving conflicts, attending to morale and organizational climate issues, handling administrative, labor management, and EEO issues, and taking disciplinary actions when other means have not been successful.

	LEF Competencies	
Conflict Management	*Influencing / Negotiating*	*Planning & Evaluating*
Customer Orientation	*Interpersonal Skills*	*Problem Solving*
Decisiveness	*Leadership*	*Self-Direction*
Flexibility	*Managing Diverse Workforce*	*Team Building*
Human Resources Management	*Oral Communication*	*Vision*

WEAK EXAMPLE

"I have been involved in selecting, training, counseling and developing personnel, planning and organizing their activities, evaluating their performance, EEO, upward mobility, and personnel management. In addition, I have worked to improve my human resources skills and those of other staff members, and to provide access to learning opportunities."1

> *1. Offers only a partial list of human resources activities. Does not describe actions or strategies used to accomplish work. General assertions parrot the Executive Core Qualification definition; they do not illustrate competence.*

GOOD EXAMPLE

"As Director of my department's Contract Policy Division, I have taken an active role in the promotion of equal employment opportunity. I have directed outreach for minority recruitment of contract specialists at universities and colleges and promoted upward mobility development positions.1 Through my direction, cooperative relationships have been established at a number of historically Black colleges and universities. As a result, minority hiring of entrance-level interns into the contract specialist training program has increased from 18 percent to 42 percent.2 To establish a high level of professionalism in the Division, I have encouraged career development opportunities, actively initiating rotational assignments and emphasizing the importance of internal training. I am the Division's representative to the Personnel Office's Executive Training Board, serve as a Total Quality Leadership Facilitator, and am an instructor for 'Prevention of Sexual Harassment' classes. To foster a partnership environment between the Division's employees and managers, I host quarterly off-site retreats. These retreats have been very successful in resolving problems and restarting communication within the staff.3 In addition, these gatherings have helped to bridge communication gaps among culturally diverse workers, enabling the entire staff to make more effective contributions to the organization's goals."4

> *1. Describes a specific activity.*
>
> *2. Describes a specific outcome.*
>
> *3. Describes an environment and specific outcome.*
>
> *4. Fosters an environment where people can work together cooperatively.*

3   PROGRAM DEVELOPMENT AND EVALUATION

The ability to establish program/policy goals and the structure and processes necessary to implement the organization's mission and strategic vision. Inherent in this process is ensuring that programs and policies are being implemented and adjusted as necessary, that the appropriate results are being achieved, and that a process for continually examining the quality of program activities is in place.

KEY CHARACTERISTICS INCLUDE:

a. Assessing policy, program, and project feasibility.

b. Formulating short- and long-term goals and objectives and integrating them into a strategic plan.

c. Structuring and organizing work and setting priorities.

d. Anticipating and identifying, diagnosing, and consulting on potential or actual problem areas relating to program implementation and goal achievement; selecting from alternative courses of corrective action; and/or taking action from developed contingency plans.

e. Setting effectiveness, efficiency, productivity, evaluation, and management/internal control standards.

f. Establishing and utilizing procedures and processes to monitor progress toward organizational objectives.

g. Taking any necessary corrective action to ensure an effective, efficient, and productive organizational unit.

LEF Competencies		
Creative Thinking	*Influencing / Negotiating*	*Self-Direction*
Customer Orientation	*Leadership*	*Team Building*
Decisiveness	*Management Controls / Integrity*	*Technology Management*
External Awareness	*Oral Communication*	*Vision*
Flexibility	*Planning & Evaluating*	*Written Communication*
Human Resources Management	*Problem Solving*	

WEAK EXAMPLE

"My organization has 176 employees.1 My responsibilities run the gamut
of administrative functions. For example, I have effected major management
improvements of my organization's computer capabilities.2 In addition, I recently
completed a detail as Special Assistant to the agency director. I performed staff
assignments in all areas of administration, including personnel, budget, management information systems, accounting, and procurement. This assignment gave
me a unique overview of many projects.3 I am closely involved in monitoring
ongoing activities, identifying both potential and present deficiencies, and making
recommendations for their ultimate improvement and correction. For example,
I updated the Agency Program System Plan, a major undertaking."4

> 1. *Number of employees supervised is not, in itself, evidence of competence.
>   Additional information is needed to show how this supervision relates to
>   the competencies being addressed.*
>
> 2. *Too general; does not illustrate how or why the candidate effected these
>   improvements.*
>
> 3. *Listing staff assignments does not illustrate specific experience in directing
>   and guiding programs, projects, or policies.*
>
> 4. *Candidate does not define competencies or experience.*

GOOD EXAMPLE

"As Director of the Food, Housing, and Recreation Services, I established an
aggressive inspection process to focus on quality control and oversee operations
at department facilities providing these services.1 This resulted in a $10 million
increase in authorized appropriated funding, and more efficient operation of our
restaurants, troop lodgings, and recreation programs.2 The Secretary praised the
inspection program as one of the best in the department. One of my initiatives
was developing formal staff assistance and oversight teams that visited each
base's services to correct problems. I achieved a similar success in another project.
I established a Staff Evaluation Team which visited each base and provided
guidance on how to improve services.3 Civilian restaurants at one base had a
loss of over $50,000 in 1991. My team's efforts lead to restaurant profits of $95,000
in 1993.

Working with the department's Food, Housing, and Recreation Advisory Board,
I developed and implemented a strategic planning process which adopted corporate
standards as well as the long- and short-range strategies to achieve improvements
in these services. These standards were keys to the successes achieved in the Gulf
War, and they are still being used to meet our food, housing, and recreational
needs at all bases."4

> 1. *Describes an activity—direction of a major project.*
>
> 2. *Describes a specific outcome.*
>
> 3. *Describes the environment.*
>
> 4. *Example of an effective management control standard.*

200

4 RESOURCES PLANNING AND MANAGEMENT

The ability to acquire and administer financial, material, and information resources. It also involves the ability to accomplish the organization's mission, support program policy objectives, and promote strategic vision.

KEY CHARACTERISTICS INCLUDE:

a. Managing the budgetary process, including preparing and justifying a budget and operating the budget under organizational and Congressional procedures.

b. Overseeing procurement and contracting procedures and processes.

c. Integrating and coordinating logistical operations.

d. Overseeing the allocation of financial resources.

e. Establishing and assuring the use of internal controls for financial systems.

f. Ensuring the development and utilization of management information systems and other technological resources that meet the organization's needs.

LEF Competencies

Conflict Management	*Human Resources Mgmt*	*Oral Communication*
Decisiveness	*Influencing / Negotiating*	*Planning & Evaluating*
External Awareness	*Leadership*	*Problem Solving*
Financial Management	*Management Controls / Integrity*	*Written Communication*
Flexibility		

WEAK EXAMPLE

"My position requires a full range of administrative support functions including real and personal property management, printing services, travel, and building management. The work involves budget, procurement, funds control, and reconciliation activities. I have a firm grasp of these activities as they relate to the duties and responsibilities of a major administrative management official."1

> 1. *No description of activities or accomplishments related to the work or illustrations of experience.*

GOOD EXAMPLE

"As director of the agency's Wind Tunnel Restoration Project, I managed a construction budget of $100 million and a research and development budget of $8 million.1 The construction budget had four different fund sources and five different funding years. To track and administer these complex budgets, in accordance with Federal guidelines, I worked closely with our agency's Director of Information Resources Management. We designed two separate ADP systems to separately track the construction and the research and development budgets. I approved ADP contracts to purchase a large scale IBM Central Processing Unit and agency-wide mainframe and microcomputer data base software.2 The systems were so successful that the agency head adopted them as the tracking models for all future budgeting projects.3

> 1. *Describes a specific activity.*
>
> 2. *Demonstrates use of management information systems and technological resources.*
>
> 3. *Describes a specific outcome.*

5 ORGANIZATIONAL REPRESENTATION AND LIAISON

The ability to explain, advocate, and negotiate with individuals and groups internally and externally. It also involves the ability to develop an expansive professional network with other organizations and organizational units.

KEY CHARACTERISTICS INCLUDE:

a. Representing and speaking for the organizational unit and its work (e.g., presenting, explaining, selling, defending, and negotiating) to those within and outside the agency (e.g., agency heads and other political and career executives; Office of Management and Budget; Congressional members, staffs, and committees; the media; clientele and professional groups).

b. Establishing and maintaining working relationships with internal organizational units (e.g., other program areas and staff support functions).

c. Developing and enhancing alliances with external groups (e.g., other agencies and governments, Congress, and clientele groups).

d. Working in groups and teams; conducting briefings and other meetings.

e. Seeing that reports, memoranda, and other documents reflect the position and work of the organizational unit.

f. Getting understanding and support from higher-level management.

LEF Competencies

Conflict Management	*Flexibility*	*Oral Communication*
Customer Orientation	*Influencing / Negotiating*	*Self-Direction*
External Awareness	*Interpersonal Skills*	*Written Communication*

203

WEAK EXAMPLE

"My current responsibilities include working effectively with high-level officials, within and outside the agency. I maintain beneficial relationships with several major departments.1 I have presented comprehensive briefing papers reflecting the viewpoints of my office and the agency in a variety of settings.2 Daily work requires persuading, selling, and negotiating. I possess the skills to effectively discharge these duties."3

> 1. *No examples of "beneficial relationships." How does the candidate maintain these relationships and what are the results?*
>
> 2. *This is a duty statement, much like those found in position descriptions. Lacks an example of how viewpoints were presented and what resulted from those presentations.*
>
> 3. *Too general; no specific evidence of talents.*

GOOD EXAMPLE

"As a task leader on the Weather Station Redesign Team, I represented the department in discussions with the Advisory Committee on the Redesign of the Weather Station, the media, Congress, contractors, and International Partner Organizations. To develop evaluation criteria and perform a needs assessment, I met with representatives from Japan and Canada.1 I presented the status and results of the program to the Advisory Committee on the Redesign of the Weather Station at several public forums with the media. For the Congressional hearings on the redesign of the Space Station, I was designated as a potential witness and provided information for the *Congressional Record*. As a representative of the department's Construction of Facility Program, I served on review committees and working groups for new construction initiatives.2 The chairperson asked me to lead the working group toward a consensus position, to be included in the overall National Facility Study. The group produced an ambitious proposal, which included the addition of new testing capability and modification of existing testing resources. The working group has completed a detailed implementation plan for the proposal."3

> 1. *Describes the environment — the variety of publics the candidate dealt with in this ECQ.*
>
> 2. *Describes a specific activity.*
>
> 3. *Describes a specific outcome.*

S tart your qualifications statement with a brief summary of your managerial experience before individually addressing the five ECQ's. The key to a well-written qualifications statement is to give your readers— executive resources staff, rating officials, selecting officials, and QRB members— the information they need to compare your experience to the ECQ's. Based on discussions with QRB members, we know that the preferred style is short, concise qualifications statements.

AN ACTIVITIES/CONTEXT/OUTCOME APPROACH

For each ECQ, provide at least one example of your experience. Keep in mind that the QRB will be looking for specific, job-related **activities**. In addition, they will be interested in the **context** and **outcomes** of these activities.

Follow these steps as you document your experience:

- First, identify specific job-related **activities** (e.g., leadership, planning, acquiring a diverse workforce, budgeting) in which you participated and describe your actions. The Key Characteristics listed under each ECQ (see Case Examples, pages 10 - 19) provide a guide to the key actions that are relevant to executive jobs.

- Next, describe the **context** or environment within which you performed these actions. Mention other individuals or groups involved in the activity (e.g., client groups, members or staff of Congress, individuals in other agencies or organizations).

- Finally, state the **outcomes** of your actions. These indicate the quality and effectiveness of your performance and demonstrate your ability to achieve results, a key requirement of executive positions.

The following example illustrates the activities/context/outcomes format.

"I supervised eight professional engineers in the development of a complex technological forecast (activity). It had to be completed very quickly in order for the client company to compete for a major Army contract (context). The forecast was completed on time, and contracting documents indicated it was a major factor in the company winning the contract (outcome)."

SOME OTHER SUGGESTIONS

In addition to the activities/context/outcomes framework, keep these points in mind when writing your qualifications statements.

- You may demonstrate competence in the ECQ's through:
    - regular supervisory/managerial responsibilities;
    - special assignments, such as task forces; or
    - as a specialist responsible for much of the technical work on a plan, budget, or other project.
- You should cite relevant formal training which enhanced the ECQ.
- You may cite relevant, non-Federal experience such as work in the private sector and volunteer and professional organizations.

LEADERSHIP EFFECTIVENESS FRAMEWORK
COMPETENCY DEFINITIONS

Conflict Management
Anticipates and seeks to resolve confrontations, disagreements, and complaints in a constructive manner.

Creative Thinking
Develops insights and solutions; fosters innovation among others.

Customer Orientation
Actively seeks customer input; ensures customer needs are met; continuously seeks to improve the quality of services, products, and processes.

Decisiveness
Takes action and risks when needed; makes difficult decisions when necessary.

External Awareness
Stays informed on laws, policies, politics, Administration priorities, trends, special interests, and other issues; considers external impact of statements or actions; uses information in decision-making.

Financial Management
Prepares and justifies budget; monitors expenses; manages procurement and contracting.

Flexibility
Adapts to change in the work environment; effectively copes with stress.

Human Resources Management
Ensures effective recruitment, selection, training, performance appraisal, recognition, and corrective/disciplinary action; promotes affirmative employment, good labor relations, and employee well-being.

Influencing/Negotiating
Networks with, and provides information to, key groups and individuals; appropriately uses negotiation, persuasion, and authority in dealing with others to achieve goals.

Interpersonal Skills
Considers and responds appropriately to the needs, feelings, capabilities and interests of others; provides feedback; treats others equitably.

Leadership
Demonstrates and encourages high standards of behavior; adapts leadership style to situations and people; empowers, motivates, and guides others.

Management Controls/Integrity
Ensures the integrity of the organization's processes; promotes ethical and effective practices.

Appendix E

OPERATING MANUAL
for
QUALIFICATION STANDARDS FOR GENERAL SCHEDULE POSITIONS

TABLE OF CONTENTS

I.   How to Use this Manual I-1

II.   General Policies and Instructions

      Table of Contents for Section II . . . . II-i

      Policies and Instructions II-1

III. Index to Qualification Standards III-1

    A.   Series Number Order III-A-1

    B.   Alphabetical Order by Title III-B-1

IV.   Qualification Standards IV-1

    A.   Group Coverage Qualification Standards
        1.   Clerical and Administrative Support Positions IV-A-1
        2.   Technical and Medical Support Positions IV-A-7
        3.   Administrative and Management Positions IV-A-13
        4.   Professional and Scientific Positions IV-A-19
        5.   Competitive Service Student Trainee Positions IV-A-25
        6.   Supervisory Positions IV-A-29
        7.   Policy Analysis and Administrative Analysis Positions IV-A-33
        8.   Positions Involving Equal Employment Opportunity
            Collateral Assignments IV-A-35
        9.   Positions Requiring Collateral Correctional Skills IV-A-37

    B.   Individual Qualification Standards and
        Occupational Requirements in Series Order IV-B-1

V.   Test Requirements V-1

VI.   Medical Requirements VI-1

VII. Technical Notes and Updates VII-1

VIII. Transmittal Sheets (as issued)

207

QUALIFICATION STANDARDS OPERATING MANUAL

**Group Coverage Qualification Standard for
Administrative and Management Positions**

OCCUPATIONAL COVERAGE

A list of the occupational series covered by this qualification standard is provided below. The occupational series marked with an asterisk have individual occupational requirements in Section IV-B of this Manual. Refer to Section V for information about occupations with test requirements.

GS-006 Correctional Institution Administration*	GS-505 Financial Management*
GS-011 Bond Sales Promotion*	GS-526 Tax Technician*
GS-018 Safety and Occupational Health Management*	GS-560 Budget Analysis
GS-023 Outdoor Recreation Planning*	GS-570 Financial Institution Examining*
GS-028 Environmental Protection Specialist	GS-669 Medical Records Administration*
GS-030 Sports Specialist*	GS-670 Health System Administration*
GS-062 Clothing Design*	GS-671 Health System Specialist*
GS-080 Security Administration	GS-672 Prosthetic Representative
GS-105 Social Insurance Administration	GS-673 Hospital Housekeeping Management*
GS-106 Unemployment Insurance*	GS-685 Public Health Program Specialist*
GS-107 Health Insurance Administration	GS-828 Construction Analyst*
GS-132 Intelligence	GS-920 Estate Tax Examining
GS-142 Manpower Development	GS-930 Hearings and Appeals
GS-160 Civil Rights Analysis	GS-950 Paralegal Specialist
GS-188 Recreation Specialist*	GS-958 Pension Law Specialist*
GS-201 Personnel Management	GS-962 Contact Representative
GS-205 Military Personnel Management	GS-965 Land Law Examining*
GS-212 Personnel Staffing	GS-967 Passport and Visa Examining*
GS-221 Position Classification	GS-990 General Claims Examining
GS-222 Occupational Analysis	GS-991 Workers' Compensation Claims Examining
GS-223 Salary and Wage Administration	GS-993 Railroad Retirement Claims Examining
GS-230 Employee Relations	GS-996 Veterans Claims Examining
GS-233 Labor Relations	GS-1001 General Arts and Information*
GS-235 Employee Development	GS-1008 Interior Design*
GS-244 Labor Management Relations Examining*	GS-1010 Exhibits Specialist*
GS-246 Contractor Industrial Relations	GS-1020 Illustrating*
GS-249 Wage and Hour Compliance*	GS-1035 Public Affairs
GS-260 Equal Employment Opportunity	GS-1040 Language Specialist*
GS-270 Federal Retirement Benefits	GS-1051 Music Specialist*
GS-301 Miscellaneous Administration and Program	GS-1054 Theater Specialist*
GS-334 Computer Specialist*	GS-1056 Art Specialist*
GS-340 Program Management	GS-1071 Audiovisual Production*
GS-341 Administrative Officer	GS-1082 Writing and Editing
GS-343 Management and Program Analysis	GS-1083 Technical Writing and Editing*
GS-346 Logistics Management	GS-1084 Visual Information*
GS-360 Equal Opportunity Compliance	GS-1101 General Business and Industry*
GS-362 Electric Accounting Machine Project Planning	GS-1103 Industrial Property Management*
GS-391 Telecommunications*	GS-1104 Property Disposal
GS-501 Financial Administration and Program	GS-1130 Public Utilities Specialist
	GS-1140 Trade Specialist*
	GS-1144 Commissary Store Management* ☞

U.S. OFFICE OF PERSONNEL MANAGEMENT

**Group Coverage Qualification Standard for
Administrative and Management Positions**

OCCUPATIONAL COVERAGE (Continued)

The occupational series marked with an asterisk have individual occupational requirements in Section IV-B of this Manual. Refer to Section V for information about occupations with test requirements.

GS-1145 Agricultural Program Specialist*
GS-1146 Agricultural Marketing*
GS-1147 Agricultural Market Reporting
GS-1150 Industrial Specialist*
GS-1160 Financial Analysis*
GS-1161 Crop Insurance Administration*
GS-1162 Crop Insurance Underwriting*
GS-1163 Insurance Examining*
GS-1165 Loan Specialist*
GS-1169 Internal Revenue Officer*
GS-1170 Realty
GS-1171 Appraising
GS-1173 Housing Management
GS-1176 Building Management
GS-1361 Navigational Information*
GS-1397 Document Analysis*
GS-1421 Archives Specialist
GS-1630 Cemetery Administration
GS-1640 Facility Management*
GS-1654 Printing Management*
GS-1670 Equipment Specialist*
GS-1702 Education and Training Technician
GS-1712 Training Instruction*
GS-1715 Vocational Rehabilitation*
GS-1801 General Inspection, Investigation, and
    Compliance*
GS-1810 General Investigating
GS-1811 Criminal Investigating*

GS-1812 Game Law Enforcement
GS-1816 Immigration Inspection
GS-1831 Securities Compliance Examining*
GS-1850 Agricultural Commodity Warehousing
    Examining*
GS-1854 Alcohol, Tobacco and Firearms
    Inspection*
GS-1864 Public Health Quarantine Inspection*
GS-1889 Import Specialist*
GS-1890 Customs Inspection*
GS-1894 Customs Entry and Liquidating*
GS-1910 Quality Assurance*
GS-1980 Agricultural Commodity Grading*
GS-2001 General Supply
GS-2003 Supply Program Management
GS-2010 Inventory Management
GS-2030 Distribution Facilities and Storage
    Management
GS-2032 Packaging
GS-2050 Supply Cataloging
GS-2101 Transportation Specialist*
GS-2110 Transportation Industry Analysis*
GS-2123 Motor Carrier Safety*
GS-2125 Highway Safety*
GS-2130 Traffic Management*
GS-2150 Transportation Operations*
GS-2161 Marine Cargo*

209

OPERATING MANUAL
for
QUALIFICATION STANDARDS FOR GENERAL SCHEDULE POSITIONS

SECTION I. HOW TO USE THIS MANUAL

This Manual (generally referred to as the *Qualification Standards Operating Manual*) contains qualification standards that have been established by the U.S. Office of Personnel Management (OPM) for General Schedule (GS) positions in the Federal Government. It is directed primarily to personnel specialists who need to determine whether applicants meet the minimum requirements for the positions being filled. The information in this Manual may also be of interest to supervisors and managers, high school and college placement officials, applicants, and others who wish to obtain information about Federal employment qualifications. However, users of this material should be aware that the broad guidelines in this Manual are not intended to provide detailed information about the specific qualification requirements for individual positions. Such information, e.g., a description of the specialized experience requirements for a particular position, is normally included in the vacancy announcement that OPM and agencies issue when they have a position to fill. Information about the work performed in General Schedule occupational series is contained in the *Handbook of Occupational Groups and Series* and the *Position Classification Standards,* and is not repeated in this Manual.

Qualification standards are intended to identify applicants who are likely to be able to perform successfully on the job, and to screen out those who are unlikely to do so. They are not designed to rank candidates, identify the best qualified applicants for particular positions, or otherwise substitute for a careful analysis of applicants' knowledge, skills, and abilities.

Users of this Manual should familiarize themselves with the general organization of the material to facilitate locating information about particular subjects or occupations. Section II, "General Policies and Instructions," is the key to understanding and using the qualification standards in this Manual. It contains basic information that applies across occupations, and should be considered an integral part of the standards themselves. The indexes (Section III), test requirements (Section V), medical requirements summary (Section VI), and technical notes (Section VII) are quick references to help users find specific information. For example, to find out whether a written or performance test is required for a particular occupation and grade level, users of this Manual should refer to Section V, "Test Requirements." "Technical Notes and Updates" and "Transmittal Sheets" should be filed as received in Sections VII and VIII, respectively. Section IV, "Qualification Standards," is the largest section of the Manual. Section IV-A includes "Group Coverage Qualification Standards" that describe common patterns of education, experience, or other requirements that apply to many different occupational series. Section IV-B, "Individual Qualification Standards and Occupational Requirements in Series Order," provides information about the minimum requirements for each occupational series. Information about test requirements is generally not included in Section IV, since it is provided separately in Section V.

The Office of Personnel Management does not stock copies of the *Operating Manual for Qualification Standards For General Schedule Positions.* It is printed and distributed by the Government Printing Office (GPO), and may be purchased from the Superintendent of Documents. The mailing address is:

Superintendent of Documents
U.S. Government Printing Office
Washington, DC 20402

The telephone number for the order desk is (202) 783-3238.

☆

210

QUALIFICATION STANDARDS OPERATING MANUAL

Group Coverage Qualification Standard for
Administrative and Management Positions

This qualification standard covers positions in the General Schedule that involve the performance of two-grade interval administrative and management work. It contains common patterns of creditable education and experience to be used in making qualifications determinations. Section IV-B of this Manual contains individual occupational requirements for some occupations that are to be used in conjunction with this standard. Section V identifies the occupations that have test requirements.

A list of the occupational series covered by this standard is provided on pages IV-A-13 and IV-A-14. This standard may also be used for two-grade interval positions other than those listed if the education and experience pattern is determined to be appropriate.

EDUCATION AND EXPERIENCE REQUIREMENTS

The following table shows the amounts of education and/or experience required to qualify for positions covered by this standard.

GRADE	EDUCATION	OR EXPERIENCE	
		GENERAL	SPECIALIZED
GS-5	4-year course of study leading to a bachelor's degree	3 years, 1 year of which was equivalent to at least GS-4	None
GS-7	1 full year of graduate level education *or* superior academic achievement	None	1 year equivalent to at least GS-5
GS-9	2 full years of progressively higher level graduate education *or* master's or equivalent graduate degree (such as an LL.B. or J.D.)	None	1 year equivalent to at least GS-7
GS-11	3 full years of progressively higher level graduate education *or* Ph.D. or equivalent doctoral degree	None	1 year equivalent to at least GS-9
GS-12 and above	None	None	1 year equivalent to at least next lower grade level

Equivalent combinations of education and experience are qualifying for all grade levels for which both education and experience are acceptable.

Some of the occupational series covered by this standard include both one- and two-grade interval work. The qualification requirements described in this standard apply only to those positions that typically follow a two-grade interval pattern. While the levels of experience shown for most positions covered by this standard follow the grade level progression pattern outlined in the table, users of the standard should refer to **E.3.***(p)* in the "General Policies and Instructions" (Section II of this Manual) for guidance on crediting experience for positions with different lines of progression.

Undergraduate Education: Successful completion of a full 4-year course of study in *any field* leading to a bachelor's degree, in an accredited college or university, meets the GS-5 level requirements for many positions covered by this standard. Others have individual occupational requirements in Section IV-B that specify that applicants must, in general, (1) have specific course work that meets the requirements for a major in a *particular field(s)*, or (2) have at least 24 semester hours of course work in the field(s) identified. Course work in fields closely related to those specified may be accepted if it clearly provides applicants with the background of knowledge and skills necessary for successful job performance. One year of full-time undergraduate study is defined as 30 semester hours or 45 quarter hours, and is equivalent to 9 months of general experience.

Superior Academic Achievement: The superior academic achievement provision is applicable to all occupations covered by this standard. See the "General Policies and Instructions" for specific guidance on applying the superior academic achievement provision.

Graduate Education: Education at the graduate level in an accredited college or university in the amounts shown in the table meets the requirements for positions at GS-7 through GS-11. Such education must demonstrate the knowledge, skills, and abilities necessary to do the work.

One year of full-time graduate education is considered to be the number of credit hours that the school attended has determined to represent 1 year of full-time

U.S. OFFICE OF PERSONNEL MANAGEMENT

Group Coverage Qualification Standard for
Administrative and Management Positions

study. If that information cannot be obtained from the school, 18 semester hours should be considered as satisfying the 1 year of full-time study requirement.

Part-time graduate education is creditable in accordance with its relationship to a year of full-time study at the school attended.

For certain positions covered by this standard, the work may be recognized as sufficiently technical or specialized that graduate study alone may not provide the knowledge and skills needed to perform the work. In such cases, agencies may use selective factors to screen out applicants without actual work experience.

General Experience: For positions for which individual occupational requirements do not specify otherwise, general experience is 3 years of progressively responsible experience, 1 year of which was equivalent to at least GS-4, that demonstrates the ability to:

1. Analyze problems to identify significant factors, gather pertinent data, and recognize solutions;
2. Plan and organize work; and
3. Communicate effectively orally and in writing.

Such experience may have been gained in administrative, professional, technical, investigative, or other responsible work. Experience in substantive and relevant secretarial, clerical, or other responsible work may be qualifying as long as it provided evidence of the knowledge, skills, and abilities (KSA's) necessary to perform the duties of the position to be filled. Experience of a general clerical nature (typing, filing, routine procedural processing, maintaining records, or other nonspecialized tasks) is not creditable. Trades or crafts experience appropriate to the position to be filled may be creditable for some positions.

For some occupations or positions, applicants must have had work experience that demonstrated KSA's in addition to those identified above. Positions with more specific general experience requirements than those described here are shown in the appropriate individual occupational requirements.

Specialized Experience: Experience that equipped the applicant with the particular knowledge, skills, and abilities to perform successfully the duties of the position, and that is typically in or related to the work

of the position to be filled. To be creditable, specialized experience must have been equivalent to at least the next lower grade level in the normal line of progression for the occupation in the organization. Applicants who have the 1 year of appropriate specialized experience, as indicated in the table, are not required by this standard to have general experience, education above the high school level, or any additional specialized experience to meet the minimum qualification requirements.

Combining Education and Experience: Combinations of successfully completed post-high school education and experience may be used to meet total qualification requirements for the grade levels specified in the table, and may be computed by first determining the applicant's total qualifying experience as a percentage of the experience required for the grade level; then determining the applicant's education as a percentage of the education required for the grade level; and then adding the two percentages. The total percentages must equal at least 100 percent to qualify an applicant for that grade level. Only graduate education in excess of the amount required for the next lower grade level may be used to qualify applicants for positions at grades GS-9 and GS-11. (When crediting education that requires specific course work, prorate the number of hours of related courses required as a proportion of the total education to be used.)

The following are examples of how education and experience may be combined. They are examples only, and are not all-inclusive.

- The position to be filled is a Quality Assurance Specialist, GS-1910-5. An applicant has 2 years of general experience and 45 semester hours of college that included 9 semester hours in related course work as described in the individual occupational requirements in Section IV-B. The applicant meets 67 percent of the required experience and 38 percent of the required education. Therefore, the applicant exceeds 100 percent of the total requirement and is qualified for the position.

- The position to be filled is a Management Analyst, GS-343-9. An applicant has 6 months of specialized experience equivalent to GS-7 and 1 year of graduate level education. The applicant meets 50 percent of

QUALIFICATION STANDARDS OPERATING MANUAL

Group Coverage Qualification Standard for Administrative and Management Positions

the required experience but none of the required education, since he or she does not have any graduate study beyond that which is required for GS-7. Therefore, the applicant meets only 50 percent of the total requirement and is not qualified for the position. (The applicant's first year of graduate study is not qualifying for GS-9.)

The position to be filled is a Music Specialist, GS-1051-11. An applicant has 9 months of specialized experience equivalent to GS-9 and 2 1/2 years of creditable graduate level education in music. The applicant meets 75 percent of the required experience and 50 percent of the required education, i.e., the applicant has 1/2 year of graduate study beyond that required for GS-9. Therefore, the applicant exceeds the total requirement and is qualified for the position. (The applicant's first 2 years of graduate study are not qualifying for GS-11.)

USING SELECTIVE FACTORS FOR POSITIONS COVERED BY THIS STANDARD

Selective factors must represent knowledge, skills, or abilities that are essential for successful job performance and cannot reasonably be acquired on the job during the period of orientation/training customary for the position being filled. For example, while the individual occupational requirements for Recreation Specialist provide for applicants to meet minimum qualifications on the basis of education or experience in any one of a number of recreational fields, a requirement for knowledge of therapeutic recreation may be needed to perform the duties of a position providing recreation services to persons with physical disabilities. If that is the case, such knowledge could be justified as a selective factor in filling the position.

Appendix F

OPM NEWS
R|E|L|E|A|S|E

FOR IMMEDIATE RELEASE
June 22, 1994

CONTACT: Mary Ann Maloney
(202) 606-1800

CUMBERSOME STANDARD FORM 171 TO BE ELIMINATED, AS RECOMMENDED BY NATIONAL PERFORMANCE REVIEW

Washington, D.C. -- U.S. Office of Personnel Management Director Jim King today announced that a new proposal will make it simpler to apply for federal jobs. The lengthy Standard Form 171, Application for Federal Employment, currently required for the vast majority of federal occupations will be eliminated, as recommended by Vice President Gore's National Performance Review.

"The intent of the proposal is to make it easier for people to apply for federal jobs," said Jim King. "The SF-171 is too cumbersome and sends the wrong message when we are trying to move to a more customer-friendly and flexible system."

"The easiest way to begin the search for a federal job will now be to review OPM's centralized list of all agency job openings and follow the simple instructions given," said Jim King.

The job list is available through OPM's Career America Connection on 912-757-3000 (telephone listing) or our Federal Job Opportunities Bulletin Board on 912-757-3100 (requires a computer and modem). Other options are to use the touch screens at OPM Federal Employment Information Centers located throughout the country or visit a local State Employment Service office. TDD numbers also are available.

The new proposal highlights OPM's commitment to simplifying the application process through computerized hiring methods. For selected jobs, applicants can apply to OPM by a telephone. For other jobs, job seekers will complete a questionnaire that is read and scored by computer. Both methods drastically reduce the time it takes an applicant to apply and the time it takes to produce a list of ranked candidates.

214

United States Office of Personnel Management

Office of Communications

Theodore Roosevelt Building
1900 E Street, NW
Room 5F12
Washington, DC 20415-0001

(202) 606-1800
FAX: (202) 606-2264

CON 151-02-1
OC-1 8/93

Appendix G

ANNUAL SALARY RATES
1995 General Schedule (GS)

STEP INCREASES 1-10									
GRADE 1	2	3	4	5	6	7	8	9	10
GS -1 12,595	13,015	13,433	13,851	14,272	14,517	14,929	15,343	15,365	15,754
2 14,161	14,498	14,968	15,365	15,534	15,990	16,447	16,903	17,360	17,816
3 15,452	15,968	16,583	16,999	17,514	18,030	18,546	19,061	19,577	20,092
4 17,346	17,924	18,502	19,080	19,658	20,236	20,813	21,391	21,969	22,547
5 19,407	20,054	20,701	21,349	21,996	22,643	23,291	23,938	24,585	25,233
6 21,632	22,353	23,074	23,795	24,516	25,237	25,958	26,679	27,400	28,121
7 24,038	24,838	25,639	26,440	27,241	28,042	28,843	29,644	30,445	31,245
8 26,662	27,509	28,396	29,283	30,170	31,057	31,944	32,837	33,718	38,605
9 29,405	30,385	31,366	32,346	33,326	34,307	35,287	36,268	37,248	38,228
10 32,382	33,462	34,542	35,622	36,702	37,782	38,862	39,942	41,022	42,102
11 35,578	36,763	37,949	39,135	40,321	41,506	42,692	43,878	45,064	46,249
12 42,641	44,063	45,484	46,905	48,326	49,747	51,169	52,590	54,001	55,432
13 50,706	52,396	54,086	55,776	57,466	59,156	60,846	62,536	64,225	65,915
14 59,920	61,917	63,914	65,911	67,908	69,905	71,902	73,899	75,896	77,893
15 70,482	72,832	75,181	77,531	79,881	82,231	84,580	86,930	89,280	91,629

Appendix H

NATIONAL PERFORMANCE REVIEW REPORTS

Hard copy of the NPR reports can be obtained from the U.S. Government Printing Office (GPO), Superintendent of Documents, P.O. 371954, Pittsburgh, PA 15250-7954. For additional information, call (202) 783-3228. Copies can also be ordered from the National Technical Information Service (NTIS) by calling: (703) 487-4650 for First Class mail service; 1-800-553-NITS for Overnight Courier; and (703) 321-8547 for FAX orders. The NTIS TDD (Hearing Impaired) line is (703) 487-4639.

Electronic versions of the NPR reports can be obtained by using a variety of different methods, including electronic bulletin boards, Internet, and a number of commercial services such as America Online, Compuserve, Genie, MCI, The Well, and MetaSystems. For a "Road Map" of where and how to obtain NPR material electronically, send a **blank** Internet e-mail message to: **npraace,esusda.gov.**

Listed below are the NPR accompanying reports:

Creating Quality Leadership and Management

Streamlining Management Control

Transforming Organizational Structures

Improving Customer Service

Mission-Driven, Results-Oriented Budgeting

Improving Financial Management

Reinventing Human Resource Management

Reinventing Federal Procurement

Reinventing Support Services

Reengineering Through Information Technology

Rethinking Program Design

Strengthening the Partnership in Intergovernmental Service Delivery

Reinventing Environmental Management

Improving Regulatory Systems

AGENCY REPORTS

Agency for International Development

Department of Agriculture

Department of Commerce

Department of Defense

Department of Education

Department of Energy

Environmental Protection Agency

Executive Office of the President

Federal Emergency Management Agency

General Services Administration

Department of Health and Human Services

Department of Housing and Urban Development

Intelligence Community

Department of the Interior

Department of Justice

Department of Labor

National Aeronautics and Space Administration

National Science Foundation/Office of Science and Technology Policy

Office of Personnel Management

Small Business Administration

Department of State/U.S. Information Agency

Department of Transportation

Department of the Treasury/Resolution Trust Corporation

Department of Veterans Affairs

Special Reports

"From Red Tape to Results/Creating a Government that Works Better & Costs Less," September 7, 1993.

"Putting Customers First/Standards for Serving the American People," September, 1994.

Glossary

Abilities: Talents and capabilities that applicants bring to the application process.

Area of Consideration: An eligibility requirement that is either "organizational" or "geographic," typically put on a federal job limiting consideration to federal or agency employees, or those who live in a specific commuting area, or opens up consideration to "all sources," which means that the job is open to the public.

Complexity: Refers to "job complexity." A factor in the analysis of a job experience that takes into consideration multiplicity of demands, and kinds of problem-solving employed.

Curriculum Vitae: Literally "life study." It is the academic "resume" format used in universities and in some scientific or academic government jobs.

Department or Agency Wide: Examples of "Areas of Consideration" which limit eligibility of some federal jobs to those in the agency or department where the job is posted.

Desirable Technical Qualifications: Many federal jobs list technical qualifications, some of which are mandatory in order to be considered, others are merely desirable, giving the applicant who has these technical qualifications an edge.

EEO (Equal Employment Opportunity): Federal law requiring that all "federally related" jobs be filled in a manner that does not discriminate on the basis of race, religion, national origin, or gender.

Executive Core Qualifications (ECQ): A set of experiences and competencies that anyone applying for Senior Executive Service status must have.

Factor Evaluation System (FES): A group of factors developed by OPM which are used in its evaluation of a candidate for a particular job.

Factor Statements: One of the many nicknames for the "Supplemental Qualification Statement" or "Selective Placement Factors."

Individual Development Plan (IDP): A plan of training and career development for a Federal employee.

Knowledge: Personal knowledge derived from education, experience, and training which must be consistent with the job knowledge requirements of target job.

KSAs (Knowledge, Skills, and Abilities): Refers to the essential elements that make up a "Supplemental Qualification Statement."

Mandatory Technical Qualification: Technical Qualification which is required for consideration for a position.

Mars (Micro-computer Assisted Rating System): A system developed by OPM to computer scan and rate applications.

Narrative Statement: One of the many names for the "Supplemental Qualification Statement."

National Performance Review (NPR): An organization set up by Vice President Al Gore to streamline the federal government's structure and procedures. NPR is the impetus behind the new federal resume.

Occupational Codes/Job Series Codes: A series of four digit codes used to designate specific federal jobs so that they can be classified and compared.

Office of Personnel Management (OPM): The office acts as the federal government's human resource branch and a personnel policy maker and coordinator for the various departments and agencies of the executive branch.

Personnel Review Process: The process of analyzing resumes to determine first, eligibility; next, appropriate skills and education; and then, merit qualifications; and ultimately, designate final candidates for consideration.

Qualification Standards for General Schedule Positions: Previously referred to as the **X-118**. This is an extensive OPM manual which gives all the standards and position requirements for government grades GS-1 through GS-15 levels (not GM or SES).

Quality Ranking Factors (QRF): The term typically applied by government personnelists to the elements "Supplemental Qualification Statement."

Resumix: A software program that reads "scannable" resumes in certain format. It is in limited use in the government, most notably the White House.

Scope and Effect: Factors describing previous work in terms of how large and how much impact the work has on the system it is performed in.

Senior Executive Service (SES): Corps of executives created in 1978 who by their skills and abilities are able to provide the top leadership in the government. They are considered above the standard GS or GM rating system, and are often appointed to their roles.

Selective Placement Factors: Listed in the Vacancy Announcements, these are the specific qualifications not absolutely required to perform a job, but significant qualifications that will affect success in a position, and therefore rated as important by personnelists in reviewing an application.

Spoils System: Previously, the Civil Service Reform winners in the political system would reward their campaign workers and supporters with government jobs as "spoils" of the victory. This happens today only at the political appointee level.

Status Applicants/Status Candidates: Terms often found in federal job announcements referring to current federal employees or former federal employees who have "reinstatement eligibility," typically career employees with a minimum of three years of service.

Statutory Position: A job in the federal government that is covered by the Civil Service statutes.

Supplemental Qualification Statement: Known by many names, "narrative, statement, factor statements, and KSAs." The supplemental qualification statement is a document that demonstrates to the reviewer that certain "knowledge, skills and abilities" identified as necessary to do a particular job are identified on a point by point basis as part of the experience of the applicant.

X-118: The old name for Qualification Standards for General Schedule Positions.

Government Forms

OF-612. The optional application for federal employment, an alternative application to either the federal resume or SF-171.

SF-171. The old standard federal resume/job application. Federal agencies may accept an SF-171 if they wish, but they may not require an SF-171 for consideration since it is no longer an "authorized form."

SF-50. Formally identified as "Notification of Personnel Action," this document serves to notify already existing employees of personnel actions or movement of personnel, such as promotions, reassignment from one agency to another or within an agency, organizational changes that affect positions, etc. These forms may be used to document federal service.

1203-AW. The form used for the MARS system at OPM. Also referred to as "Qualifications and Availability Form (Form C)."

OF-510. The OPM brochure that specifies the standards and requirements for the federal resume.

DD-214. Certificate of Release or Discharge from Active Duty required in order to prove Honorable Discharge or eligibility for veterans' preference.

SF-15. Form needed to claim "service-related disability" for veterans' preference.

Biographies of Contributing Authors

MICHAEL DOBSON has been Executive Writer for The Resume Place in Washington, DC, where he specialized in writing SF-171s and resumes for executives and technical professionals. He was President, Michael Dobson & Associates, a career counseling firm whose clients included numerous presidential appointees and SES managers. In addition to federal employment with the Smithsonian Institution and a series of senior management positions in private industry, Dobson is currently a Management Consultant for SkillPath, Inc. and Dun & Bradstreet Business Education Services.

SHARON A. HARVEY Quality Consultant, Management Analyst, for the Office of Administrative Assistant (OAA) to the Secretary of the Army, Resource Services-Washington and Headquarters Services-Washington. Over 10 years with the federal government as analyst, consultant/facilitator, and program manager; 4 years with state and local governments as program manager, trainer, and volunteer services coordinator. Began Total Army Quality efforts in 1990-91, working extensively within OAA activities, US Army Corps of Engineers, Military District of Washington, the National Guard Bureau, and outside the Army arena for US Coast Guard and US Navy activities. TQM certification, 1993; Member, American Society for Quality Control; American Society for Training and Development; Capital Area Network for Organizational Effectiveness (C.A.N.O.E.).

JO LEE LOVELAND LINK has been affiliated with The Resume Place as a Senior Career Consultant where she specialized in career transition SF-171s and resumes for mid-career transitions for senior executives, retiring military officers and individuals creating new careers after reorganizations and downsizing. Ms. Loveland Link is currently an organizational consultant in private practice. She frequently consults at federal agencies on reinvention, team development, and leadership training. Together with her husband and business partner, she presents their original simulation, *Flying Chaos, Inc.*, which addresses the impact of accelerated change and turbulence on people and organizations. Ms. Loveland Link holds an Advanced Certificate in Applied Behavior Science and Organization Development through the Mid-Atlantic Association of Training and Consulting, and has a B.S. from the State University of New York.

EDWARD J. LYNCH, Ph.D. currently serves as a professional staff member with the Subcommittee on Civil Service of the House Committee on Government Reform and Oversight. He is also professor and lecturer on immigration policy at the Institute of World Politics. He served in senior policy and public affairs positions during the Reagan and Bush administrations, including the Immigration and Naturalization Service, the Federal Aviation Administration, the President's Commission on Privatization, and the Environmental Protection Agency. His articles have been published in *The Public Interest, Policy Review, The Los Angeles Times, The Washington Post,* and *The Christian Science Monitor.*

PAUL RADDE, Ph.D. is a practicing psychologist and career counselor who has conducted psychotherapy and counseling sessions after hours at The Resume Place in Washington, D.C., since 1985. Dr. Radde is also an author, professional speaker, and management and organizational consultant. He has addressed corporate, government and association audiences nationwide, as well as in Russia, Denmark, Portugal, and Mexico. Dr. Radde is an expert and contributing author on seating arrangement, has written two books on management, Supervising: A Guide For All Levels, as well as The Supervision Transition! An Employee Guide for Choosing and Moving Into A Supervisory Position; and has just released a work on Thrival! Functioning Fully With Supreme Confidence: Six Essential Steps to Thriving.

About the Author and the Company

Kathryn Troutman founded The Resume Place as a resume typeset-design service when there were no memory typewriters or computers. She typeset the resumes on an IBM composer, changing the "font" numerous times per resume. Business grew fast in the early 70's because people did not have access to quality type. The Resume Place grew from a typesetting service to a writing service very soon, as Ms. Troutman recognized that the clients needed help with writing and targeting their resumes toward their objective.

Today The Resume Place specializes in writing for upwardly-mobile and career change clients who need help translating their current experience toward their future goals.

Kathryn has made resume writing an art - writing and formatting each resume to suit the client's background, goals, experience, and special abilities.

Author, Kathryn Troutman and sister Bonny Day manage the Resume Place offices in Baltimore and Washington.

The Resume Place is the oldest resume writing service in Washington, DC assisting professional clients through four Presidents since 1971. The Nation's Capital is a unique city in that professionals are affected by economics and politics - which cause frequent resume writing and updating.

Currently Kathryn writes for and manages two offices, in Baltimore, where she lives, and in Washington, DC, where she founded the business.

Ms. Troutman currently writes resumes for all industries and levels of clients from students to White House and Congressional Committee professional staff, to corporate executives. She has been successful in recruiting outstanding senior executive writers (five of whom contributed chapters to this book). The Resume Place has written and typeset resumes for more than 60,000 clients in the 24 years in business.

An excellent and interesting public speaker, Ms. Troutman has presented many seminars and workshops on resume and 171 writing, on owning a business, managing business and home, for federal government, associations and corporations. She is also a frequent guest on radio talk shows. She has had numerous articles published in newspapers about her business and career accomplishments.

She was a founding board member of the National Association of Women Business Owners, a keynote speaker at the Federal Women's Program in Port Hueneme, California, and a frequent speaker at FEW Training Conferences.

Kathryn attended the University of Maryland, majoring in English and writing. She manages a career and a family of three children, Christopher, age 20; Emily, age 16; and Lauren, age 13. The children are career-minded and are very supportive of their mother's entrepreneurship.

The Resume Place is a family business with Bonny as Manager and Bonita Kraemer, (former English teacher and newspaper editor), mother, as proofreader and editor. The family atmosphere and support has been an important part of this long-running successful business.

Occupational Outlook Handbook, 1996-1997

By the U.S. Department of Labor

*The best-selling job information
book of all time!*

The best source of information on growth projections, salaries, education and training required, the nature of work—and more-for the jobs that 85 percent of Americans hold.

- **JIST's best-selling title**

- **A highly successful book for more than 50 years**

- **Updated every two years—an incredible resource!**

- **Explains education and training needed for every job**

- **Valuable salary information**

- **1996-1997 Edition first shipped April 1996**

Occupational Outlook Handbook

Developed by U.S. Department of Labor, Bureau of Labor Statistics

The most accurate and up-to-date resource for career information.

Nearly 250 occupations are described in detail covering about 90 percent of all workers. Interesting, readable descriptions outline:

- ✓ Required Skills
- ✓ Working Conditions
- ✓ Employment Opportunities
- ✓ Training and Advancement
- ✓ Earnings
- ✓ Related Occupations
- ✓ Much More!

1996 1997

Career Reference
8.5 x 11, 505 pp.

Paper: 1-56370-277-0 • $16.95

Hard: 1-56370-278-9 • $21.95

The Very Quick Job Search, 2nd Edition

Get a Better Job in Half the Time!

By J. Michael Farr

More than 120,000 copies sold

"I gave a copy of this to my daughter, and she got a job. It lays everything out, exactly what you need to do. My daughter said, 'It's the best thing since sliced bread!' "
        —Dr. Pat Schwallie-Giddis, Assistant Executive Director, American Vocational Association

How effective is the advice presented by Mike Farr, one of the founders of the self-directed job search movement, in this classic book? In a demonstration program in a city with an unemployment rate over 24 percent, 96 percent of the job seekers found jobs in an average of 2.4 weeks using these techniques!

- **Proven, effective advice for students, job changers, job seekers, employers, educators, and counselors**

- **Author's career books have sold more than 1.5 million copies**

- **The latest information on market trends and results-oriented job search techniques**

- **Includes a special annotated bibliography listing many additional resources**

- **Author is a popular guest on radio talk shows**

- **First shipped in December 1995, and already in its second printing**

PUBLICITY

Author maintains an extensive nationwide seminar schedule

Direct mail advertising to more than one million consumers

National broadcast publicity

Careers/Job Search
7.5 x 9.5, Paper, 501 pp.

1-56370-181-2 • $14.95

Call 1-800-JIST-USA

The Quick Interview & Salary Negotiation Book

Dramatically Improve Your Interviewing Skills in Just a Few Hours!

By J. Michael Farr

"In short punchy style, this book lives up to its claim that it will 'dramatically improve your interviewing skills in just a few hours.'"

—Orange County Register

This book could literally be worth thousands of dollars in salary increases! America's leading author of job search books shares simple, fast, effective techniques for improving interviewing skills, handling unusual and difficult interview situations, negotiating salaries and pay increases, and much more.

- **Great advice for students, job changers, displaced professionals, and others**

- **Graphic icons make information immediate and easy to follow**

- **Includes average earnings information for hundreds of jobs**

- **Tips on job seeking, resumes, and preparing for interviews**

- **Author's books have sold more than 1.5 million copies**

- **Author is a popular guest on radio talk-shows**

PUBLICITY

Author maintains an extensive nationwide seminar schedule

National broadcast publicity

Careers
7.5 x 9.5, Paper, 379 pp.

1-56370-162-6 • $12.95

Using the Internet and the World Wide Web in Your Job Search, 2nd Edition

By Fred E. Jandt & Mary B. Nemnich

"If you're looking for a job on the Internet, this is the book to buy!"

—Northern Computer Users Group Newsletter

"... JIST has another 'hit' on its hands ... job site addresses and real case histories make this one of the most comprehensive and user-friendly web roadmaps on the market today."

—Drema Howard, Ph.D., Director, Career Resource Center, University of South Florida

In just a few short years, the Internet has become the most important business and personal communications tool since the telephone. There are thousands of job opportunities online and this book shows how to find them, with expert advice on everything from getting connected to getting the job.

- **An invaluable reference for any job seeker with Internet access and all employers who wish to recruit online**
- **Lists specific World Wide Web sites for job seekers and potential employers**
- **Updated advice on electronic resume preparation, plus how to include photographs and voice with resume**
- **Real stories of online job search success**
- **Covers all major online services, Internet job databases, and the World Wide Web**

Nearly 80% of college students expect to use the World Wide Web to find a job

Includes FREE software that helps readers create electronic resumes and upload them to the Internet!

PUBLICITY

National print publicity

Author lectures and bookstore events

Computer bulletin board promotion

Special co-op advertising and ad-slicks

Direct mail advertising to more than one million consumers

Careers/Computers
7.5 x 9.5, Paper, 300 pp.

1-56370-292-4 • $16.95

Previous ISBN 1-56370-173-1

Gallery of Best Resumes

A Collection of Quality Resumes by Professional Resume Writers

By David F. Noble, Ph.D.

A one-of-a-kind "idea book" of exceptional resumes for all job seekers

"This book is superior in both its content and presentation. In my opinion, it is a highly valuable source for direction, instruction, and reference for any level or profession of employment seeker."
–Barbara A. Aversalo, CEO, Business Assistance Associate

" ... an impressive survey for any who wants a comprehensive volume."
–Midwest Book Review

Editor and business communications professor David Noble invited members of the Professional Association of Resume Writers to submit their best designs for review. This book is the result—a "best of the best" collection of 200 top resumes, plus invaluable resume writing and job search tips from the experts.

- **Perfect idea-starter for all job seekers, regardless of age or employment experience**
- **Includes selection of resumes printed on special paper to enhance eye appeal**
- **A wide selection of resumes in many occupational categories, plus expert writing and design tips**
- **Also includes 25 top cover letters**
- **More than 25,000 copies sold ... a JIST best-seller**

Resumes
8.5 x 11, Paper, 400 pp.
1-56370-144-8 • $16.95

Dare to Change Your Job and Your Life

By Carole Kanchier, Ph.D.

A breakthrough for people ready to take charge of their careers—and their lives

"... a well-written, well-balanced book ... I strongly recommend this book to anyone seeking a new career or a new meaning in their life's work."

—Warren Farrell, Ph.D., author of *The Myth of Male Power* and *Why Men Are the Way They Are*

Corporate downsizing, a changing economic base, and the aging of America have made this a time of reflection and uncertainty for millions across the nation. Here's help: Dr. Carole Kanchier's hands-on, thought-provoking, and practical guide to life and career enrichment.

- **A proven self help approach to developing a more meaningful career and a more fulfilling life**

- **Appeals to a wide audience of readers of all ages, backgrounds, and occupations**

- **Practical advice based on interviews with more than 5,000 adults**

- **Easy-to-read, interactive format**

PUBLICITY

Print publicity

National broadcast publicity

Author lectures and bookstore events

Careers/Job Search
6 x 9, Paper, 332 pp.

1-56370-224-X • $14.95

JIST Products and Resources That Help America Work

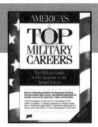

Getting the Job You Really Want, 3rd Edition
A Step-by-Step Guide

By J. Michael Farr

Over 150,000 copies sold

"This book is a very, very valuable addition to our collection"
　　　　　—Amy Wells, Versa Care, Attleboro, MA

The best book of its kind!

Getting the Job You Really Want is a unique, interactive job search and career planning guide. This book helps the reader through the entire career selection and job search process. Used extensively in programs across North America.

- **More than one million people have used these step-by-step techniques to find jobs**

- **Helps all types of job-seekers—career changers, students, and white-collar professionals**

- **Interactive format and great graphics**

- **Author is a popular guest on radio talk-shows**

PUBLICITY

Author maintains extensive nationwide seminar schedule

Direct mail advertising to more than one million consumers

National broadcast publicity

Job Search
Workbook: 8.5 x 11, Paper, 204 pp.

1-56370-092-1 • $9.95

Instructor's Guide: 8.5 x 11, Paper, 64 pp.

1-56370-196-0 • $12.95

Call 1-800-JIST-USA

JIST Customer Information

JIST specializes in publishing the very best results-oriented career and self-directed job search methods. For sixteen years we have been a leading publisher in career assessment devices, books, videos, and software. We continue to strive to make our materials the best there are so that people can stay abreast of what's happening in the labor market, and so they can clarify and articulate their skills and experiences for themselves as well as for prospective employers. **Our products are widely available through your local bookstores, wholesalers, and distributors.**

The World Wide Web

For more occupational or book information, get on-line and see our web site at **http://www.jist.com/jist**. Advance information about new products, services, and training events is continually updated.

Quantity Discounts Available!

Quantity discounts are available for businesses, schools and other organizations.

The JIST Guarantee

We want you to be happy with everything you buy from JIST. If you aren't satisfied with a product, return it to us within 30 days of purchase along with the reason for the return. Please include a copy of the packing list or invoice to guarantee quick credit to your order.

How to Order

For your convenience, the last page of this book contains an order form.

24-Hour Consumer Order Line:
Call toll free 1-800-547-8872
Please have your credit card (VISA, MC or AMEX) information ready!

Mail: Mail your order to the address listed on the order form: JIST Works, 720 North Park Avenue, Indianapolis, IN 46202-3490

Fax: Toll free 1-800-547-8329

JIST Order Form

Please copy this form if you need more lines for your order.

Purchase Order #: _____

Billing Information

Organization Name: _____
Accounting Contact: _____
Street Address: _____
_____
_____
City, State, Zip: _____
Phone Number: (   ) _____

Shipping Information (if different from above)

Organization Name: _____
Contact: _____
Street Address: (we canNOT ship to P.O. boxes) _____
_____
City, State, Zip: _____
Phone Number: (   ) _____

Phone: 1-800-547-8872
1-800-JIST-USA
Fax: 1-800-547-8329

Credit Card Purchases: VISA_____   MC_____   AMEX_____
Card Number: _____
Exp. date: _____
Name as on card: _____
Signature: _____

Quantity	Product Code	Product Title	Unit Price	Total

	Subtotal	
	+Sales Tax Indiana residents add 5% sales tax.	
	+Shipping / Handling Add $3.00 for the first item and an additional $.50 for each item thereafter.	
	TOTAL	

JIST Works, Inc.
720 North Park Avenue
Indianapolis, IN 46202

JIST thanks you for your order!

The Resume Place

Federal Resume Critique - $75.00

One hour written review and critique covering OF-510 compliance, scannability, target, language, and format (not proofreading).

Professional resume writing staff will provide the following assessment of your federal resume:

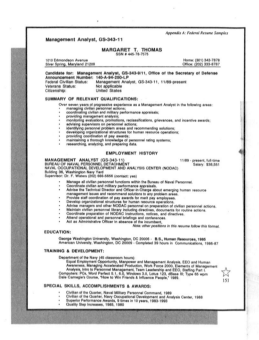

1. Analysis of your federal resume based on your announcement or objectives.

2. A written sheet with suggestions and criticisms; ideas for accomplishments; areas to highlight important skills, etc.

3. A resume mark-up with recommendations for improved presentation and format, including typestyle, margins, headings, quality of presentation.

4. Review to ensure your federal resume is in compliance with the OF-510.

5. Review to ensure optimum scanning of content and format.

Please include:

1. Your federal resume (hard copy or PC or Macintosh disk).

2. A sample or current job announcement (if possible); or information on the type and level of position you are seeking.

3. Check or credit card number for $75.00.

Complete federal resume writing and design services are available at **$75.00 per hour.**

Mail or fax resume for federal resume critique, estimate or writing to the following address:

The Resume Place • 310 Frederick Road • Baltimore, MD 21228
Tel: (410) 744-4324 • Fax: (410) 744-0112